GOOD
HOUSEKEEPING

400 FLAT-TUMMY
RECIPES & TIPS

GOOD
HOUSEKEEPING

400
FLAT-TUMMY
RECIPES & TIPS

HEARST
books

HEARSTBOOKS

An Imprint of Sterling Publishing Co., Inc.
1166 Avenue of the Americas
New York, NY 10036

ISBN 978-1-61837-238-3

The Good Housekeeping Cookbook Seal guarantees that the recipes in this publication meet the strict standards of the Good Housekeeping Research Institute. The Institute has been a source of reliable information and a consumer advocate since 1900, and established its seal of approval in 1909. Every recipe in this publication has been triple-tested for ease, reliability, and great taste by the Institute.

Distributed in Canada by Sterling Publishing Co., Inc.
c/o Canadian Manda Group, 664 Annette Street
Toronto, Ontario, M6S 2C8, Canada
Distributed in Australia by NewSouth Books
45 Beach Street, Coogee, NSW 2034, Australia

For information about custom editions, special sales, and premium and corporate purchases, please contact Sterling Special Sales at 800-805-5489 or specialsales@sterlingpublishing.com.

Manufactured in China

2 4 6 8 10 9 7 5 3 1

sterlingpublishing.com

goodhousekeeping.com

CONTENTS

Orange Granita (page 462)

FOREWORD

Delicious recipes that also help give you a flat tummy? It's not impossible! Far from it, in fact, *400 Flat-Tummy Recipes & Tips* is full of ideas for breakfasts, lunches, dinners, and snacks that will keep belly bulge under control—and keep you satisfied with the great-tasting food you've come to expect from *Good Housekeeping*.

Produced with the guidance of *Good Housekeeping's* registered dietician Jaclyn London, this book includes recipes that are brimming with flat-tummy all-stars—ingredients that actually help your midsection look sleeker and flatter. And if you need to drop a few pounds to help the cause, you've come to the right place, because these recipes are chosen to fall within calorie guidelines that can help you lose up to 2 pounds each week. We've kept your health in mind, too, with good-for-you limits on saturated fat and sodium.

And you'll keep hunger pangs at bay with these recipes. They contain plenty of lean protein and fiber to keep you feeling full. Herbs and spices add flavor without calories, and certain fruits and vegetables act as diuretics to help you get rid of belly bulge-causing fluids. We've also included foods that contain flat-tummy-promoting probiotics and prebiotics—gut friendly bacteria and the fibers that feed them. It turns out that a happier gut is a flatter gut!

All of these recipes have been triple-tested and include complete nutritional information. Plan your meals and snacks using this book and you can count on looking and feeling great—and enjoying every bite.

—SUSAN WESTMORELAND
Food Director, *Good Housekeeping*

Roasted Sweet and Sour Brussels Sprouts (page 417)

INTRODUCTION

SECRETS TO A FLAT TUMMY

For many of us, eliminating belly bulge is a major challenge. Intestinal issues or food allergies can cause gas, and PMS can lead to uncomfortable, water-retaining bloat. If you're overweight (especially if you're post-menopausal), you may carry extra pounds around your middle. Plus, some people are genetically predisposed to be shaped like apples rather than pears. Whatever the reason for a protruding tummy, struggling with clothes that no longer fit quite right is a pain. Plus it's a bummer to know you don't look your best. *Good Housekeeping 400 Flat-Tummy Recipes & Tips* is a great guide to help eliminate belly bloat in the most delicious and healthy way. This collection of fabulous recipes and helpful tips will assist you in being your best self and reaching your personal weight-loss goals.

But desiring a sleek midsection isn't just a matter of vanity. Managing bulk around your middle is essential to good health. A large waistline is one of five risk factors for metabolic syndrome (along with high triglycerides, low HDL—or "good"—cholesterol, high blood pressure, and high fasting blood sugar). It also raises your risk factors for heart disease, diabetes, and stroke. This excess weight is also linked to dementia, including Alzheimer's, and lifestyle-related cancers caused by diet, stress, obesity, and physical inactivity, among others.

Interestingly, the culprit behind these risk factors isn't necessarily the soft fat—called subcutaneous fat—that lies just below the skin. Instead, it's the visceral fat deep within your abdomen, surrounding the liver, intestines, and other organs, that produces proteins that lead to problems with inflammation, blood pressure, and insulin resistance. This is also the type of fat implicated in cardiovascular disease, dementia, asthma, breast cancer, and colorectal cancer. As a general rule, if a woman has a waist that's 35 inches or larger, she probably has too much visceral fat.

If your belly bulge is caused by temporary bloating, it's probably a result of overeating, gas, or retaining water. Following the guidelines below—particularly when it comes to eating beans and cruciferous vegetables—may help you feel better. If the problem is ongoing, see your doctor. You could have an obstruction in your digestive tract, Irritable Bowel Syndrome, Celiac disease, a food allergy or sensitivity, or a more serious problem, including cancer.

Whether the cause of your less-than-svelte tummy is extra pounds, or bloat caused by water retention or gas, *Good Housekeeping* is here to help. Every recipe in this book includes at least one (and often many more) flat-tummy all-stars. These foods contain nutrients that help battle belly bulge.

What's more, every recipe in this book falls within nutritional guidelines that will help you lose up to 2 pounds a week, if that's your goal. (Note: These guidelines are for women who weigh 150 pounds; if you weigh more or less, you may need to adjust your food intake.) For example, so that you can follow a sensible and steady diet of 1,600 calories a day, our breakfast recipes are 300 calories or less; lunch weighs in at 400 calories or less; dinner at 500 calories or less, and you'll still have room for two 200-calorie snacks. If you find after a few days that you feel too hungry, add one or two more snacks to your daily routine. (You can find recipes for yummy snacks like kale chips or roasted garbanzo beans in chapter 5. Or, check the sidebar, "Flat-Tummy Noshes," on page 15 for quick, healthy snacks.) Our recipes also contain less than 500 to 600 milligrams of sodium to minimize bloating, along with less than 6 grams of saturated fat for heart health.

FLAT-TUMMY ALL-STARS

In each recipe, we highlight one or more ingredients specially chosen to slim down your middle. You'll find ingredients that fill you up without excess calories and fat; help battle fluid-retention caused by too much sodium; add flavor with a minimum of calories; feed the good bacteria in your gut; and regulate overall gut health.

BEANS AND LENTILS: These high-fiber foods are healthful flat-tummy all-stars, but they can result in bloating. Introduce them gradually into your diet if you're not used to eating them regularly.

BROWN RICE, WHITE POTATOES, AND SWEET POTATOES: If you've been a carb-phobe in recent years, it's time to welcome some carbohydrates back into your meal plan. Whole grains, like brown rice, and both white and sweet potatoes contain potassium, which is helpful for de-bloating. Plus, they're ultra-rich in fiber—a key component if you're looking to drop some weight, since it helps satisfy hunger.

FISH (INCLUDING SHELLFISH) AND OTHER LEAN PROTEINS: When it comes to healthy sources of protein, it doesn't get any better than fish. Salmon, tuna, and sardines are filled with important omega-3 fats. These fats are loaded with bloat-battling potassium, which can help counteract the effects of sodium. They're also high in lean protein, helping to keep hunger pangs at bay and to curb cravings without excess calories and fat. Lean cuts of beef, pork, chicken, and egg whites are also flat-tummy favorites. Keep in mind that an entrée serving should contain no more than 6 grams of saturated fat (the recipes in this book have been chosen with that guideline in mind).

FRESH HERBS: Basil, cilantro, rosemary, tarragon, mint, and more introduce flavor to dishes without adding extra calories and sodium. Grow your own herb garden in the summer months for a fresh supply, or search out fresh herbs at your supermarket.

FRUITS AND VEGETABLES: It's hardly a news flash that fruits and vegetables are healthy foods. Five servings of fruits and vegetables each day is the hallmark of any healthy eating plan. The phytonutrients they contain are immune-boosting, plus they include filling fiber, and many provide bloat-reducing potassium, making them flat-tummy superstars. Naturally sweet and delicious, fruits also provide extra hydration, and low-sugar fruits like raspberries and blueberries deliver a boost of vitamin C. Bananas, loaded with potassium, are another good choice. Vegetables containing omega-3s, such as leafy greens, squash, and cauliflower, are especially helpful. Other veggies are great, too: mushrooms, carrots, tomatoes, and cucumber are all filled with water, which can help you stay hydrated due to their high

H_2O content. Ultra-nutritious cruciferous vegetables, like broccoli, cabbage, and Brussels sprouts, are all-stars, too, but they can cause bloat, so be sure to add them to your diet slowly if you're not used to eating them regularly.

GINGER AND TURMERIC: Whether fresh or powdered, these robustly flavored spices have been linked to reducing inflammation, are loaded with antioxidants, and deliver flavor without additional sodium or processed sugar.

LOW-FAT DAIRY PRODUCTS: Incorporating dairy into your everyday routine has been correlated with weight loss, and dairy can also serve as a lean, affordable source of protein to add to any meal. We suggest having two servings daily of reduced-fat milk or cheese.

NATURAL DIURETICS: Citrus, such as orange, lemon, and grapefruit, plus leeks, fennel, dandelion, and asparagus, helps to rid the body of excess fluid, promoting a flatter, sleeker tummy. Tea and coffee are diuretics as well, and coffee also helps with regularity. Aim for three 8-ounce cups a day, but skip the sugar (it's okay to drink coffee or tea with milk). Contrary to common wisdom, caffeine drinks will not lead to dehydration unless you consume more than 400 milligrams of caffeine a day.

POLY- AND MONOUNSATURATED FATS: Not all fat is bad and it is needed in your diet to help absorb nutrients. Opt for plant-based oils like olive, canola, or sesame oil when cooking. Add foods like nuts, nut butters, avocados, chia seeds, and flax seeds to your meals as well. These mineral-rich foods have been linked to a slew of positive health effects, including reducing waist circumference, lowering blood pressure, and improving cholesterol levels. Remember, a healthy portion of nuts is 1 ounce a day.

PREBIOTICS: Prebiotics are specialized plant fibers that feed the good bacteria that live in your digestive tract, helping it proliferate. Not only does this help promote a flat tummy by creating a "friendlier" environment for your digestion and absorption of nutrients, but a recent Oxford University study shows that prebiotics may help reduce anxiety and depression. Artichokes, garlic, onions, leeks, asparagus, bananas, jicama, oats, and other 100% whole-grain foods are prebiotics.

PROBIOTIC FOODS: Fermented foods, like miso and sauerkraut, contain probiotics or friendly bacteria that help to boost immunity, regulate gut function, and banish bloat. Unsweetened Greek yogurt is another probiotic-containing food we love: Thick, creamy, and delicious, it is also packed with protein to keep cravings at bay.

TOFU AND EDAMAME: These soy products deliver ample amounts of satisfying protein with little saturated fat.

VINEGAR: This flavorful liquid is a calorie-free way to add tang to dishes and a great dressing for salad. Lightly dress a salad with vinegar with or without a splash of olive oil.

WATER: Drink lots! Eight cups daily helps keep bloat at bay. (When you don't drink enough, your body hoards water.) But avoid carbonated water; those bubbles can actually promote bloat rather than reduce it.

WHOLE GRAINS: All kinds of whole grains (whole wheat, oats, buckwheat) are included in this book. They're mineral-rich, which helps counterbalance salt in your diet. Plus, whole grains are filling, which can help offset any cravings for sweets.

ALL-STAR HABITS

What you eat matters a lot, but so do behaviors. Incorporate these three practices into your day:

EXERCISE: High-five! You're eating right, so now it's time to get your body moving at least 30 minutes a day. Try a combo of heart-pumping cardio (walking briskly, jogging, Zumba class!) and lifting weights to stay healthy and strong. Sound daunting? Don't worry: No need to do 30 minutes all at once. Break your activity into bite-size chunks: Go for a lunchtime stroll; take the stairs instead of the elevator; contract those abs in the car. Commit to be fit with small changes every day.

Ready for a little fat-melting magic? Try something called high-intensity interval training (HIIT), alternating between fast and slow bursts of activity. Research shows that as little as one minute of all-out exercise three times a week can improve your fitness. Try this: Pedal a stationary bike for 3, 20-second bursts, with two minutes of catch-your-breath biking in between.

MINDFUL EATING: Pay attention to what goes in your mouth. Keep a food diary, if it helps you focus, and try to avoid eating while reading or watching television.

POSTURE: Mom was right, as usual. Sitting up straight engages stomach muscles, which help in toning them. Plus, good posture aids in reducing acid reflux. One other benefit: Your tummy will automatically appear flatter!

FLAT-TUMMY FAILS

Steer clear of these traps:

CHEWING GUM: You swallow air when you chew, causing—you guessed it—bloat.

CARBONATED BEVERAGES: Along with carbonated water, mentioned above, sodas also contain bubbles that bloat.

SYNTHETIC SUGAR ALCOHOLS, SUCH AS SORBITOL, AND FAKE SWEETENERS: They're found in processed foods, like beverages and diet desserts. Aim to avoid these as much as possible.

Follow these steps and you'll enjoy foods that are healthy and delicious—and you can look forward to being in the best shape of your life!

FLAT-TUMMY NOSHES

Each of the following snacks has about 100 calories, which means you can help yourself to three or four of them a day!

SWEET

½ small apple with 2 teaspoons of peanut butter

1 cup blueberries

½ medium cantaloupe

1 cup grapes

1 cup mango slices

2 cups raspberries

2½ cup strawberries

SAVORY

17 almonds

2 tablespoons each mashed avocado and chopped tomatoes stuffed in ½ mini whole-grain pita

40 baby carrots with 4 tablespoons salsa for dipping

13 cashews

45 steamed edamame pods (green soybeans)

3 tablespoons hummus with 1 small red pepper, sliced for dipping

20 roasted peanuts

30 pistachios

9 walnut halves

4 ounces full-fat Greek yogurt topped with ¼ cup fruit or chopped tomato

Tropical Smoothie Bowl (page 45)

1 | BREAKFASTS

Jump-start your day with a satisfying, filling breakfast. Starting your morning with a complete meal ensures that you will be fueled for the day's activities. These 300-calorie breakfasts are filled with flat-tummy all-stars.

This is also a great time to have foods high in protein, which, like fiber, helps you feel full throughout the morning. To help you do that, this chapter is brimming with egg dishes including prebiotic-packed vegetables like the Asparagus Frittata (page 21) or topped with flavorful fresh herbs like the Tofu Scramble with Chopped Tomatoes and Chives (page 28). Blueberries, raspberries, and bananas are delicious additions to unsweetened, plain yogurt in the Fruity Yogurt Parfait (page 43) or blend them together for a tasty, on-the-go smoothie. Replace sugary syrup on your breakfast and try the Whole-Grain Berry Pancakes (page 49) with pureed berries for a natural sweetener. And if you are looking to indulge a bit, Grab-and-Go Cranberry Granola Bars (page 59) are also health-conscious treats with fiber, protein, and antioxidants that also satisfy any sweet tooth.

BASIC OMELETS

A well-made omelet can be a quick supper or a satisfying breakfast. Mix up a batch of eggs, prepare your fillings, and you're ready for quick assembly-line production. For lower-fat omelets, use 4 large eggs and 8 egg whites.

TOTAL TIME: 7 minutes, plus preparing filling
MAKES: 4 servings

Filling of choice (page 19)
8   large eggs
½   cup water
½   teaspoon salt
4   teaspoons butter

1. Prepare filling. In medium bowl, with wire whisk, beat eggs, water, and salt.

2. In nonstick 10-inch skillet, melt 1 teaspoon butter over medium-high heat. Pour ½ cup egg mixture into skillet. Cook, gently lifting edge of eggs with heat-safe rubber spatula and tilting pan to allow uncooked eggs to run underneath, until eggs are set, about 1 minute. Spoon one-fourth of filling over half of omelet. Fold unfilled half of omelet over filling and slide onto warm plate. Repeat with remaining butter, egg mixture, and filling. If desired, keep omelets warm in 200°F oven until all omelets are cooked.

Each serving (without filling): About 183 calories, 13g protein, 1g carbohydrate, 14g total fat (5g saturated), 0g fiber, 455mg sodium

EGG-WHITE OMELET

Drop 4 grams of saturated fat by making your omelet with egg whites.

TOTAL TIME: 7 minutes, plus preparing filling
MAKES: 1 serving

Filling of choice (optional)
2	tablespoons nonfat (0%) milk
1	tablespoon all-purpose flour
4	large egg whites
⅛	teaspoon salt
¼	teaspoon turmeric (optional)
2	teaspoons olive oil

1. Prepare filling below, if using.

2. Blend 2 tablespoons nonfat milk and 1 tablespoon all-purpose flour until smooth. Whisk in 4 large egg whites, ⅛ teaspoon salt, and ¼ teaspoon turmeric, if using.

3. In nonstick 8-inch skillet, heat 2 teaspoons olive oil over medium heat. Add egg-white mixture and cook until just set, about 2 minutes. Spoon filling, if using, over half of omelet. Continue as for Basic Omelets (page 18).

Each serving (without filling): About 186 calories, 16g protein, 9g carbohydrate, 9g total fat (1g saturated), 0g fiber, 543mg sodium

FLAT-TUMMY FILLINGS

Slice or dice any of the following vegetables for added nutrients in your omelet. Add your prepared vegetables to a skillet coated with nonstick spray. Sauté until vegetables soften or onions become translucent. Remove from heat but keep warm until ready to add to your omelet.

SUGGESTED FLAT-TUMMY ALL-STAR FILLINGS

Mushrooms, red and/or yellow peppers, onion, green onion
Top with salsa or chopped basil or chives for added flavor!

SPINACH AND CHEESE OMELET

Good-for-you spinach and low-fat cheese make omelets even more delicious.

TOTAL TIME: 15 minutes

MAKES: 4 servings

1	(10-ounce) bag prewashed spinach
½	cup (2 ounces) reduced-fat Cheddar cheese
8	large eggs
½	cup water
½	teaspoon salt
1	teaspoon butter

1. Wash, dry, and remove tough stems from spinach. In 3-quart saucepan, cook over high heat until just wilted; drain. When cool enough to handle, squeeze out excess liquid from spinach and coarsely chop. Shred cheese. Set aside.

2. In medium bowl, with wire whisk, beat eggs, water, and salt. In 10-inch skillet, melt butter over medium-high heat. Pour ½ cup egg mixture into skillet. Cook, gently lifting edge of eggs with heat-safe rubber spatula and tilting pan to allow uncooked eggs to run underneath, until eggs are set, about 1 minute.

3. Spoon spinach and cheese over half of omelet. Fold unfilled omelet half over filling and slide onto warm plate. Repeat three times.

Each serving: About 205 calories, 18g protein, 3g carbohydrate, 13g total fat (5g saturated), 1g fiber, 538mg sodium

ASPARAGUS FRITTATA

A frittata is an Italian omelet in which the ingredients are mixed with the eggs, rather than folded inside. The frittata is often slipped under the broiler to brown the top.

ACTIVE TIME: 15 minutes **TOTAL TIME:** 25 minutes
MAKES: 4 servings

8	large eggs
1/3	cup low-fat (1%) milk
1/2	teaspoon salt
1/8	teaspoon freshly ground pepper
1	tablespoon olive oil
1	pound asparagus, cut into 1-inch pieces
4	green onions, thinly sliced

1. Preheat oven to 375°F. In medium bowl, with wire whisk, beat eggs, milk, salt, and pepper until well blended.

2. In oven-safe nonstick 10-inch skillet (if skillet is not oven-safe, wrap handle with a double layer of foil), heat oil over medium-high heat. Stir in asparagus; cook 4 minutes. Reduce heat to medium, add onions, cook 2 minutes, stirring. Spread vegetable mixture in skillet. Pour in egg mixture and cook, without stirring, until it begins to set around edge, 3 to 4 minutes.

3. Place skillet in oven; bake until frittata is set, 8 to 10 minutes. To serve, loosen frittata from skillet and slide onto warm platter; cut into 4 wedges.

Each serving: About 210 calories, 16g protein, 7g carbohydrate, 13g total fat (4g saturated), 3g fiber, 401mg sodium

SPINACH SCRAMBLE

Using prewashed bagged spinach makes this easy recipe even easier.

TOTAL TIME: 10 minutes

MAKES: 1 serving

Nonstick cooking spray

½	red pepper, chopped
1	cup spinach, chopped
2	eggs, beaten
1	tablespoon feta cheese, crumbled

1. In a nonstick skillet coated with cooking spray, sauté pepper until tender.

2. Add spinach and cook until just wilted, about 1 minute. Stir in two beaten eggs and cheese and cook, stirring frequently, until eggs are firm and cooked through.

Each serving: About 200 calories, 15g protein, 6g carbohydrate, 12g total fat (5g saturated), 2g fiber, 255mg sodium

TIP

Switch up your scramble and trade the spinach and peppers for freshly chopped chives.

BROCCOLI CHEDDAR SCRAMBLE

Thawed frozen broccoli is perfect for this dish.

TOTAL TIME: 10 minutes
MAKES: 1 serving

2	eggs
½	cup frozen broccoli florets, thawed
1	tablespoon low-fat Cheddar cheese, shredded

Salt and pepper, to taste

1. Scramble 2 eggs with ½ cup thawed, frozen broccoli florets.

2. Just before eggs are fully cooked, top with 1 tablespoon shredded low-fat cheddar cheese. Add salt and pepper to taste.

Each serving: About 175 calories, 16g protein, 5g carbohydrate, 10g total fat (3g saturated), 2g fiber, 340mg sodium

THE NUTRITIONAL BENEFITS OF EGGS

Eggs got a bum rap for years. Yes, the yolk of an egg does contain cholesterol, but as many studies can attest, if eaten in moderation, eggs do not increase an individual's cholesterol level. Plus, eggs offer so many nutritional benefits. Along with a boost of protein, a single egg is a good source of selenium, a mineral that provides protection to antioxidants; iodine, vital to thyroid function; and energy-producing vitamin B_2.

SOUTHWESTERN RICE AND CORN FRITTATA

Not just for breakfast, this hearty, one-skillet dish is perfect for a weeknight supper or a Sunday brunch. Or cut the frittata into smaller wedges and serve it as a game-day snack.

ACTIVE TIME: 25 minutes   **TOTAL TIME:** 45 minutes
MAKES: 6 servings

1	package (8 to 9 ounces) precooked whole-grain brown rice (scant 2 cups)
4	teaspoons olive oil
1	small onion, chopped
1	jalapeño chile, seeded and finely chopped
1	garlic clove, finely chopped
1	cup frozen corn kernels
8	large eggs
1/4	cup nonfat (0%) milk
1/4	cup loosely packed fresh cilantro leaves, chopped
1/2	teaspoon salt
1/2	cup low-fat Mexican cheese blend, shredded

Prepared salsa for serving (optional)

1. Cook brown rice as label directs.

2. Meanwhile, preheat oven to 400°F. In oven-safe nonstick 10-inch skillet, heat 2 teaspoons oil over medium heat until hot. Add onion and cook 4 to 5 minutes or until lightly browned, stirring occasionally. Stir in jalapeño and garlic; cook 30 seconds, stirring. Add corn and cook 1 minute or until corn is thawed, stirring occasionally. Transfer corn mixture to bowl.

3. In large bowl, with wire whisk, beat eggs, milk, cilantro, and salt until well blended. Stir in rice, corn mixture, and cheese.

4. In same skillet, heat remaining 2 teaspoons oil over medium heat until hot. Pour in egg mixture; cover and cook 3 minutes or until egg mixture starts to set around the edge.

5. Remove cover and place skillet in oven; bake 20 minutes or until knife inserted 2 inches from edge comes out clean. Remove frittata from oven; let stand 5 minutes.

6. To serve, loosen frittata from skillet; slide onto warm platter. Cut into wedges; serve with salsa if you like.

Each serving: About 255 calories, 14g protein, 22g carbohydrate, 13g total fat (4g saturated), 2g fiber, 390mg sodium

CALIFORNIA FRITTATA

This frittata, accompanied by salsa, crisp jicama sticks, and 100% whole-grain corn tortillas, makes for a substantial meal that's high in fiber and low in fat. An egg substitute may be used instead of eggs, if you prefer.

ACTIVE TIME: 30 minutes **TOTAL TIME:** 1 hour, 5 minutes
MAKES: 4 servings

3	small potatoes
1	tablespoon olive oil
1½	cups thinly sliced onions
1	zucchini (6 ounces), thinly sliced
1	cup cremini mushrooms, thinly sliced
2	ripe plum tomatoes (6½ ounces), each cored, halved, and thinly sliced
½	teaspoon kosher salt
½	teaspoon ground black pepper
1	cup spinach or Swiss chard, shredded
1	tablespoon fresh basil leaves, slivered (optional)
2	large eggs
3	large egg whites
½	jicama (8 ounces), peeled and cut into matchsticks
2	teaspoons fresh lime juice
3	tablespoons feta cheese, crumbled (optional)
2	tablespoons fresh flat-leaf parsley, chopped
¾	cup bottled salsa
4	(6-inch) 100% whole-grain corn tortillas

1. Preheat oven to 350°F. In saucepan, heat potatoes with enough water to cover to a boil over high heat. Reduce heat to low; cover and simmer until fork-tender, 15 to 20 minutes. Drain and cool. Cut into ¼-inch-thick slices.

2. In cast-iron skillet or another heavy oven-safe skillet, heat oil over medium. Add onions and cook until softened, about 5 minutes. Add potatoes, zucchini, mushrooms, and tomatoes, and season with salt and pepper; cook, stirring gently, until zucchini begins to soften, 2 to 3 minutes. Add spinach and, if using, basil, and cook until spinach wilts, 1 to 2 minutes.

3. In bowl, with wire whisk or fork, mix eggs and egg whites. With spatula, stir vegetables while pouring eggs into skillet. Transfer skillet to oven and bake until eggs are set, 3 to 5 minutes.

4. While frittata bakes, sprinkle jicama sticks with lime juice; set aside.

5. When frittata is done, scatter feta cheese, if using, and parsley on top. Cut into 4 pieces and serve with salsa, tortillas, and jicama sticks.

Each serving: About 265 calories, 11 g protein, 38g carbohydrate, 7g total fat (1g saturated), 8g fiber, 140 mg sodium

THREE QUICK BREAKFASTS

FRUIT AND CHEESE

Slice medium apple and top with 1 ounce reduced-fat Cheddar cheese (such as Cabot 50% Reduced Fat sharp Cheddar); serve with ¼ cup almonds.

Each serving: About 370 calories, 16g protein, 34g carbohydrate, 23g total fat (4g saturated), 9g fiber, 172mg sodium

EGG ROLL-UP

Fill a 100% whole-grain corn tortilla with 1 scrambled egg or egg substitute. Microwave 1 slice Canadian bacon about 1 minute on High. Chop, and add to tortilla with ½ cup raw baby spinach, and roll up.

Each serving: About 185 calories, 14g protein, 13g carbohydrate, 8g total fat (2g saturated), 2g fiber, 329mg sodium

PB AND B

Spread 1 slice whole-grain bread with 1½ tablespoons peanut butter, add slices from ½ banana. Drizzle with 1 teaspoon honey and fold over.

Each serving: About 285 calories, 9g protein, 36g carbohydrate, 14g total fat (3g saturated), 5g fiber, 202mg sodium

TOFU SCRAMBLE WITH CHOPPED TOMATOES AND CHIVES

Serve this nondairy scramble with whole-grain toast or in a 100% whole-grain corn tortilla.

TOTAL TIME: 15 minutes
MAKES: 4 servings

1	(14- to 16-ounce) package of firm tofu
3	tablespoons olive oil
1	large garlic clove, finely chopped
¼	cup fresh chives, snipped

Pinch of cayenne pepper

½	teaspoon ground turmeric
1	large ripe tomato, seeded and chopped
½	teaspoon salt
1	tablespoon fresh lemon juice

1. Rinse tofu and press with clean towel to absorb excess water. Place in bowl and mash into small pieces with fork.

2. In nonstick 12-inch skillet, heat oil over medium until hot. Stir in garlic, chives, cayenne, and turmeric; cook 2 minutes, stirring.

3. Add mashed tofu, tomato, and salt; raise heat and simmer 5 minutes. Remove from heat and stir in lemon juice. Serve immediately.

Each serving: About 190 calories, 9g protein, 5g carbohydrate, 15g total fat 9 (2g saturated), 2g fiber, 297mg sodium

WILD RICE SPINACH EGG BOWL

Bring whole grains and fresh greens to the breakfast table.

TOTAL TIME: 5 minutes
MAKES: 1 serving

Nonstick cooking spray
1	large egg
⅛	teaspoon black pepper
2	cups baby spinach

Salt to taste
1	(12-ounce) container Minute Rice Multi-Grain Medley

1. Spray 12-inch nonstick skillet with nonstick cooking spray; heat on medium. To one side, add egg; cook 3 minutes. Sprinkle egg with black pepper. Then, to other side of skillet, add spinach and pinch of salt.

2. Cover; cook 3 minutes or until spinach wilts and egg white sets.

3. Heat rice as label directs; top with spinach, then egg.

Each serving: About 305 calories, 14g protein, 47g carbohydrate, 10g total (2g saturated fat), 9g fiber, 530mg sodium

HEALTHY MAKEOVER SPINACH QUICHE

Quiche, a French bistro classic, is a perfect one-dish meal, but it can leave you feeling less than svelte. Replace a portion of white flour with whole wheat, and use nonfat milk instead of cream, to bid adieu to 25 grams of fat, reduce the calories by half, and quadruple the fiber. Bon appétit!

ACTIVE TIME: 35 minutes **TOTAL TIME:** 1 hour, 20 minutes
MAKES: 6 servings

³⁄₄	cup all-purpose flour
¹⁄₂	cup whole wheat flour
³⁄₈	teaspoon salt
4	tablespoons cold butter, cut into pieces
¹⁄₄	cup low-fat (1%) buttermilk
	Nonstick cooking spray
3	large egg whites
1	(6- to 8-ounce) leek, white and light green parts only, sliced into half-moons
¹⁄₂	teaspoon fresh thyme leaves, chopped
6	ounces (about 6 cups) baby spinach
2	large eggs
1¹⁄₂	cups nonfat (0%) milk
1	teaspoon Dijon mustard
¹⁄₄	teaspoon ground black pepper
1	ounce goat cheese, softened

1. In food processor, pulse both flours and ¼ teaspoon salt until combined. Add butter; pulse until coarse crumbs form. Add buttermilk; pulse just until blended. If dough does not stay together when pinched, add ice water, 1 tablespoon at a time, pulsing after each addition, just until dough holds together. Shape into disk. Wrap in plastic; refrigerate 20 minutes or overnight. (If chilled overnight, let stand 30 minutes at room temperature before rolling.)

2. Preheat oven to 400°F. Spray 9-inch glass pie plate with cooking spray. On lightly floured surface, with floured rolling pin, roll dough into 12-inch round; place in pie plate. Gently press against bottom and up side without stretching; trim edge. Prick holes in crust with fork. Line with foil; fill with pie weights or dried beans. Bake 15 minutes or until beginning to set. Remove 1 tablespoon egg white from rest of whites; set remainder aside. Remove foil with weights; brush

bottom of crust with 1 tablespoon egg white. Bake 5 to 6 minutes or until golden brown and dry to the touch. Cool completely on wire rack.

3. Meanwhile, coat 12-inch skillet with cooking spray; heat on medium. Add leek, thyme, and remaining ⅛ teaspoon salt. Cook 3 to 4 minutes or until soft, stirring occasionally. Add spinach; cook 5 minutes or until mixture is very soft and dry, stirring frequently. Let cool.

4. In large bowl, whisk whole eggs, milk, and remaining egg whites. Stir in mustard, leek mixture, and pepper. Spread bottom of crust with goat cheese; place pie plate in jelly-roll pan. With strips of foil, cover crust edges to prevent overbrowning. Pour egg mixture into crust; bake 32 to 35 minutes or until knife inserted in center comes out clean. Cool on wire rack 15 minutes to serve.

Each serving: About 250 calories, 11g protein, 26g carbohydrate, 11g total fat (6g saturated), 2g fiber, 339mg sodium

CRUSTLESS TOMATO AND RICOTTA PIE

Serve this delicious cross between a frittata and a quiche for brunch or dinner, as well as for a hearty breakfast.

ACTIVE TIME: 20 minutes   **TOTAL TIME:** 55 minutes
MAKES: 6 servings

1	(15-ounce) container low-fat ricotta cheese
3	large eggs, plus 2 egg whites
¼	cup freshly grated Pecorino-Romano cheese
½	teaspoon salt
⅛	teaspoon coarsely ground black pepper
¼	cup low-fat (1%) milk
1	tablespoon cornstarch
½	cup loosely packed fresh basil leaves, chopped
1	pound ripe tomatoes (about 3 medium), thinly sliced

1. Preheat oven to 375°F. In large bowl, whisk ricotta, eggs, cheese, salt, and pepper.

2. In measuring cup, stir milk and cornstarch until smooth; whisk into cheese mixture. Stir in basil.

3. Pour mixture into nonstick 10-inch skillet with oven-safe handle. Arrange tomatoes on top, overlapping slices if necessary. Bake pie 35 to 40 minutes or until lightly browned on top, set around edge, and puffed at center. Let stand 5 minutes before serving.

Each serving: About 190 calories, 15g protein, 10g carbohydrate, 10g total fat (5g saturated), 2g fiber, 380mg sodium

BREAKFAST TORTILLA STACK

Need a breakfast that will keep you full all morning long? Top a 100% whole-grain corn tortilla with fluffy eggs, fat-free refried beans, and flavorful salsa.

ACTIVE TIME: 25 minutes   **TOTAL TIME:** 30 minutes
MAKES: 4 servings

1	cup ice water
¼	cup red onion, chopped
2	(6 to 8 ounce) ripe medium tomatoes, chopped
¼	cup loosely packed fresh cilantro leaves, chopped
4	large eggs
4	large egg whites
⅛	teaspoon salt
⅛	teaspoon ground black pepper
	Nonstick cooking spray
1	cup fat-free refried beans
¼	teaspoon ground chipotle chile
4	(7-inch) 100% whole-grain corn tortillas

1. In ice water, soak chopped onion 10 minutes; drain well. In small bowl, combine onions, tomatoes, and cilantro; set aside.

2. In medium bowl, with wire whisk or fork, beat whole eggs, egg whites, salt, and pepper until blended.

3. Spray nonstick 10-inch skillet with cooking spray; heat on medium 1 minute. Pour egg mixture into skillet; cook about 5 minutes or until egg mixture is set but still moist, stirring occasionally.

4. Meanwhile, in microwave-safe small bowl, mix beans and chipotle chile. Cover with vented plastic wrap; heat in microwave on High 1 minute or until hot.

5. Place stack of tortillas between damp paper towels on microwave-safe plate; heat in microwave on High 10 to 15 seconds to warm. To serve, layer each tortilla with eggs, beans, and salsa.

Each serving: About 230 calories, 16g protein, 27g carbohydrate, 6g total fat (2g saturated), 6g fiber, 450mg sodium

HUEVOS RANCHEROS

Fast and flavorful, these Mexican-inspired baked eggs are ideal for brunch. Baking rather than frying the tortilla cups keeps the calories and fat in check.

ACTIVE TIME: 15 minutes   **TOTAL TIME:** 40 minutes
MAKES: 4 servings

4	(6-inch) 100% whole-grain corn tortillas

Nonstick cooking spray

1	(16-ounce) jar mild, low-sodium salsa
1	cup canned black beans, rinsed and drained
1	cup frozen corn kernels
3	green onions, sliced
1	teaspoon ground cumin
4	large eggs
1/4	cup loosely packed fresh cilantro leaves, thinly sliced
1/2	avocado, sliced into thin wedges

1. Preheat oven to 350°F. On 15½ x 10½-inch jelly-roll pan, invert four 6-ounce custard cups. With kitchen shears, make four evenly spaced 1-inch cuts, from edge toward center, around each tortilla. Lightly spray both sides of tortillas with cooking spray and drape each over a custard cup. Bake tortilla cups 8 minutes or until golden and crisp.

2. Meanwhile, in nonstick 12-inch skillet, combine salsa, beans, corn, green onions, and cumin; heat to boiling over medium heat. Cover and cook 3 minutes to blend flavors.

3. With large spoon, make four indentations in salsa mixture, spaced evenly around skillet. One at a time, break eggs into cup and gently pour into indentations. Cover and simmer 8 to 10 minutes or until eggs are set or cooked to desired doneness.

4. To serve, set each tortilla cup on plate. Spoon egg with some salsa mixture into each tortilla cup. Spoon any remaining salsa mixture around and on eggs in cups. Sprinkle with cilantro; serve with avocado wedges.

Each serving: About 300 calories, 13g protein, 39g carbohydrate, 10g total fat (2g saturated), 9g fiber, 450mg sodium

SOUTH OF THE BORDER BREAKFAST WRAP

Take this wrap on the go for those busy mornings.

TOTAL TIME: 5 minutes
MAKES: 1 serving

1	large egg
1	large egg white
2	tablespoons cilantro, chopped, plus additional for garnish
¼	teaspoon chili powder
⅛	teaspoon salt
1	large sprouted whole-grain tortilla
¼	cup grape tomatoes
⅙	ripe avocado

1. In medium bowl, whisk egg, egg white, cilantro, chili powder, and ⅛ teaspoon salt.

2. In 8-inch nonstick skillet on medium, cook egg mixture 3 minutes or until almost set, stirring frequently.

3. Place tortilla on large plate. Cover with damp paper towel; microwave 30 seconds on high.

4. Add eggs to tortilla along with tomatoes, avocado, and cilantro leaves, if desired.

Each serving: About 300 calories, 17g protein, 31g carbohydrate, 14g total fat (3g saturated), 8g fiber, 590mg sodium

BANANA-BERRY SMOOTHIE

A little ginger and tart pineapple juice add a kick to this sweet but healthy blend of banana and berries.

TOTAL TIME: 5 minutes
MAKES: 2 servings

1	small banana
6	ounces pineapple juice
½	cup ice
6	ounces (1 cup) blueberries
6	ounces (1 cup) raspberries or blackberries
2	teaspoons honey
1	teaspoon fresh ginger, peeled and grated

In blender, puree banana, pineapple, ice, blueberries, raspberries or blackberries, honey, and ginger until smooth.

Each serving: About 210 calories, 3g protein, 51g carbohydrate, 1g total fat (0g saturated), 9g fiber, 6mg sodium

WHY YOU SHOULD BUY WHOLE FRUITS, RATHER THAN JUICE

You'll feel fuller on fewer calories and get more healthy fiber from the actual fruit. A cup of apple juice, for example, has no fiber and more than 100 calories, but a cup of sliced apple (about one small apple) has 75 calories and more than 3 grams of fiber.

JUMP-START SMOOTHIE

This smoothie would be great with a variety of other fruit, too. Substitute the strawberries or blueberries with frozen blackberries, raspberries, or mango.

TOTAL TIME: 5 minutes

MAKES: 1 serving

1	cup frozen strawberries
½	cup frozen blueberries
½	cup fresh orange juice
2	teaspoons fresh ginger, peeled and chopped
¼	cup plain, unsweetened Greek yogurt
2	ice cubes

1. In blender, combine strawberries, blueberries, orange juice, ginger, yogurt, and ice cubes.

2. Blend until smooth, scraping down side of container occasionally.

Each serving: About 210 calories, 8g protein, 38g carbohydrate, 4g total fat (2g saturated), 5g fiber, 27mg sodium

WHY GREEK YOGURT?

Greek yogurt has become popular in many Americans diets. It has a texture similar to sour cream, but with the added health benefit of live bacteria, including Lactobacillus bulgaricus and Streptococcus thermophiues, along with a healthy dose of protein—10 grams a serving. Plus, Greek yogurt can be heated to high temperatures without curdling. To get its thick, creamy texture, the yogurt is strained, removing the whey or milky liquid. Greek yogurt can be found in the dairy aisle of your local supermarket.

FRUITY YOGURT PARFAIT

Start your day with a colorful, healthy dish featuring two flat-tummy all-stars—yogurt and a variety of mixed berries, kiwi, and blueberries.

TOTAL TIME: 5 minutes
MAKES: 1 serving

1	cup frozen mixed berries
2/3	cup low-fat plain, unsweetened Greek yogurt
1	tablespoon flaxseed
1/8	teaspoon vanilla extract
1/2	kiwi, peeled and chopped
1/4	cup fresh blueberries
3	tablespoons whole grain fruit and nut granola

1. In food processor or blender, pulse frozen berries, yogurt, flaxseed, and vanilla extract until smooth.

2. Transfer yogurt mixture to bowl; top with kiwi, blueberries, and fruit and nut granola.

Each serving: About 300 calories, 18g protein, 46g carbohydrate, 7g total fat (3g saturated), 7g fiber, 78mg sodium

WILL SKIPPING BREAKFAST HELP YOU LOSE WEIGHT?

No. In fact, it's the opposite! Not eating meals can lead to weight gain. A recent British study that tracked 6,764 people found that breakfast skippers gained twice as much weight over the course of four years as breakfast eaters. Another research group analyzed government data on 4,200 adults. They found that women who ate breakfast tended to eat fewer calories over the course of the day.

SUNRISE SMOOTHIE

Banana bread isn't the only yummy recipe for bananas!

TOTAL TIME: 5 minutes
MAKES: 4 servings

1	large banana
2	cups ice
2	cups frozen pineapple
1	cup orange juice
½	cup low-fat vanilla yogurt

Puree banana, ice, pineapple, orange juice, and yogurt until smooth.

Each serving: About 120 calories, 3g protein, 28g carbohydrate, 1g total fat (0g saturated), 2g fiber, 21mg sodium

FLAT-TUMMY ALL-STAR: BANANAS

Bananas are available year-round. Yellow bananas are supermarket staples, but red and small yellow bananas are also available in some areas.

If you want to eat bananas right away, buy solid yellow bananas with some brown flecks. Bananas that are somewhat green will ripen within a few days at room temperature. To hasten ripening, store in a closed paper bag at room temperature.

After they ripen, bananas can be refrigerated for two or three days. (The skins will darken, but the fruit inside will remain ripe and fresh.) For longer storage, mash the fruit with a little lemon juice, pack into freezer containers (leaving ½-inch headspace), and freeze. Thaw in the refrigerator before using.

To prepare bananas, peel and slice or cut them up, depending on use. If they aren't to be eaten immediately, sprinkle with a little lemon juice to prevent browning.

TROPICAL SMOOTHIE BOWL

Top this fruity smoothie with chopped almonds, shredded coconut, fresh kiwi, mango, and blueberries. (See photograph on page 16.)

TOTAL TIME: 5 minutes
MAKES: 2 servings

1	banana, sliced and frozen
1	cup frozen mango chunks
1	cup frozen pineapple chunks
1	cup unsweetened almond milk

In blender, pulse banana, mango, and pineapple with almond milk until smooth but still thick, stopping and stirring occasionally. Add more liquid if needed. Pour into 2 bowls. Top as desired.

Each serving: About 180 calories, 3g protein, 43g carbohydrate, 2g total fat (0g saturated), 5g fiber, 90mg sodium

ORANGE-PEACH SMOOTHIE BOWL

Load this breakfast smoothie bowl with toppings and eat it with a spoon.

TOTAL TIME: 5 minutes
MAKES: 2 servings

1	banana, sliced and frozen
1½	cup frozen peaches
½	cup low-fat plain, unsweetened Greek yogurt
¾	cup orange juice

Blend banana, peaches, and Greek yogurt with orange juice. Pour into 2 bowls. Top as desired.

Each serving: About 175 calories, 8g protein, 36g carbohydrate, 2g total fat (1g saturated), 3g fiber, 25mg sodium

STEEL-CUT OATMEAL

If you haven't tried steel-cut oats, you're in for a deliciously chewy, full-flavored treat. We've included several tasty variations.

ACTIVE TIME: 5 minutes   **TOTAL TIME:** 30 minutes
MAKES: 4 servings

3	cups water
1	cup steel-cut oats

Pinch of salt

In medium saucepan, combine water, oats, and salt. Bring to boiling over high heat. Reduce heat and cover. Simmer until water is absorbed and oats are tender but still chewy, 20 to 25 minutes, stirring occasionally.

Each serving: About 75 calories, 3g protein, 14g carbohydrate, 1g total fat (0g saturated), 2g fiber, 35mg sodium

BLUEBERRY-ALMOND OATMEAL

In small bowl, mix **1 cup fresh blueberries**, **¼ cup toasted and chopped almonds**, and **4 teaspoons honey**. Divide topping among servings of oatmeal.

Each serving: About 95 calories, 3g protein, 17g carbohydrate, 2g total fat (0g saturated), 2g fiber, 35 mg sodium

TIP

Serve plain oatmeal or any of the variations with one hard-boiled egg (80 calories) and one-half red or pink grapefruit (50 calories) for a satisfying, 205- to 320-calorie start to your day.

APPLE-CINNAMON OATMEAL

Melt **1 tablespoon butter** in medium skillet over medium-high heat. Add **2 peeled, cored, and diced apples**. Reduce heat to medium; cook apples until tender, about 8 minutes, stirring a few times. Stir in **¼ teaspoon ground cinnamon**. Divide apples among servings of oatmeal and sprinkle each bowl with **1 tablespoon brown sugar**.

Each serving: About 190 calories, 3g protein, 37g carbohydrate, 4g total fat (2g saturated), 3g fiber, 59mg sodium

OATMEAL MIX-INS

Oatmeal with snazzy mix-ins have become popular at fast food restaurants. Try re-creating these winning breakfasts at home, with these yummy additions. Prepare 1 cup cooked plain oatmeal (regular, quick, or instant) with water as package label directs and add:

MIX-INS	CALORIES
¼ cup shredded apple and a few pinches of pumpkin-pie spice	182 total calories
½ banana	53 total calories
1 tablespoon dried cranberries and 1 tablespoon chopped walnuts	72 total calories
1 tablespoon sunflower seeds	51 total calories
1 tablespoon honey and ½ teaspoon prepared chai spice blend—or your own combo of cardamom, cinnamon, ginger, cloves, and black pepper	230 total calories

WHOLE-GRAIN BERRY PANCAKES

Raspberry puree is a healthy alternative to maple syrup, and just as delicious.

ACTIVE TIME: 30 minutes **TOTAL TIME:** 40 minutes

MAKES: 4 servings

¼	cup old-fashioned oats
¾	cup low-fat (1%) buttermilk
½	cup white whole wheat flour
1	teaspoon baking powder
¼	teaspoon baking soda
½	teaspoon pumpkin pie spice
⅛	teaspoon salt
1	large egg
1	tablespoon canola oil
2	teaspoons vanilla

Walnuts, for serving

Berries, for serving

Pureed raspberries, for serving

1. Soak oats in buttermilk 20 minutes. In large bowl, whisk flour, baking powder, baking soda, pumpkin pie spice, and salt. Whisk egg, canola oil, and vanilla into oat mixture until just combined.

2. Heat 12-inch nonstick skillet on medium. Working in batches, pour batter by ¼-cupfuls onto hot skillet. Cook until tops are bubbly and edges look dry. Turn; cook until undersides are golden.

3. Serve with walnuts, berries, and pureed raspberries.

Each serving (without toppings): About 155 calories, 6g protein, 19g carbohydrate, 6g total fat (1g saturated), 1g fiber, 268mg sodium

BUTTERMILK PANCAKES WITH OATMEAL AND PECANS

Who doesn't love fluffy hot pancakes with warm maple syrup? To make this down-home favorite healthier, we added oats to the batter and cooked the pancakes in a nonstick skillet brushed with oil.

TOTAL TIME: 25 minutes

MAKES: 8 servings

³/₄	cup (3 ounces) pecans
2	cups low-fat (1%) buttermilk
1¹/₂	cups quick-cooking oats, uncooked
¹/₂	cup all-purpose flour
1	teaspoon baking soda
¹/₂	teaspoon salt
2	large eggs
2	tablespoons confectioners' sugar
2	tablespoons vegetable oil
1	cup maple or maple-flavor syrup
¹/₄	teaspoon ground cinnamon, or to taste

Fresh fruit for garnish (optional)

1. In nonstick 12-inch skillet over medium heat, toast pecans until golden brown. Cool slightly; coarsely chop.

2. In large bowl, combine buttermilk, oats, flour, baking soda, salt, eggs, and 1 tablespoon confectioners' sugar, and stir just until flour is moistened; stir in toasted pecans.

3. Place same skillet over medium until hot; brush lightly with oil. Pour batter by ¹/₄ cups into hot skillet, making 2 or 3 pancakes per batch. Cook until bubbles form on top of pancakes and then burst; edges will look dry. With wide spatula, flip pancakes and cook until undersides are golden. Transfer to platter in low oven to keep warm. Repeat until all batter is used, brushing skillet with more oil as necessary.

4. In small saucepan over medium, heat maple syrup until very warm. In cup, mix cinnamon with remaining 1 tablespoon confectioners' sugar. Sprinkle pancakes with cinnamon-sugar and serve with warm maple syrup and fresh fruit, if desired.

Each serving (2 pancakes): About 330 calories, 8g protein, 50g carbohydrate, 15g total fat (2g saturated), 3g fiber, 388mg sodium

BUCKWHEAT PANCAKES

Buckwheat flour adds a wonderfully nutty flavor to these buttermilk pancakes.

TOTAL TIME: 30 minutes

MAKES: 7 servings

½	cup all-purpose whole wheat flour
½	cup buckwheat flour
1	tablespoon sugar
2	teaspoons baking powder
½	teaspoon baking soda
¼	teaspoon salt
1¼	cups low-fat (1%) buttermilk
3	tablespoons butter, melted and cooled
1	large egg, lightly beaten

Vegetable oil for brushing pan

1. In large bowl, combine both flours, sugar, baking powder and soda, and salt. Add buttermilk, melted butter, and egg; stir just until flour is moistened.

2. Heat griddle or 12-inch skillet over medium-low until drop of water sizzles when sprinkled on hot surface; brush lightly with oil. Pour batter by scant ¼ cups onto hot griddle, making 2 or 3 pancakes per batch. Cook until tops are bubbly and edges look dry, 2 to 3 minutes. With wide spatula, flip pancakes and cook until undersides brown, 2 to 3 minutes longer. Transfer to platter in low oven to keep warm.

3. Repeat with remaining batter, brushing griddle with more oil as necessary.

Each serving: About 150 calories, 5g protein, 17g carbohydrate, 8g total fat (4g saturated), 2g fiber, 412mg sodium

> **TIP**
> It's best to store buckwheat flour in the refrigerator to keep it from going rancid.

THREE-INGREDIENT BANANA PANCAKES

These tasty hotcakes are a cinch to whip up.

TOTAL TIME: 25 minutes
MAKES: 4 servings

2	very ripe large bananas
3	large eggs
¾	cup self-rising flour

Sliced bananas for garnish

1. In blender, puree bananas until smooth. Add eggs; pulse until combined. Pulse in flour until just incorporated.

2. Lightly grease griddle or nonstick 12-inch skillet; heat on medium 1 minute.

3. Drop batter onto hot griddle. Cook pancakes 2 to 3 minutes or until bubbles start to form and edges look dry. With spatula, turn; cook 1 to 2 minutes more until puffy and underside is golden brown (keep warm on cookie sheet in 225°F oven).

4. Serve with sliced bananas.

Each serving: About 200 calories, 8g protein, 33g carbohydrate, 4g total fat (2g saturated), 2g fiber, 335mg sodium

PUFFY APPLE PANCAKES

When you want pancakes, these skillet-browned apples, topped with a light batter and baked, are a great low-calorie option.

TOTAL TIME: 45 minutes

MAKES: 6 servings

2	tablespoons butter
½	cup, plus 2 tablespoons sugar
¼	cup water
6	medium (about 2 pounds) Granny Smith or Newtown Pippin apples, peeled, cored, and each cut into 8 wedges
3	large eggs
¾	cup low-fat (1%) milk
¾	cup all-purpose whole wheat flour
¼	teaspoon salt

1. Preheat oven to 425°F. In 12-inch skillet with oven-safe handle, heat butter, ½ cup sugar, and water to boiling over medium-high heat. Add apple wedges; cook about 15 minutes, stirring occasionally, until apples are golden and sugar mixture begins to caramelize.

2. Meanwhile, in blender on medium speed or in food processor with knife blade attached, blend eggs, milk, flour, salt, and remaining 2 tablespoons sugar until batter is smooth.

3. When apple mixture in skillet is golden and lightly caramelized, pour batter over apples. Place skillet in oven; bake pancake 15 minutes or until puffed and golden. Serve immediately.

Each serving: About 295 calories, 7g protein, 54g carbohydrate, 7g total fat (4g saturated), 4g fiber, 162mg sodium

HEALTHY MAKEOVER FRENCH TOAST

Our slimmed-down take on this Sunday-morning family favorite is practically saintly. Using low-fat milk and egg whites gives it half the fat of traditional French toast. And it's très easy to make!

ACTIVE TIME: 10 minutes   **TOTAL TIME:** 23 minutes
MAKES: 4 servings

2	large egg whites
1	large egg
¾	cup low-fat (1%) milk
¼	teaspoon vanilla extract
2	teaspoons butter
8	slices firm whole-wheat bread

1. Preheat oven to 200°F. In pie plate, with whisk, beat egg whites, egg, milk, and vanilla until blended. In 12-inch nonstick skillet, melt 1 teaspoon butter on medium heat.

2. Dip bread slices, one at a time, in egg mixture, pressing bread lightly to coat both sides well. Place 3 or 4 slices in skillet, and cook 3 to 4 minutes or until lightly browned; flip and cook 3 to 4 minutes on second side.

3. Transfer French toast to cookie sheet; keep warm in oven. Repeat with remaining butter, bread slices, and egg mixture.

Each serving (2 slices): About 300 calories, 12g protein, 46g carbohydrate, 9g total fat (2g saturated), 6g fiber, 460mg sodium

SPICED BANANA-CHOCOLATE MUFFINS

These muffins are a great way to start the day. Or, grab one as an energy-boosting snack!

ACTIVE TIME: 15 minutes
TOTAL TIME: 35 minutes
MAKES: 18 muffins

2	cups old-fashioned oats
1¼	cups whole wheat flour
½	cup brown sugar
2	tablespoons chia seeds
2	teaspoons baking powder
¾	teaspoon baking soda
½	teaspoon salt
½	teaspoon ground cinnamon
¼	teaspoon ground ginger
1¼	cups mashed banana
1	cup low-fat (1%) buttermilk
2	tablespoons vegetable oil
1	large beaten egg
2	ounces bittersweet chocolate (60% to 70% cacao), melted

1. Preheat oven to 400°F. Line 18 muffin-pan cups with paper liners.

2. In a large bowl, whisk oats, flour, sugar, chia seeds, baking powder, baking soda, salt, cinnamon, and ginger. In medium bowl, stir together bananas, buttermilk, oil, and egg. Fold banana mixture into flour mixture. Divide among 18 cups in muffin pan.

3. Bake 20 to 25 minutes or until toothpick inserted into centers of muffins comes out clean. Cool on wire rack 10 minutes. Remove muffins from pan; cool completely on wire rack.

4. Drizzle tops with melted chocolate.

Each serving (2 muffins): About 300 calories, 6g protein, 48g carbohydrate, 8g total fat (2g saturated), 6g fiber, 430 mg sodium

GRAB-AND-GO CRANBERRY GRANOLA BARS

With this simple and delicious DIY granola bar recipe on hand, you won't ever be tempted to skip breakfast again.

ACTIVE TIME: 10 minutes   **TOTAL TIME:** 40 minutes
MAKES: 16 bars

Nonstick cooking spray
2   cups old-fashioned oats
½   cup honey
½   cup vegetable oil
2   tablespoons water
2   large egg whites
2   tablespoons packed light brown sugar
1   teaspoon ground cinnamon
½   teaspoon salt
¾   cup wheat germ, toasted
¾   cup chopped walnuts
¾   cup dried cranberries

1. Preheat oven to 325°F. Spray 13 x 9-inch metal baking pan with nonstick cooking spray. Line pan with foil, leaving 2-inch overhang; spray foil. Spread 2 cups old-fashioned oats on plate; microwave on high, in 1-minute intervals, 4 to 5 minutes or until fragrant and golden, stirring occasionally. Let cool. In large bowl, whisk honey, vegetable oil, water, egg whites, light brown sugar, ground cinnamon, and ½ teaspoon salt until well blended. Fold in oats and toasted wheat germ, chopped walnuts, and dried cranberries; transfer to prepared pan. Using wet hands, press into even layer.

2. Bake 28 to 30 minutes or until golden. Cool in pan on wire rack. Using foil, transfer to cutting board; cut into 16 bars. Store in airtight container at room temperature up to 4 days or freeze up to 1 month.

Each bar: About 215 calories, 5g protein, 25g carbohydrate, 12g total fat (1g saturated), 3g fiber, 80mg sodium

Kale Caesar Pasta Salad *(page 65)*

2 | MAIN-DISH SALADS

Come midday, you need an extra boost of energy. Enter the healthy, hearty salad. Veggie-focused, salads deliver a ton of fuel, especially when topped with lean protein like chicken breast and filling fibers like whole grains and beans. Plus the combination of protein, fiber, and vegetables will keep you feeling full throughout the day and reduce the risk of grazing throughout the afternoon.

The salads in this chapter all contain lots of flat-tummy all-stars—leafy greens, crunchy veggies, lean proteins like chicken, fish, beans, and low-fat dairy. Plus dishes like Balsamic-Roasted Pork with Berry Salad (page 84) include delicious and juicy fruit.

But don't forget the dressing! Plant-based poly- and monounsaturated fats are in olive oil, which is the base for many dressings. These fats can also be found in avocados, nuts, and seeds (all great toppings for a salad) and are important to incorporate in your diet. For more complex flavors, combine healthy oils with vinegars to make tangy, low-calorie dressings. Plus, vinegars have been proven to lower blood sugar and assist in weight loss. Drizzle on!

DIJON BEAN AND VEGGIE SALAD

This easy-to-toss-together salad will keep your calories low and your fiber and satisfaction levels high.

TOTAL TIME: 5 minutes
MAKES: 1 serving

½	cup canned kidney beans, rinsed and drained
½	cup canned garbanzo beans, rinsed and drained
½	cup cucumbers, sliced
½	cup tomatoes, sliced
½	cup carrots, sliced
2	teaspoons extra-virgin olive oil
2	teaspoons cider vinegar
1	teaspoon Dijon mustard
1	garlic clove, minced
¼	teaspoon ground cumin
¼	teaspoon ground black pepper

In medium bowl, combined kidney and garbanzo beans. Add cucumbers, tomatoes, and carrots. Toss with olive oil, cider vinegar, mustard, garlic, cumin, and black pepper.

Each serving: About 345 calories, 14g protein, 47g carbohydrate, 12g total fat (2g saturated), 13g fiber, 495mg sodium

GARBANZO BEAN SALAD

Low in fat and high in protein, beans are a quick, delicious route to a healthy lunch at home.

TOTAL TIME: 5 minutes
MAKES: 3 servings

1	(15-ounce) can garbanzo beans, rinsed and drained
1	red pepper, chopped
1	(15¼-ounce) can corn kernels, drained
⅓	cup cilantro leaves, chopped
2	tablespoons ranch dressing

In medium bowl, combine garbanzo beans, red pepper, corn, cilantro, and ranch dressing. Stir and serve.

Each serving: About 245 calories, 9g protein, 36g carbohydrate, 7g total fat (1g saturated), 8g fiber, 437mg sodium

> **TIP**
> Make this salad a meal by serving it over a bed of greens and topping with ½ cup ripe avocado, cubed. On the side, enjoy an orange.

WARM WILD MUSHROOM AND LENTIL SALAD

This earthy salad gives your meal a French flair.

ACTIVE TIME: 10 minutes   **TOTAL TIME:** 30 minutes
MAKES: 6 servings

1	pound mixed wild mushrooms, sliced
¼	cup olive oil
2	cloves garlic, crushed with press
¼	teaspoon salt
12	ounces lentils, cooked
1	cup parsley
¼	small red onion, very thinly sliced
⅔	cup balsamic vinaigrette

1. Toss mushrooms with olive oil, garlic, and salt. Roast on large baking sheet at 450°F for 20 minutes or until crisp.

2. Toss lentils with mushrooms, parsley, red onion, and balsamic vinaigrette.

Each serving: About 380 calories, 17g protein, 42g carbohydrate, 18g total fat (2g saturated), 16g fiber, 358mg sodium

KALE CAESAR PASTA SALAD

Whip up this slimmer dinner in no time. This easy salad is under 500 calories. (See photograph on page 60.)

ACTIVE TIME: 15 minutes   **TOTAL TIME:** 30 minutes

MAKES: 6 servings

1	pound whole-wheat bowtie pasta
6	tablespoons light mayonnaise
1/3	cup grated Parmesan cheese
3	tablespoons lemon juice
1	tablespoon Dijon mustard
1	tablespoon extra-virgin olive oil
1	clove garlic, crushed with press
1/2	teaspoon salt
1/2	teaspoon pepper
1	large bunch of kale, stemmed and chopped
8	medium radishes, cut into quarters

1. Cook pasta as label directs.

2. In a large bowl, whisk together the mayonnaise, Parmesan, lemon juice, Dijon, olive oil, garlic, salt, and pepper. Add kale, tossing to combine.

3. While cooked pasta is still hot, add to the kale mixture. Let cool slightly. Stir in the radishes and serve.

Each serving: About 370 calories, 14g protein, 61g carbohydrate, 10g total fat (2g saturated), 7g fiber, 422mg sodium

ROASTED WINTER VEGGIE SALAD

Acorn squash and chickpeas are the super-carb stars of this great vegetarian dish.

ACTIVE TIME: 25 minutes   **TOTAL TIME:** 45 minutes
MAKES: 4 servings

1	medium acorn squash
1	medium red pepper
1	medium red onion
$\frac{1}{2}$	teaspoon cayenne pepper
5	tablespoons olive oil
$\frac{1}{2}$	teaspoon salt
8	ounces small shiitake mushrooms
$\frac{1}{4}$	cup lemon juice
1	tablespoon Dijon mustard
1	large bunch kale
1	(15-ounce) can garbanzo beans
$\frac{1}{2}$	cup salted almonds

1. Preheat oven to 425°F. Cut acorn squash in half lengthwise. With spoon, scrape out seeds, and membrane; discard. Thinly slice the squash.

2. In a large bowl, combine squash, red pepper, onion, cayenne, 2 tablespoons oil, and ¼ teaspoon salt. Arrange in a single layer on 2 large rimmed baking sheets, leaving half of the sheet empty. Roast 10 minutes, stirring once.

3. Meanwhile, in the same bowl, toss mushrooms with 2 tablespoons oil. Arrange in a single layer in empty side of the pan in oven. Roast vegetables together 15 to 20 minutes or until mushrooms are crisp and squash is tender, stirring once.

4. In a very large bowl, whisk lemon juice, mustard, remaining 1 tablespoon oil, and ¼ teaspoon salt. Add kale, garbanzo beans, and almonds, tossing until well coated. Add all roasted vegetables except squash to bowl, tossing. To serve place squash on top of the salad.

Each serving: About 455 calories, 14g protein, 42g carbohydrate, 29g total fat (3g saturated), 12g fiber, 600mg sodium

CURRIED CHICKEN WITH MANGO-CANTALOUPE SLAW

A sprightly slaw adds color and crunch to grilled chicken.

ACTIVE TIME: 25 minutes   **TOTAL TIME:** 35 minutes plus marinating
MAKES: 4 servings

3	limes
1	(6-ounce) container plain, unsweetened Greek yogurt
1	teaspoon curry powder
1	teaspoon fresh ginger, peeled and grated
1	teaspoon salt
1/4	teaspoon crushed red pepper
4	medium (1¼-pound) skinless, boneless chicken-breast halves
2	cups cantaloupe, rind removed, cut into 2 x ¼-inch matchstick strips
2	cups mango, peeled and cut into 2 x ¼-inch matchstick strips
1/2	cup loosely packed fresh cilantro leaves, chopped
1	head Boston lettuce

1. From 1 or 2 limes, grate ½ teaspoon peel and squeeze 2 tablespoons juice. In large bowl, with wire whisk, whisk 1 tablespoon lime juice and ¼ teaspoon lime peel with yogurt, curry powder, ginger, ¾ teaspoon salt, and ⅛ teaspoon crushed red pepper. Add chicken, turning to coat with marinade. Cover and let stand 15 minutes at room temperature or 30 minutes in refrigerator, turning occasionally.

2. Meanwhile, prepare slaw: In medium bowl, with rubber spatula, gently stir cantaloupe and mango with cilantro, 1 tablespoon lime juice, ¼ teaspoon lime peel, ¼ teaspoon salt, and ⅛ teaspoon crushed red pepper; set aside. Makes about 4 cups.

3. Prepare outdoor grill for direct grilling over medium heat. Grease grill rack. Remove chicken from marinade; discard marinade. Place chicken on hot rack. Cover and grill, 10 to 12 minutes, turning once, until instant-read thermometer registers 165°F. Transfer chicken to cutting board; cool slightly, then cut into long thin slices. Cut remaining lime into wedges.

4. To serve, arrange lettuce leaves on dinner plates; top with chicken and slaw. Garnish with lime wedges.

Each serving chicken with ½ cup slaw: About 225 calories, 32g protein, 14g carbohydrate, 5g total fat (2g saturated), 2g fiber, 331mg sodium

HONEY-MUSTARD CHICKEN SALAD

This simple, tasty salad is great for lunch or a light dinner.

TOTAL TIME: 5 minutes
MAKES: 1 serving

3	cups mixed greens
½	cup sweet onion, sliced
½	cup cucumbers, sliced
½	cup carrots, shredded
½	cup grape tomatoes
2	tablespoons reduced-fat Cheddar or Monterey Jack, shredded
2	tablespoons honey-mustard dressing
1	cup boneless skinless chicken breast, chopped or sliced

Toss greens with vegetables and top with dressing, chicken, and cheese.

Each serving: About 500 calories, 52g protein, 26g carbohydrate, 21g total fat (5g saturated), 5g fiber, 396mg sodium

BUY PREPREPPED PRODUCE

With already peeled, cut, and washed fruit and veggies on hand, you'll be less likely to turn to unhealthy choices. While they cost more than whole produce, they're hassle-free and time-saving.

PREWASHED SALAD GREENS: It's easy to eat salads more often when all you have to do is dump and dress. Look for darker greens and mixed greens, which pack more nutrition per bite.

PRECUT FRUIT: If you're counting on fruit to help you through a sweet craving, it's got to be ready when the need strikes. Be sure to purchase packages without added sugar. Precut fruit can also reduce the chance that you'll buy a whole fruit and forget it in your crisper.

PRECUT SLAW: Talk about versatility in a bag! Look for plain, precut veggie slaw (sans the fatty dressing, of course) and try it sautéed with a little oil for a quick side dish, mix it with veggies for a stir-fry, or use it to bulk up homemade or canned soups.

CHICKEN AND RASPBERRY SALAD

This satisfying, healthful salad features grilled avocado, a buttery counterpart to fresh berries and grilled chicken.

TOTAL TIME: 45 minutes, plus chilling
MAKES: 4 servings

2	tablespoons fresh lemon juice
2	tablespoons plain, unsweetened Greek yogurt
1	tablespoon pure honey
1	teaspoon Dijon mustard

Salt

Pepper

1	teaspoon poppy seeds
1	pound skinless, boneless chicken-breast halves
1½	teaspoon olive oil
1	avocado, cut in half with pit removed
1	pint raspberries
1	(6-ounce) package mixed greens
¼	cup sliced toasted almonds

1. Prepare outdoor grill for direct grilling on medium.

2. In bowl, whisk lemon juice, yogurt, honey, Dijon, and ⅛ teaspoon each salt and pepper. Stir in poppy seeds. Cover; refrigerate dressing up to 1 day.

3. With meat mallet, pound chicken to an even ½-inch thickness. Rub 1 teaspoon oil over chicken; sprinkle with ¼ teaspoon each salt and pepper. Rub cut sides of avocado with remaining ½ teaspoon oil. Place chicken and avocado on grill. Cook chicken 8 to 10 minutes or just until no longer pink, turning once. Grill avocado 3 to 5 minutes or until grill marks appear, turning once. Let both rest 5 minutes. Discard avocado peel; slice. Slice chicken.

4. In bowl, toss raspberries with 1 tablespoon dressing. In large bowl, toss greens with remaining dressing; divide among plates. Top with raspberries, chicken, avocado, and almonds.

Each serving: About 330 calories, 28g protein, 20g carbohydrate, 17g total fat (3g saturated), 9g fiber, 281mg sodium

DIET TRAP:
NOT EATING ENOUGH PRODUCE

Researchers at Pennsylvania State University randomly assigned 97 obese women to two groups. One group was counseled to simply reduce their fat intake, while the other was told to lower the fat and eat more water-rich foods, particularly fruits and vegetables. After one year, all the women had lost weight, but the second group had dropped 3.3 more pounds on average, with a total average loss of 17 pounds.

The difference: Produce-aisle foods are fiber-packed and filling and they're also low-cal. Plus, the second group focused on what they *could* eat as opposed to what they needed to avoid.

SPINACH AND STRAWBERRY SALAD

Chicken and walnuts boost this salad into the entrée category.

TOTAL TIME: 10 minutes
MAKES: 6 servings

1	pound strawberries
3	tablespoons lime juice
2	teaspoons honey
1	teaspoon extra-virgin olive oil

Salt

Pepper

1	(5-ounce) container baby spinach
10	ounces cooked skinless chicken breast, sliced or shredded
¾	cup walnuts

1. In blender, puree ¾ cup strawberries with lime juice, honey, oil, ¼ teaspoon salt, and ⅛ teaspoon freshly ground black pepper. Transfer dressing to large serving bowl.

2. To bowl with dressing, add spinach, chicken, and remaining strawberries; toss to coat. Sprinkle salad with walnuts to serve.

Each serving: About 220 calories, 18g protein, 11g carbohydrate, 13g total fat (1g saturated), 3g fiber, 140mg sodium

STOP THE CART FOR SPINACH

Spinach nutritionally outscores even the much-praised broccoli with its long list of vitamins and minerals. This leafy wonder is also one of the richest sources of lutein, a plant chemical that protects against age-related blindness. It's convenient, too: Just open a bag of prewashed spinach for salads or sandwiches. Or pop it right in the microwave for two to three minutes for a convenient side dish. To economize, cook a package of frozen spinach, which is just as nutritious.

AUTUMN SQUASH SALAD

Roast two pears and cut into chunks for a sweet addition.

ACTIVE TIME: 10 minutes   **TOTAL TIME:** 50 minutes
MAKES: 4 servings

2	(20-ounce) containers chopped butternut squash
1	pound skinless, boneless chicken thighs
1	tablespoon olive oil
½	teaspoon salt
½	teaspoon pepper
1	(5-ounce) container mixed greens
3	tablespoons lemon juice
1	ounce goat cheese, crumbled

On 2 large rimmed baking sheets, toss butternut squash and chicken thighs with oil and salt and pepper. Bake at 425°F 40 minutes or until squash is tender. Chop chicken; toss with squash, mixed greens, lemon juice, and goat cheese. Season with salt and pepper to taste.

Each serving: About 325 calories, 24g protein, 35g carbohydrate, 12g total fat (3g saturated), 6g fiber, 376mg sodium

PASTA SALAD WITH CHICKEN AND MIXED VEGGIES

This is a great recipe for using frozen vegetables.

ACTIVE TIME: 10 minutes   **TOTAL TIME:** 25 minutes

MAKES: 1 serving

3	ounces cooked skinless chicken breast, cubed
½	cup thawed frozen mixed vegetables
½	cups chopped cherry tomatoes
¼	cup garbanzo beans
1	cup cooked whole-wheat rotini
1	teaspoon extra-virgin olive oil
1	teaspoon red wine vinegar
Salt	
Pepper	

Combine chicken, mixed vegetables, tomatoes, and garbanzo beans with rotini. Toss with olive oil, vinegar, and salt and pepper to taste.

Each serving: About 430 calories, 37g protein, 47g carbohydrate, 11g total fat (2g saturated), 9g fiber, 295mg sodium

WALDORF SALAD

Pick up a rotisserie chicken and some broccoli slaw at the grocery store and you've got this salad practically made!

TOTAL TIME: 5 minutes
MAKES: 1 serving

1½	cups broccoli slaw
1	cup chopped or shredded skinless, boneless, white breast meat or ¾ cup dark meat from a rotisserie chicken
1	cup chopped Granny Smith apple
¼	cup halved seedless grapes
1	tablespoon chopped walnuts
1	tablespoon crumbled blue cheese
3	tablespoons plain, unsweetened Greek yogurt
1	tablespoon lemon juice
⅛	teaspoon ground black pepper
2	cups mixed greens

Combine slaw, chicken, apple, grapes, walnuts, and blue cheese. Stir in yogurt, lemon juice, and pepper. Serve over mixed greens.

Each serving: About 465 calories, 52g protein, 36g carbohydrate, 14g total fat (4g saturated), 8g fiber, 607mg sodium

MEDITERRANEAN COUSCOUS

Here's another recipe that's super-fast when you start with a rotisserie chicken.

TOTAL TIME: 5 minutes
MAKES: 1 serving

³/₄	cup cooked whole-wheat couscous
¹/₂	cup low-sodium cannellini beans, rinsed and drained
¹/₄	cup chopped red onion
¹/₂	cup halved grape tomatoes
¹/₂	cup chopped or shredded skinless, boneless white breast meat (or ¹/₃ cup dark meat) from a rotisserie chicken
3	tablespoons lemon juice
1	teaspoon extra-virgin olive oil
2	tablespoons chopped fresh basil
2	tablespoons crumbed feta cheese

Ground black pepper
Sea salt

Combine couscous with beans, onion, tomatoes, and chicken. Drizzle with lemon juice and olive oil, and sprinkle basil and feta cheese on top. Season with pepper and a sprinkle of sea salt.

Each serving: About 500 calories, 39g protein, 82g carbohydrate, 8g total fat (3g saturated), 15g fiber, 325mg sodium

CHICKEN AND RICE SALAD

Put leftover brown rice from dinner to work at lunch the next day.

TOTAL TIME: 5 minutes
MAKES: 1 serving

1/2	cup cooked brown rice
3/4	cup diced cooked chicken breast
1/3	cup shredded carrots
1/2	cup chopped broccoli
1	teaspoon sesame oil
2	tablespoons lemon juice
1	garlic clove, minced
2	teaspoons low-sodium soy sauce

Combine rice, chicken, carrots, and broccoli. Toss with sesame oil, lemon juice, garlic, and soy sauce.

Each serving: About 330 calories, 35g protein, 30g carbohydrate, 9g total fat (2g saturated), 3g fiber, 452mg sodium

EASY CHICKEN PANZANELLA SALAD

If you like, substitute a rotisserie chicken for the cooked breasts.

ACTIVE TIME: 10 minutes   **TOTAL TIME:** 30 minutes

MAKES: 4 servings

1	large leek, chopped
1	(8-ounce) loaf rustic whole-wheat bread, torn into chunks
3½	tablespoons extra-virgin olive oil
2	tablespoons lemon juice
2	tablespoons grainy mustard
Kosher salt	
3	large ripe tomatoes, chopped
4	cups shredded cooked chicken breast
½	cup fresh parsley

1. On large rimmed baking sheet, toss leeks, bread, and 2½ tablespoons olive oil. Bake in 450°F oven 15 minutes or until bread is toasted and leeks are golden.

2. In large bowl, whisk lemon juice, grainy mustard, remaining olive oil, and salt to taste. Add tomatoes; toss. Add chicken, parsley, toasted bread, and leeks. Toss to combine.

Each serving: About 525 calories, 51g protein, 39g carbohydrate, 19g total fat (3g saturated), 5g fiber, 519mg sodium

WATERCRESS AND PEACH SALAD WITH TURKEY

The addition of deli turkey (or ham, if you prefer) transforms this fresh and colorful summer salad into a meal.

TOTAL TIME: 20 minutes, plus marinating
MAKES: 4 servings

3	limes
$1/2$	teaspoon Dijon mustard
2	tablespoons extra-virgin olive oil
$1/2$	teaspoon salt
$1/4$	teaspoon coarsely ground black pepper
4	(2 pounds) ripe large peaches, peeled, pitted, and cut into wedges
2	(8-ounce) bunches watercress, tough stems discarded
8	ounces sliced deli turkey, cut crosswise into $1/4$-inch strips

1. From limes, grate $1/2$ teaspoon peel and squeeze 3 tablespoons juice.

2. In medium bowl, with wire whisk, mix $1/4$ teaspoon lime peel and 2 tablespoons lime juice with mustard, 1 tablespoon oil, $1/4$ teaspoon salt, and $1/8$ teaspoon pepper. Gently stir in peaches; let stand 15 minutes.

3. Just before serving, in large bowl, toss watercress and turkey with remaining $1/4$ teaspoon lime peel, 1 tablespoon lime juice, 1 tablespoon oil, $1/4$ teaspoon salt, and $1/8$ teaspoon pepper. Transfer watercress mixture to platter; top with peach mixture.

Each serving: About 205 calories, 20g protein, |17g carbohydrate, 7g total fat (1g saturated), 3g fiber, 360mg sodium

SMOKED TURKEY SALAD WITH BLUEBERRIES

Blueberries make an unusual, but delicious partner for the tomatoes and smoked turkey in this red, white, and blue salad.

ACTIVE TIME: 10 minutes   **TOTAL TIME:** 40 minutes
MAKES: 4 servings

2	green onions
1	small head Boston lettuce
1	piece smoked turkey (about 1 pound dark turkey meat)
2	medium ripe tomatoes
1	cup fresh blueberries

Lime slices (optional)
Balsamic vinegar or prepared salad dressing (optional)

1. At least 30 minutes before assembling salad, cut green onions lengthwise into thin strips. Cut strips across into 3-inch lengths. Drop in small bowl of ice water and refrigerate 15 minutes to curl.

2. Divide lettuce among 4 chilled plates. Arrange smoked turkey, tomatoes, blueberries, and drained green onion curls on lettuce. If desired, cut lime slices crosswise to within ¼ inch of edge and twist for garnish. Pass balsamic vinegar or prepared salad dressing to serve on salad, if desired.

Each serving (without dressing): About 218 calories, 35g protein, 9g carbohydrate, 4g total fat (2g saturated), 2g fiber, 83mg sodium

BALSAMIC-ROASTED PORK WITH BERRY SALAD

Satisfying and slimming, this salad pairs roasted pork tenderloin with potassium-rich produce—including strawberries, blackberries, and baby spinach—which helps keep blood pressure in check. Bonus: The berries' vitamin C assists in warding off wrinkles. Toss with a no-fuss mustard vinaigrette that whisks together in seconds.

ACTIVE TIME: 25 minutes   **TOTAL TIME:** 35 minutes
MAKES: 4 servings

4	tablespoons balsamic vinegar
2	tablespoons extra-virgin olive oil
3	teaspoons Dijon mustard
2	teaspoons packed fresh oregano leaves
2	bulbs fennel, each cut into ¼-inch-thick slices
1	small red onion
1	pork tenderloin (about 1 pound)
Salt	
Pepper	
1	pound strawberries
¼	cup packed fresh basil leaves
1	(5-ounce) package prewashed baby spinach
½	pint blackberries

1. Preheat oven to 450°F.

2. In large bowl, with wire whisk, stir together 3 tablespoons balsamic vinegar, 1 tablespoon oil, 2 teaspoons mustard, and oregano. Add fennel, tossing until well coated. Arrange on outer edges of 18 x 12-inch jelly-roll pan. To same bowl, add onions, tossing until well coated. Arrange onions in center of pan. Add pork to same bowl and toss until coated; place on top of onions.

3. Sprinkle pork and vegetables with ¼ teaspoon salt and ⅛ teaspoon freshly ground black pepper. Roast 18 to 22 minutes or until meat thermometer inserted in thickest part of pork registers 140°F. Let pork stand 5 minutes.

4. While pork roasts, hull and slice strawberries. Finely chop basil; place in large bowl.

5. In bowl with basil, whisk together remaining 1 tablespoon balsamic vinegar, 1 tablespoon oil, 1 teaspoon mustard, and ⅛ teaspoon salt until well combined. Thinly slice pork. Add fennel, onion, spinach, and strawberries to bowl with dressing, tossing until well mixed. Divide among 4 serving plates. Top with blackberries and pork.

Each serving: About 315 calories, 26g protein, 30g carbohydrate, 1g total fat (2g saturated), 10g fiber, 480mg sodium

THAI BEEF SALAD

This hearty salad makes a great one-dish meal. Steak is marinated in an Asian-style dressing before it's grilled and served on top of a watercress salad tossed with mint, cilantro, radishes, and red onion.

ACTIVE TIME: 30 minutes   **TOTAL TIME:** 40 minutes, plus marinating
MAKES: 4 servings

2	tablespoons sugar-free Asian fish sauce
1	tablespoon zero-calorie sweetener
1	pound beef top round steak, ³/₄ inch thick
2	limes
3	tablespoons vegetable oil
¹/₄	teaspoon crushed red pepper
¹/₄	teaspoon coarsely ground black pepper
2	bunches watercress, tough stems discarded
1	cup loosely packed fresh mint leaves
1	cup loosely packed fresh cilantro leaves
1	bunch radishes, each cut in half and thinly sliced
¹/₂	small red onion, thinly sliced

1. In 8-inch or 9-inch square glass baking dish, stir 1 tablespoon fish sauce and half of sweetener. Add steak, turning to coat; marinate 15 minutes at room temperature or 1 hour in refrigerator, turning occasionally.

2. Prepare outdoor grill for direct grilling over medium heat.

3. Meanwhile, from limes, with vegetable peeler, remove peel in 2 x ³/₄-inch strips. With sharp knife, cut enough peel crosswise into matchstick-thin strips to equal 1 tablespoon. Squeeze limes to yield 3 tablespoons juice. In small bowl, make dressing by whisking lime juice, oil, crushed red pepper, black pepper, and the remaining 1 tablespoon fish sauce and half of sweetener until blended.

4. In large bowl, toss watercress, mint, cilantro, radishes, onion, and lime peel; cover and refrigerate until ready to serve.

5. Place steak on hot grill rack. Cover grill and cook steak 10 to 15 minutes for medium-rare or to desired doneness, turning over once. (Instant-read thermometer inserted horizontally into center of steak should register 145°F.) Transfer steak to cutting board; let stand 10 minutes to set juices for easier slicing. Cut steak diagonally into thin strips.

6. Add steak and dressing to watercress mixture and toss until well coated.

Each serving: About 310 calories, 28g protein, 7g carbohydrate, 23g total fat (4g saturated), 2g fiber, 295mg sodium

TIP

A "secret ingredient" in Southeast Asian cooking, Asian fish sauce is a thin, translucent, salty brown liquid extracted from salted, fermented fish. We suggest using a sugar-free version such as Red Boat Fish Sauce.

SOY-BRAISED BEEF AND TOMATO-MINT SALAD

A slow cooker makes this Asian take on brisket oh so easy.

ACTIVE TIME: 15 minutes **TOTAL TIME:** 6 hours, 15 minutes
MAKES: 6 servings

3	pounds beef brisket, trimmed of excess fat and cut into 1-inch chunks
5	cloves garlic, chopped
¼	cup brown sugar
¼	cup rice vinegar
¼	cup low-sodium soy sauce
3	tablespoons fish sauce
½	teaspoon pepper
1	pint grape tomatoes, cut into halves
1	small red onion
½	cup mint leaves
Brown rice	

1. In 7- to 8-quart slow-cooker bowl, combine beef brisket, garlic, brown sugar, rice vinegar, soy sauce, fish sauce, and pepper.

2. Cook on Low 6 to 8 hours or until tender; toss with grape tomatoes, red onion, and mint leaves. Serve with steamed brown rice.

Each serving: About 225 calories, 26g protein, 10g carbohydrate, 8g total fat (3g saturated), 1g fiber, 553mg sodium

GINGERY STEAK AND CORN SALAD WITH GINGER DIJON VINAIGRETTE

Corn is the secret weapon in this killer salad.

TOTAL TIME: 10 minutes
MAKES: 4 servings

Ginger Dijon Vinaigrette

½ cup toasted sesame oil
½ cup rice vinegar
⅓ cup Dijon mustard
1 tablespoon fresh ginger, peeled and grated
Kosher salt
Black pepper

Salad

1 pound grilled lean cut steak
8 cups baby kale
2 cups sliced cucumbers
2 cups fresh corn kernels

1. Make the Ginger Dijon Vinaigrette: Shake sesame oil, rice vinegar, Dijon, ginger, salt, and pepper.

2. Make the Salad. Drizzle ginger vinaigrette over steak, baby kale, cucumbers, and corn.

Each serving (2 tablespoons dressing per serving): About 395 calories, 29g protein, 19g carbohydrate, 23g total fat (6g saturated), 4g fiber, 306mg sodium

GREEK STEAK SALAD

Grilled, broiled, or sautéed flank steak is the key ingredient in this hearty salad.

TOTAL TIME: 10 minutes
MAKES: 1 serving

1	ounce cubed cooked flank steak
2	cups mixed greens
1/2	cup halved cherry tomatoes
1/2	cup chopped cucumber
2	tablespoons crumbled feta cheese
2	tablespoons olives
2	teaspoons red wine vinegar
2	teaspoons extra-virgin olive oil

Salt and pepper, to taste

1   (4-inch-wide) whole wheat pita

Mix steak, greens, tomatoes, cucumber, cheese, olives, vinegar, oil, salt, and pepper. Serve with pita.

Each serving: About 320 calories, 16g protein, 25g carbohydrate, 19g total fat (5g saturated), 5g fiber, 593mg sodium

STEAK SALAD WITH CHARRED GREEN ONIONS AND BEETS

Sous vide is French for "under vacuum" and hyperskilled chefs use the technique to cook meat or fish to perfection.

ACTIVE TIME: 15 minutes   **TOTAL TIME:** 35 minutes

MAKES: 4 servings

1	pound boneless top loin beefsteak (2 inches thick)
1	tablespoon vegetable oil
1/2	bunch green onions, halved
3/4	teaspoon flaky sea salt
1	(5-ounce) package mixed greens
1/2	small head radicchio, leaves separated and torn
4	cooked beets, quartered
1/4	cup red wine vinegar
1	tablespoon extra-virgin olive oil
1/4	teaspoon pepper
1	ounce blue cheese, crumbled

1. In 8-quart saucepot, set up *sous vide* device as package directs. Add water and set temperature to 130°F on device. Place steak in gallon-size resealable plastic bag; seal tightly, pushing out excess air. Place bag in hot water. Cook 2 hours. Remove bag from water. Remove steak from bag; pat dry.

2. In 10-inch skillet, heat oil on medium-high until very hot. Add green onions; cook 2 minutes or until lightly charred, turning. Add steak to skillet. Cook 2 minutes, turning frequently. Transfer to cutting board; sprinkle with 1/2 teaspoon flaky sea salt and thickly slice.

3. In large bowl, toss greens, radicchio, beets, vinegar, olive oil, 1/4 teaspoon flaky sea salt, and pepper. Transfer to platter. Top with steak, onions, and blue cheese.

Each serving: About 250 calories, 23g protein, 9g carbohydrate, 14g total fat (4g saturated), 2g fiber, 609mg sodium

MEDITERRANEAN TUNA SALAD

This recipe calls for long, sweet, thin-skinned English cucumbers, which don't need to be peeled.

TOTAL TIME: 5 minutes
MAKES: 2 servings

1	English cucumber, cut into ¼-inch chunks
2	(5-ounce) cans flaked chunk light tuna in water, drained
6	pitted Kalamata olives, chopped
2	small tomatoes, chopped
3	tablespoons olive oil vinaigrette
4	cups greens

In a large bowl, combine cucumber, tuna, olives, tomatoes, and vinaigrette. Stir until blended. Serve over greens.

Each serving: About 270 calories, 30g protein, 11g carbohydrate, 15g total fat (2g saturated), 4g fiber, 600mg sodium

HEALTHY MAKEOVER TUNA SALAD

Our lower-fat, lower-calorie version is packed with crunchy, flavorful vegetables and opts for light mayo.

TOTAL TIME: 15 minutes
MAKES: 4 servings

2	(5-ounce) cans of light tuna in water
2	medium stalks celery, chopped
1	medium carrot, chopped
½	medium (4- to 6-ounce) red pepper, chopped
¼	cup light mayonnaise
3	tablespoons plain, unsweetened Greek yogurt
1	tablespoon fresh lemon juice
¼	teaspoon ground black pepper

In medium bowl, combine tuna, celery, carrot, red pepper, mayonnaise, yogurt, lemon juice, and black pepper.

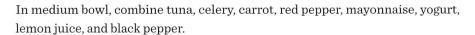

Each serving: About 135 calories, 16g protein, 67g carbohydrate, 6g total fat (1g saturated), 1g fiber, 340mg sodium

NIÇOISE SALAD

Shake up this salad's shallot vinaigrette in a mason jar.

TOTAL TIME: 15 minutes
MAKES: 4 servings

Shallot Vinaigrette

½ cup extra-virgin olive oil
1 tablespoon grainy mustard
3 tablespoons red wine vinegar
3 tablespoons lemon juice
1 medium shallot, finely chopped
1 teaspoon sugar
Kosher salt
Black pepper

Nicoise Salad

2 (5-ounce) cans oil-packed tuna
¼ cup oil-packed olives
4 hard-boiled eggs, quartered
1½ cups cherry tomatoes, halved
6 cups mixed greens

1. Make the Shallot Vinaigrette: Shake olive oil, mustard, vinegar, lemon juice, shallot, sugar, salt, and pepper.

2. Make the Niçoise Salad. Drizzle shallot vinaigrette over tuna, olives, eggs, cherry tomatoes, and mixed greens.

Each serving: About 490 calories, 21g protein, 10g carbohydrate, 43g total fat (8g saturated), 2g fiber, 610mg sodium

LIME TUNA AND BLACK BEAN SALAD

Tuna takes a Southwestern twist in this low-calorie lunch.

TOTAL TIME: 5 minutes
MAKES: 1 serving

3	cups mixed greens
$1/2$	cup sliced cucumbers
$1/2$	cup sliced sweet onion
$1/3$	cup corn
$1/3$	cup canned low-sodium black beans, rinsed and drained
$1/4$	avocado, peeled, pitted, and sliced
1	tablespoon extra-virgin olive oil
$1/2$	tablespoon lime juice
1	(3-ounce) can or pouch tuna

Toss greens with cucumbers, onion, corn, beans and avocado. Whisk together olive oil and lime juice. Toss greens with dressing and top with tuna.

Each serving: About 480 calories, 30g protein, 38g carbohydrate, 19g total fat (3g saturated), 16g fiber, 425mg sodium

SWEET AND SAVORY SALMON SALAD

Give tuna salad a rest and try this other healthful favorite fish, mixed with fruit, and veggies.

TOTAL TIME: 5 minutes
MAKES: 1 serving

3	cups mixed greens
½	cup sliced cucumbers
½	cup sliced strawberries
¼	cup mandarin oranges
2	tablespoons dried cranberries
1	tablespoon sliced almonds
2	tablespoons red wine vinaigrette
1	(3-ounce) can or pouch salmon

Toss greens with cucumber, strawberries, oranges, cranberries, and almonds. Toss with vinaigrette and top with salmon.

Each serving: About 380 calories, 24g protein, 40g carbohydrate, 16g total fat (3g saturated), 6g fiber, 597mg sodium

SCANDINAVIAN SHRIMP SALAD

Enjoy this tart and creamy salad for a special lunch.

TOTAL TIME: 5 minutes

MAKES: 4 servings

1	(13- to 14-ounce) English cucumber, thinly sliced
12	ounces large shrimp, cooked and shelled
1/2	cup low-fat plain, unsweetened Greek yogurt
1/4	teaspoon freshly grated lemon peel
2	tablespoons fresh lemon juice
2	tablespoons chopped fresh dill
1/4	teaspoon ground black pepper

Lettuce

In large bowl, combine cucumber, shrimp, yogurt, lemon peel, and juice, dill, and pepper. Stir to combine. Serve on lettuce.

Each serving: About 115 calories, 18g protein, 6g carbohydrate, 2g total fat (1g saturated), 1g fiber, 665mg sodium

CRAB COBB SALAD

This lightened version of the traditional Cobb salad features lump crab-meat and a luscious but low-calorie yogurt dressing.

TOTAL TIME: 30 minutes
MAKES: 4 servings

1	cup plain low-fat plain, unsweetened Greek yogurt
¼	cup loosely packed fresh chives, snipped
1	tablespoon Dijon mustard
¼	teaspoon salt
¼	teaspoon freshly ground black pepper
2	romaine hearts, torn
8	ounces lump crabmeat
2	large tomatoes, seeded and chopped
1	ripe avocado, pitted, peeled, and chopped

1. In a small bowl, with wire whisk, stir yogurt, chives, Dijon, salt, and pepper until well combined.

2. In a large bowl, toss romaine with half of dressing. In small bowl, gently stir half of remaining dressing into crabmeat.

3. Divide romaine among 4 serving plates. Arrange tomatoes, avocado, and crabmeat in rows over romaine. Spoon remaining dressing over salads and serve.

Each serving: About 200 calories, 19g protein, 12g carbohydrate, 9g total fat (2g saturated), 6g fiber, 473mg sodium

SPEEDY SEED REMOVAL

Seeding and chopping tomatoes and avocados doesn't have to be a slippery business. Just follow these tips and you'll be surprised how easily you can do it.

TOMATO: Halve tomato and gently dig out the seeds with your fingers. Or cut it into quarters, and use a paring knife to slice out the pulp and seeds using a scooping motion. In this method, you'll lose more flesh, but you're also sure to get all the seeds. Chop tomato as recipe directs.

AVOCADO: Cut avocado lengthwise in half, cutting around the seed. Twist the two halves to separate them. To remove the seed, give it a whack with the blade of the knife so it is slightly embedded in the seed; cup the avocado in your hand as you twist and lift the seed out. With your fingers, gently peel away the skin from the avocado and discard. Slice or chop the avocado as recipe directs.

TIP: Avocado flesh darkens quickly when exposed to air; toss with lemon or lime juice to avoid discoloration, or press plastic wrap onto the cut surfaces.

WARM LENTIL SALAD WITH SHRIMP, APPLES, AND MINT

This heart-healthy salad is chock-full of fiber, thanks to crisp Golden Delicious apples and a nutty lentil base.

ACTIVE TIME: 20 minutes   **TOTAL TIME:** 30 minutes
MAKES: 4 servings

3	tablespoons extra-virgin olive oil
3	tablespoons apple cider vinegar
1½	teaspoons salt
¼	teaspoon coarsely ground black pepper
1	pound fresh or frozen medium shrimp, thawed, shelled, and deveined
1	cup lentils, rinsed and picked through
6	cups water
1	small onion, chopped
½	cup loosely packed fresh mint leaves, chopped
1	Golden Delicious apple, cored and cut into ½-inch chunks
1	stalk celery, thinly sliced

1. In small bowl, whisk together oil, vinegar, salt, and pepper. Spoon 2 tablespoons dressing into medium bowl. Add shrimp; toss to coat.

2. In 4-quart saucepan, combine lentils, water, onion, and 2 tablespoons mint; heat to boiling on high. Reduce heat to low; cover and simmer 12 to 15 minutes or until lentils are tender but still hold their shape. Drain well.

3. Meanwhile, heat 12-inch skillet on medium-high until hot. Add shrimp and cook 4 to 5 minutes or until shrimp turn opaque. Remove from heat; stir in 1 tablespoon mint.

4. Stir shrimp, apple, celery, and remaining mint and dressing into lentils.

Each serving: About 410 calories, 37g protein, 37g carbohydrate, 13g total fat (2g saturated), 17g fiber, 475mg sodium

CITRUSY SHRIMP-STUFFED AVOCADOS

This South American fare fuses Chinese, Japanese, and Latin cuisine.

TOTAL TIME: 15 minutes
MAKES: 4 servings

1	small shallot, finely chopped
¼	cup low-fat mayonnaise
3	tablespoons plain, unsweetened Greek yogurt
3	tablespoons lime juice
2	tablespoons orange juice
¼	teaspoon salt
1	pound cooked, shelled shrimp, chopped
1	cup grape tomatoes, halved
1	Serrano chile, thinly sliced
2	ripe avocados, halved, pits removed

Cilantro, for garnish

1. In small bowl, whisk shallots, mayonnaise, yogurt, lime juice, orange juice, and salt.

2. In large bowl, toss shrimp, tomatoes, chile, and half of dressing. Refrigerate 20 minutes or up to 2 hours.

3. To serve, spoon into avocado halves and drizzle with remaining dressing. Garnish with cilantro.

Each serving: About 340 calories, 32g protein, 15g carbohydrate, 18g total fat (2g saturated), 8g fiber, 542mg sodium

FLAT-TUMMY INGREDIENT: GREENS

Salad greens fall into two basic categories: delicate and tender or assertive and slightly bitter. Tender greens, such as lettuce, are served alone or combined with other vegetables. There are four types of lettuce: crisphead varieties are crisp and mild-flavored and stand up well to thicker dressings; butterhead is sweet-tasting and delicate and should be served with an appropriately light-bodied dressing; loose-leaf is tender but has a slightly stronger leafy flavor than butterhead; long-leaf has long, firm, crisp leaves and is another candidate for rich, thick dressings.

Stronger-flavored greens (including members of the chicory family) are usually combined with sweeter lettuces for a well-balanced salad. The mild bitterness of these greens contrasts nicely with the natural sweetness of the lettuces. Greens such as radicchio and Belgian endive are also invaluable as color elements in the salad palette.

Here are the basic characteristics of the different greens to help you make the right choice at the market.

ARUGULA: Peppery arugula is also known as rugula or rocket. The older and larger the leaves, the more assertive the flavor. The leaves can be very gritty, so rinse them thoroughly.

BABY GREENS: Available in bags or in bulk at many supermarkets, this combination of very young, tender salad greens is an Americanization of the French salad mix known as mesclun.

BELGIAN ENDIVE: A member of the chicory family, Belgian endive is appreciated for its crisp texture and slightly bitter flavor. The leaves should be very white, graduating to pale yellow tips.

BIBB LETTUCE: Also called limestone lettuce, it has cup-shaped leaves and is best with mild vinaigrettes.

BOSTON LETTUCE: A loose-leaf lettuce with tender floppy leaves, it is sometimes called butterhead lettuce.

CHICORY: Although chicory is an entire family of mildly bitter greens, Americans use the term to identify a dark green variety with fringed leaves. It is also known as curly endive.

CHINESE CABBAGE: A tightly formed head of white leaves with wide stalks.

DANDELION: Tart greens that make a pungent addition to a salad. Some cooks gather the wild variety in the spring.

ESCAROLE: Sharp-tasting escarole should have curly leaves with firm stems that snap easily.

FRISÉE: A delicate, pale green variety of chicory with curly, almost spiky leaves.

ICEBERG LETTUCE: A lettuce that is best appreciated for its refreshing crisp texture rather than for its mild flavor. Cut out the core before rinsing the leaves.

MÂCHE: Also called lamb's lettuce, this green has a nutty taste and tiny tender leaves. Use within one day; it wilts easily.

MESCLUN: From the Provençal word for "mixture," true mesclun is made up of wild baby greens from the hillsides of southern France, and often includes herbs and edible flowers. Here, it is commonly a mix of sweet lettuces and bitter greens such as arugula, dandelion, frisée, mizuna, oak leaf, mâche, sorrel, and radicchio.

MIZUNA: A small, feathery, delicately flavored green of Japanese origin.

NAPA CABBAGE: Very similar to, and interchangeable with, Chinese cabbage, but shorter and rounder.

OAK LEAF: A variety of Boston lettuce with ruffled leaves. Green oak leaf is uniformly green, whereas red oak leaf has dark red tips.

RADICCHIO: The most common radicchio is round with white-veined, ruby-red leaves. Radicchio di Treviso has long, narrow red leaves that form a tapered head.

RADISH SPROUTS: Innocent-looking sprouts with tiny clover-shaped heads that pack a peppery punch.

ROMAINE: Its long, crisp, dark green leaves and slightly nutty flavor make romaine the preferred lettuce for Caesar salad.

SPINACH: Whether dark green and crinkled or flat, spinach needs to be washed thoroughly to remove all the grit. Baby spinach has very tender edible stems.

WATERCRESS: This green adds crisp texture and a mildly spicy flavor to salads. It is very perishable, so use within one or two days of purchase.

Butternut-Apple Soup (page 114)

3 | SOUPS, STEWS & CHILIS

Researchers have found that people who begin their meal with a broth-based soup can reduce their total calorie intake by a whopping 20 percent. They speculate that it's because a bowl of low-calorie, broth-based soup satisfies hunger—especially soup high in fiber and protein—which helps you feel full.

This chapter is full of comforting soups, stews, and chilis that you can still enjoy while eating for a flat tummy. Brimming with fruits and vegetables that are chock-full of nutrients, along with lean meats that pack a protein punch, the recipes in this chapter will help stave off hunger and help you slim down.

Enjoy Potato and Leek Soup (page 124) on a chilly day or Manhattan Clam Chowder (page 128) when you crave a lighter version of a beloved recipe. If looking for something hearty, consider Pork and Peppers Ragu (page 138). Many of these soups use a blender to whip up a meal. Ladle up Spring Pea Soup (page 118) or Apple and Parsnip Soup (page 111) for a flavorful starter. Plus, if you're pressed for time, consider taking out your slow-cooker for Chipotle Beef Chili (page 132). Perfect for busy workdays, this chili is easy—just pop the ingredients in the pot before you leave, and come home to a fragrant, bloat-busting dinner!

CHILLED TUSCAN-STYLE TOMATO SOUP

The lush summer flavors of Tuscany shine in this refreshing, easy-to-make cold tomato soup. We blend cubes of country bread in with the tomatoes, giving this soup a thicker body and a velvety mouth-feel.

TOTAL TIME: 15 minutes, plus chilling
MAKES: 4 servings

1	teaspoon olive oil
1	clove garlic
2	cups (1-inch cubes) country-style whole-wheat bread
3	pounds ripe tomatoes
¼	cup fresh basil leaves, plus more for garnish
1	teaspoon sugar
½	teaspoon salt

1. In small skillet, heat oil on medium until hot. Add garlic and cook 1 minute, stirring. Remove skillet from heat.

2. In food processor with knife blade attached, pulse bread until coarsely chopped. Add tomatoes and garlic; pulse until soup is almost pureed. Pour soup into bowl; stir in chopped basil, sugar, and salt. Cover and refrigerate until well chilled, at least 2 hours or overnight. Garnish each serving with basil leaves.

Each serving: About 125 calories, 5g protein, 25g carbohydrate, 2g total fat (0g saturated), 5g fiber, 384mg sodium

APPLE AND PARSNIP SOUP

This creamy soup takes delicious advantage of autumn's bounty. The puree is light, yet rich and flavorful with no need for cream.

ACTIVE TIME: 15 minutes   **TOTAL TIME:** 20 minutes

MAKES: 6 servings

1	(32-ounce) package low-sodium chicken broth
2	cups water
1	tablespoon olive oil
1/2	cup shallots, finely chopped
1	stalk celery, finely chopped
2	pounds (4 to 6 medium) McIntosh or Braeburn apples, peeled, cored, and chopped
1	pound parsnips, peeled and chopped
1/4	teaspoon dried thyme
1/2	teaspoon salt
1/4	teaspoon ground black pepper

Roasted, hulled pumpkin seeds for garnish

1. In covered 2-quart saucepan, heat chicken broth and water to boiling over high heat.

2. Meanwhile, in 5- to 6-quart saucepot, heat oil over medium heat. Add shallots and celery, and cook about 5 minutes or until softened and lightly browned. Add apples, parsnips, thyme, salt, and ground black pepper, and cook 1 minute.

3. Add hot broth mixture to saucepot; cover and heat to boiling over high heat. Reduce heat to low and simmer, covered, 6 to 7 minutes or until parsnips are very tender.

4. Spoon one-third of soup into blender; cover, removing center part of lid to let steam escape. Lay a paper towel over top and puree until smooth. Pour puree into bowl. Repeat with remaining mixture. Return to saucepot to reheat. Garnish with pumpkin seeds to serve.

Each serving: About 165 calories, 4g protein, 30g carbohydrate, 4g total fat (1g saturated), 5g fiber, 222mg sodium

TIP
If you have an immersion blender, use it to puree soup right in the pot.

ROASTED-PEPPER YOGURT SOUP

Roasting enhances the sweetness of the red and yellow peppers that combine with the yogurt in this silky smooth spring soup.

ACTIVE TIME: 30 minutes   **TOTAL TIME:** 1 hour, 20 minutes
MAKES: 6 servings

4	large sweet red peppers
2	large sweet yellow peppers
1	tablespoon olive oil
2¼	cups low-fat plain, unsweetened Greek yogurt
1	cup water
2	tablespoons balsamic vinegar
½	teaspoon salt

1. Heat oven to 375°F. Brush peppers with olive oil; place on rimmed baking sheet and roast, turning several times, 25 to 30 minutes or until skins wrinkle and blacken in spots. With tongs, place peppers into brown-paper bag; close bag and set aside 20 minutes. Then peel, halve, and seed roasted peppers.

2. In blender or food processor fitted with chopping blade, puree peppers until smooth. Add 2 cups yogurt, the water, vinegar, and salt; process until well combined.

3. In small bowl, stir remaining ¼ cup yogurt until smooth. Divide soup among 6 serving bowls. Garnish center of each bowl of soup with 2 teaspoons yogurt.

Each serving: About 125 calories, 10g protein, 16g carbohydrate, 3g total fat (1g saturated), 1g fiber, 203mg sodium

MISO SOUP

A light, spicy broth brimming with fresh vegetables and chunks of good-for-you tofu.

ACTIVE TIME: 35 minutes
TOTAL TIME: 55 minutes
MAKES: 6 servings

1	tablespoon vegetable oil
2	large carrots
2	cloves garlic
1	small onion
1	tablespoon ginger, peeled and grated
$\frac{1}{2}$	small head Napa cabbage, cut crosswise into slices
1	tablespoon seasoned rice vinegar
$\frac{1}{4}$	teaspoon coarsely ground black pepper
6	cups water
1	package firm tofu
$\frac{1}{4}$	cup red miso
2	green onions

1. In 5-quart Dutch oven, heat oil over medium heat. Add carrots, garlic, onion, and ginger and cook, stirring occasionally, about 10 minutes or until onions are lightly browned.

2. Add cabbage, vinegar, pepper, and water; heat to boiling over high heat. Reduce heat to low; cover and simmer 20 minutes or until vegetables are tender.

3. Stir in tofu and miso; heat through, about 2 minutes. Sprinkle with green onions to serve.

Each serving: About 130 calories, 9g protein, 11g carbohydrate, 6g total fat (1g saturated), 3g fiber, 594mg sodium

> **TIP**
> Miso comes in a variety of flavors, colors, and textures that fall into three basic categories: red, which has a strong flavor; golden, which is mild; and white, which is mellow and slightly sweet. Miso can be purchased in health food stores and Oriental markets.

BUTTERNUT-APPLE SOUP

Nothing can match a pureed vegetable and cream soup for texture and this subtly sweet combination of squash and apples just proves the point. (See photograph on page 108.)

ACTIVE TIME: 15 minutes   **TOTAL TIME:** 1 hour
MAKES: 8 servings

2	tablespoons vegetable oil
1	small onion, chopped
2	medium (1³/₄ pounds each) butternut squash, peeled, seeded, and cut into ³/₄-inch pieces
³/₄	pound (2 medium) Golden Delicious apples, peeled, cored, and coarsely chopped
1	(14¹/₂ ounce) can low-sodium vegetable broth
1¹/₂	cups water
1	teaspoon freshly chopped fresh thyme or ¹/₄ teaspoon dried thyme
1	teaspoon salt
¹/₈	teaspoon coarsely ground black pepper
1	cup half-and-half or light cream

1. In 4-quart saucepan, heat oil over medium heat. Add onion and cook until tender and golden, about 10 minutes. Stir in squash, apples, broth, water, thyme, salt, and pepper; heat to boiling over high heat. Reduce heat to low; cover and simmer, stirring often, until squash is very tender, 20 to 25 minutes.

2. Spoon one-third of squash mixture into blender; cover, with center part of cover removed to let steam escape, and puree until smooth. Pour puree into bowl. Repeat with remaining mixture.

3. Return puree to saucepan; stir in half-and-half. Heat through over medium heat, stirring occasionally (do not boil).

Each serving: About 165 calories, 3g protein, 27g carbohydrate, 7g total fat (2g saturated), 4g fiber, 301mg sodium

CHILLED CUCUMBER SOUP

Greek yogurt is the luscious, creamy secret behind this simple chilled cucumber soup recipe.

TOTAL TIME: 10 minutes

MAKES: 4 servings

1¼	pound seedless cucumbers
1	cup low-fat plain, unsweetened Greek yogurt
4	cups ice cubes
½	teaspoon salt
1	tablespoon chopped fresh dill
1	tablespoon fresh lemon juice
12	large cooked shrimp, shelled

1. In blender, puree cucumbers, yogurt, ice cubes, and salt until very smooth.

2. Stir in dill and lemon juice. Divide among 4 bowls and top each with 3 large shelled cooked shrimp.

Each serving: About 80 calories, 11g protein, 6g carbohydrate, 1g total fat (0g saturated), 2g fiber, 425mg sodium

HONEYDEW AND LIME SOUP

This chilled soup starts a summer meal off with a refreshing mix of surprising flavors. Choose a melon that is fully ripe for a smooth consistency.

TOTAL TIME: 10 minutes, plus chilling

MAKES: 6 servings

1	(5-pound) honeydew melon, chilled, cut into 1-inch chunks (about 8 cups)
¼	cup fresh lime juice
¼	cup loosely packed fresh cilantro leaves
1	teaspoon jalapeño hot sauce
⅛	teaspoon salt

In blender, pulse melon with lime juice, cilantro, hot sauce, and salt until pureed. Transfer soup to large bowl or pitcher; cover and refrigerate 2 hours or until chilled. Stir before serving.

Each serving: About 85 calories, 1g protein, 23g carbohydrate, 0g total fat (0g saturated), 2g fiber, 80mg sodium

SWEET BEET SOUP

Tart Granny Smith apples brighten up this sweet and savory soup.

ACTIVE TIME: 15 minutes   **TOTAL TIME:** 40 minutes
MAKES: 4 servings

1	tablespoon olive oil
1	medium onion, thinly sliced
½	teaspoon plus a pinch of salt
1	pound cooked beets, refrigerated
1	Granny Smith apple, peeled, cored, and chopped
2	cups lower-sodium vegetable or chicken broth

Plain, unsweetened Greek yogurt, for garnish
Dill, for garnish

1. In 10-inch skillet, heat oil on medium-high. Add onion and a pinch of salt. Cook 5 minutes or until browned and starting to soften, stirring frequently. Let cool.

2. To blender, add beets, apple, broth, onion, and ½ teaspoon salt. Blend until smooth. Refrigerate until cold about 3 hours. To serve, garnish with yogurt and dill.

Each serving: About 130 calories, 3g protein, 22g carbohydrate, 4g total fat (1g saturated), 3g fiber, 531mg sodium

SPRING PEA SOUP

As bright and green as the season, this soup has a fresh flavor that complements any celebratory meal. If you can't find edible flowers, garnish with pea shoots or a sprig of mint.

ACTIVE TIME: 12 minutes **TOTAL TIME:** 45 minutes
MAKES: 10 servings

2	tablespoons butter
³/₄	cup shallots, thinly sliced
1	(32 ounce) carton low-sodium chicken broth
2	cups water
2	(16-ounce) bags frozen peas, thawed
1	(8-ounce) large all-purpose potato, peeled and cut into 1-inch chunks
¹/₂	cup loosely packed fresh mint leaves, chopped
³/₄	teaspoon salt
¹/₄	teaspoon ground black pepper
3	tablespoons fresh lemon juice
10	nasturtium edible flowers for garnish (optional)

1. In 4-quart saucepan, heat butter on medium-low until melted. Add shallots and cook 10 to 12 minutes or until very tender.

2. Add broth, water, peas, potato, half of chopped mint, salt, and pepper; heat to boiling on high. Reduce heat to medium; simmer mixture 10 minutes, stirring occasionally.

3. Spoon half of mixture into blender; cover, removing center part of lid to let steam escape. Lay a paper towel on top and puree until smooth. Pour puree into medium bowl. Repeat with remaining mixture. Return soup to saucepan, and reheat on medium if necessary. Stir in lemon juice and remaining mint.

4. To serve, spoon soup into 10 serving bowls; garnish with nasturtiums, if using.

Each serving: About 120 calories, 6g protein, 19g carbohydrate, 3g total fat (1g saturated), 5g fiber, 475mg sodium

TIP
Nasturtiums and other edible flowers can be found in the produce section of better supermarkets and at farmers' markets.

SWEET POTATO SOUP

Sweet potatoes, loaded with vitamin A in the form of beta-carotene, form the base of this hearty, vivid orange soup. Avocado adds healthy, skin-softening fats, which also aid the body's absorption of beta-carotene.

ACTIVE TIME: 25 minutes **TOTAL TIME:** 45 minutes
MAKES: 6 servings

2	tablespoons olive oil
1	onion, finely chopped
1	red pepper, finely chopped
3	garlic cloves, finely chopped
1½	teaspoons ground cumin
½	teaspoon smoked paprika
¼	teaspoon ground cinnamon
1	teaspoon salt
1	(32-ounce) carton low-sodium vegetable broth
2	pounds sweet potatoes, peeled and cut into ½-inch chunks
2	(15-ounce) cans low-sodium black beans, rinsed and drained
2	cups water
¼	teaspoon ground black pepper
1	Hass avocado, thinly sliced
¼	cup packed fresh cilantro leaves
1	lime, cut into wedges

1. In 5- to 6-quart saucepot, heat oil on medium. Add onion and red pepper; cook 5 minutes, stirring. Stir in garlic, cumin, paprika, cinnamon, and ½ teaspoon salt. Cook 2 minutes, stirring.

2. Add broth, sweet potatoes, beans, water, and black pepper. Heat to boiling on high. Reduce heat to medium; simmer 15 minutes.

3. Transfer 3 cups of soup to blender. Puree until smooth; return to pot. Stir in remaining ½ teaspoon salt. Serve, garnished with avocado, cilantro, and lime wedges.

Each serving: About 330 calories, 11g protein, 53g carbohydrate, 8g total fat (1g saturated), 13g fiber, 600mg sodium

BLACK BEAN SOUP

A 15-ounce can of black beans is the start of this delicious lunch or light dinner.

ACTIVE TIME: 10 minutes   **TOTAL TIME:** 20 minutes
MAKES: 6 servings

1	cup salsa

Pinch of allspice

2	(15-ounce) cans low-sodium black beans
3	cups low-sodium chicken broth
1	cup plain, unsweetened Greek yogurt

In large nonstick saucepan, combine salsa and allspice and cook over medium heat for 3 minutes. Stir in drained and rinsed black beans and chicken broth; raise heat to medium-high and bring to boil. Reduce heat and simmer 10 minutes. Use immersion blender or potato masher to coarsely mash beans in the pot. Top with a dollop of Greek yogurt.

Each serving: About 200 calories, 15g protein, 29g carbohydrate, 3g total fat (1g saturated), 11g fiber, 489mg sodium

QUICK CREAM OF BROCCOLI SOUP

Frozen vegetables are picked and processed so quickly they often retain more nutrients than fresh ones. Many frozen vegetables are easily transformed into a satisfying soup. If broccoli is not one of your favorites, try one of the variations.

ACTIVE TIME: 5 minutes   **TOTAL TIME:** 20 minutes
MAKES: 4 servings

1	tablespoon butter
1	medium onion, chopped
1	(10-ounce) package frozen chopped broccoli
1	(14½-ounce) can low-sodium chicken broth
¼	teaspoon dried thyme
⅛	teaspoon salt
⅛	teaspoon ground black pepper

Pinch of ground nutmeg
Pinch of cayenne pepper (optional)

1½	cups low-fat (1%) milk
2	teaspoons fresh lemon juice

1. In 3-quart saucepan, melt butter over medium heat. Add onion and cook, stirring occasionally, until tender, about 5 minutes. Add frozen broccoli, broth, thyme, salt, pepper, nutmeg, and cayenne, if using; heat to boiling over high heat. Reduce heat and simmer 10 minutes.

2. Spoon half of mixture into blender; cover, with center part of cover removed to let steam escape, and puree until smooth. Pour into bowl. Repeat with remaining mixture.

3. Return puree to saucepan; stir in milk. Heat through, stirring often (do not boil). Remove from heat and stir in lemon juice.

Each serving: About 110 calories, 7g protein, 12g carbohydrate, 5g total fat (3g saturated), 3g fiber, 174mg sodium

VEGETABLE VARIATIONS

QUICK CREAM OF CORN SOUP

Prepare as directed (page 122) but substitute **1 (10-ounce) package frozen whole-kernel corn** for broccoli; if you like, add ¾ **teaspoon chili powder** after cooking onion and cook 30 seconds before adding broth.

QUICK CREAM OF PEA SOUP

Prepare as directed (page 122) but substitute **1 (10-ounce) package frozen peas** for broccoli; if you like, add ¼ **teaspoon dried mint leaves** with broth.

QUICK CREAM OF ASPARAGUS SOUP

Prepare as directed (page 122) but substitute **1 (10-ounce) package frozen asparagus** for broccoli; if you like, add ¼ **teaspoon dried tarragon** with broth.

POTATO AND LEEK SOUP

By cutting out the heavy cream that is traditionally in this recipe, we reduced both the total fat and saturated fat by 4 grams each.

ACTIVE TIME: 15 minutes   **TOTAL TIME:** 45 minutes
MAKES: 6 servings

1½	pounds (3 large) leeks
1	tablespoon olive oil
1	tablespoon butter
12	ounces all-purpose potatoes, peeled and cut into ½-inch pieces
2	(14- to 14½-ounce) cans low-sodium chicken broth
1	sprig, plus 1 tablespoon chopped fresh dill for garnish
½	teaspoon salt
⅛	teaspoon ground black pepper
1	cup low-fat (1%) milk
2	teaspoons fresh lemon juice

1. Cut off roots and trim dark green tops from leeks. Discard any tough outer leaves. Cut each leek lengthwise in half, then crosswise into ¼-inch-wide slices. Rinse leeks thoroughly in large bowl of cold water, swishing to remove sand. Transfer leeks by hand to colander to drain. Repeat process, changing water several times, until all sand is removed.

2. In 4-quart saucepan, heat oil and butter on medium until butter melts. Add leeks and cook 8 to 10 minutes or until tender, stirring occasionally. Stir in potatoes, broth, dill sprig, salt, and pepper. Cover and heat to boiling on high. Reduce heat to low; simmer 15 minutes or until potatoes are very tender.

3. Ladle potato mixture into blender in 3 batches; cover, removing center part of lid to let steam escape. Lay a paper towel on top and puree until smooth. Pour each batch of puree into bowl. Return to same saucepan and stir in milk; heat through. Stir in lemon juice and serve, garnishing with chopped dill.

Each serving: About 150 calories, 6g protein, 21g carbohydrate, 6g total fat (2g saturated), 2g fiber, 250mg sodium

GAZPACHO WITH CILANTRO CREAM

Recipes for this full-flavored, uncooked tomato-based soup abound. Ours is topped with a dollop of cilantro-spiked Greek yogurt, a tasty combination.

TOTAL TIME: 30 minutes, plus chilling

MAKES: 4 servings

2	(8-ounce) medium cucumbers, peeled
1	yellow pepper
¼	small red onion
2	pounds (5 medium) ripe tomatoes, peeled, seeded, and chopped
½	to 1 small jalapeño chile, seeded
3	tablespoons fresh lime juice
2	tablespoons extra-virgin olive oil
¾	plus ⅛ teaspoon salt
¼	cup plain, unsweetened Greek yogurt
1	tablespoon low-fat (1%) milk
4	teaspoons chopped fresh cilantro

1. Chop half of 1 cucumber, half of yellow pepper, and all of onion into ¼-inch pieces; set aside. Cut remaining cucumbers and yellow pepper into large pieces.

2. In blender or in food processor with knife blade attached, puree large pieces of cucumber and yellow pepper, tomatoes, jalapeño, lime juice, oil, and ¾ teaspoon salt until smooth. Pour puree into bowl; add cut-up cucumber, yellow pepper, and onion. Cover and refrigerate until well chilled, at least 6 hours or up to overnight.

3. Prepare cilantro cream: In small bowl, stir yogurt, milk, cilantro, and remaining ⅛ teaspoon salt until smooth. Cover and refrigerate.

4. To serve, top soup with dollops of cilantro cream.

Each serving: About 140 calories, 4g protein, 14g carbohydrate, 8g total fat (1g saturated), 2g fiber, 450mg sodium

INDIAN LENTIL STEW WITH SWEET POTATOES AND SPINACH

We love the warm flavor that garam masala brings to our lentil stew. This essential component of Indian and other South Asian cuisines is a sweet aromatic blend of dry-roasted ground spices that may include coriander, green and black cardamom, cinnamon, cloves, bay leaves, nutmeg or mace, ginger, black pepper, and cumin.

ACTIVE TIME: 25 minutes **TOTAL TIME:** 1 hour
MAKES: 6 servings

1½	cups brown basmati rice
1	tablespoon vegetable oil
1	large onion, chopped
2	tablespoons fresh ginger, peeled and minced
1½	teaspoons garam masala
1	garlic clove, chopped
4	cups water
2	cups green lentils, picked over and rinsed
1	pound sweet potatoes, peeled and cut into ½-inch chunks
1	(14½-ounce) can diced tomatoes
1	(14½-ounce) can low-sodium vegetable broth
½	teaspoon salt
1	(9-ounce) bag fresh spinach or 1 (10-ounce) package frozen leaf spinach, thawed and squeezed dry

1. Prepare rice as labels directs.

2. Meanwhile, in 6-quart saucepot, heat oil over medium heat until hot. Add onion and cook until tender and lightly browned, 8 to 10 minutes, stirring occasionally. Stir in ginger, garam masala, and garlic, and cook 1 minute. Add water, lentils, sweet potatoes, tomatoes with their juice, broth, and salt; heat to boiling over high heat.

3. Reduce heat to low; cover and simmer until lentils and sweet potatoes are tender, about 25 minutes, stirring occasionally.

4. Add spinach to stew; heat through. Serve stew with brown rice.

Each serving: About 460 calories, 20g protein, 88g carbohydrate, 6g total fat (0g saturated), 15g fiber, 414mg sodium

If you do not have garam masala and cannot find it at your local grocery store, replace the ingredient with $1\frac{1}{2}$ teaspoons curry powder plus $\frac{1}{4}$ teaspoon ground cinnamon.

MANHATTAN CLAM CHOWDER

Chowder clams are flavorful but tough and must be chopped after cooking. Substitute cherrystone clams, if you like; there's no need to chop them.

ACTIVE TIME: 30 minutes   **TOTAL TIME:** 1 hour, 20 minutes, plus cooling
MAKES: 12 servings

5	cups water
3	dozen chowder or cherrystone clams, scrubbed
1	teaspoon olive oil
1	large (12-ounce) onion, finely chopped
2	large carrots, peeled and finely chopped
2	stalks celery, finely chopped
1	pound (3 medium) all-purpose potatoes, peeled and finely chopped
1/2	bay leaf
1 1/4	teaspoons dried thyme
1/4	teaspoon ground black pepper
1	(28-ounce) can plum tomatoes
2	tablespoons chopped fresh parsley
1/2	teaspoon salt

1. In nonreactive 8-quart saucepot, heat 1 cup water to boiling over high heat. Add clams; heat to boiling. Reduce heat; cover and simmer until clams open, 5 to 10 minutes, transferring clams to bowl as they open. Discard any clams that have not opened.

2. When cool enough to handle, remove clams from their shells and coarsely chop. Strain clam broth through sieve lined with paper towels into bowl.

3. In same clean saucepot, heat olive oil over medium heat; add onion and cook until tender, 5 minutes. Add carrots and celery; cook 5 minutes.

4. Add clam broth to vegetable mixture in saucepot. Add potatoes, remaining 4 cups water, bay leaf, thyme, and pepper; heat to boiling. Reduce heat; cover and simmer 10 minutes. Add tomatoes with their liquid, breaking them up with side of spoon, and simmer 10 minutes longer.

5. Stir in chopped clams and heat through. Discard bay leaf and sprinkle with parsley. Taste for seasoning; add salt as needed.

Each serving: About 105 calories, 9g protein, 15g carbohydrate, 1g total fat (0g saturated), 2g fiber, 576mg sodium

MUSSELS IN SAFFRON-TOMATO BROTH

Serve steaming bowls of these mussels with hunks of country-style bread to sop up all the savory juices.

ACTIVE TIME: 20 minutes **TOTAL TIME:** 50 minutes

MAKES: 4 servings

3	tablespoons olive oil
2	garlic cloves, crushed with side of chef's knife
1	small bay leaf
1/2	teaspoon loosely packed saffron threads
1/8	to 1/4 teaspoon crushed red pepper
1	(14 1/2-ounce) can no-salt-added diced tomatoes
1	(8-ounce) bottle clam juice
1/2	cup dry white wine
5	dozen medium mussels, scrubbed and debearded

1. In nonreactive 8-quart saucepot, heat oil over medium heat. Add garlic and cook until golden. Add bay leaf, saffron, and crushed red pepper; cook, stirring, 1 minute.

2. Add tomatoes with their liquid, clam juice, and wine; heat to boiling over high heat. Reduce heat; cover and simmer 20 minutes.

3. Add mussels; heat to boiling over high heat. Reduce heat to medium; cover and simmer until mussels open, about 5 minutes, transferring mussels to bowl as they open. Discard bay leaf and any mussels that have not opened. To serve, transfer mussels and broth to large soup bowls.

Each serving: About 219 calories, 16g protein, 10g carbohydrate, 13g total fat (2g saturated), 590mg sodium

THREE-BEAN SWEET-POTATO CHILI

This stick-to-your-ribs dish proves vegetarian fare can be just as hearty and filling as meaty meals.

ACTIVE TIME: 20 minutes **TOTAL TIME:** 1 hour
MAKES: 6 servings

1¼	pounds sweet potatoes
2	tablespoons, plus 2 cups water
2	tablespoons vegetable oil
1	medium onion
2	chipotle chiles in adobo
3	cloves garlic
1	tablespoon ground cumin
2	teaspoons chili powder
¼	teaspoon salt
2	(14-ounce) cans diced tomatoes
1	(15-ounce) can pureed tomatoes
2	cups frozen shelled edamame
1	(14-ounce) can no-salt-added pinto beans
1	(14-ounce) can no-salt-added black beans

Reduced-fat shredded Cheddar cheese, optional, for garnish
Plain, unsweetened Greek yogurt, optional, for garnish

1. In microwave-safe glass baking dish, combine sweet potatoes and 2 tablespoons water. Cover with vented plastic wrap and microwave on High 12 minutes, or until tender.

2. Meanwhile, in 5-quart saucepot, heat oil on medium. Add onion, chipotles, garlic, cumin, chili powder, and salt. Cook 5 minutes, stirring occasionally. Add tomatoes and 2 cups water. Heat to simmering on high. Simmer 15 minutes, stirring occasionally.

3. Add sweet potatoes to pot along with edamame, pinto beans, and black beans. Cook 2 to 5 minutes, or until beans are hot. To serve, garnish with Cheddar and Greek yogurt, if desired.

Each serving: About 325 calories, 15g protein, 51g carbohydrate, 8g total fat (0g saturated), 14g fiber, 630mg sodium

CHIPOTLE BEEF CHILI

This super-satisfying main dish is perfect for potlucks and other casual parties. The chili can be made a day ahead and refrigerated. To reheat, transfer it to a Dutch oven and heat it on medium until it comes to a simmer; reduce the heat to low, cover, and simmer 20 minutes to heat through.

ACTIVE TIME: 25 minutes   **TOTAL (SLOW COOK) TIME:** 6 hours on High
MAKES: 10 servings

2	(15- to 19-ounce) cans black, pinto, or red beans
1	(7-ounce) can chipotle chiles in adobo
1	(28-ounce) can diced fire-roasted tomatoes
1	large (10- to 12-ounce) onion, finely chopped
1	medium (6- to 8-ounce) green pepper, finely chopped
2	garlic cloves, crushed with garlic press
2½	pounds beef chuck, cut into 1-inch chunks
1	tablespoon ground cumin
½	tablespoon dried oregano
⅛	teaspoon salt
⅛	teaspoon ground black pepper
½	cup (2 ounces) low-fat Monterey Jack cheese, shredded
½	cup plain, unsweetened Greek Yogurt
½	cup packed fresh cilantro leaves, coarsely chopped
1	lime, cut into wedges

1. In large colander, drain beans. Rinse well and drain again. Remove 1 chile from can of chipotle chiles in adobo and finely chop. Place in large bowl with 1 teaspoon adobo. Reserve another 2 teaspoons adobo for cooked chili, and reserve remaining chiles and adobo for another use.

2. To large bowl with chiles and adobo, add tomatoes, onions, green peppers, and garlic; mix well. In another large bowl, combine beef, cumin, oregano, salt, and pepper.

3. In 7-quart slow-cooker bowl, spread a generous layer of tomato mixture. Add beef, then beans to slow-cooker bowl and top with remaining tomato mixture. Cover slow cooker with lid and cook as manufacturer directs on High setting 6 hours.

4. Using slotted spoon, transfer solids to large serving bowl. Transfer cooking liquid from slow-cooker bowl to 4-cup liquid measuring cup. Remove and discard fat. Pour off all but 2 cups cooking liquid. Stir reserved adobo into cooking liquid in cup; pour over chili and stir to combine. Serve with low-fat Monterey Jack, Greek yogurt, cilantro, and limes alongside.

Each serving: About 290 calories, 32g protein, 25g carbohydrate, 8g total fat (3g saturated), 8g fiber, 575mg sodium

KIDNEY BEAN CHILI

Grab a couple of cans of beans and you can whip up this lean, hearty stew with a minimum of fuss.

ACTIVE TIME: 15 minutes   **TOTAL TIME:** 30 minutes
MAKES: 5 servings

8	ounces lean ground turkey
1	small onion, chopped
2	teaspoons chili powder
2	(15-ounce) cans low-sodium kidney beans, drained and rinsed
1	(14-ounce) can diced tomatoes with green chiles
1	cup water

In large nonstick saucepan, cook turkey and onion until turkey is browned and onion is tender, about 10 minutes. Stir in chili powder and cook 1 minute. Stir in kidney beans, tomatoes with green chiles, and water. Heat to boiling over medium-high heat; reduce heat to low and simmer 15 minutes, stirring occasionally.

Each serving: About 220 calories, 19g protein, 28g carbohydrate, 4g total fat (1g saturated), 8g fiber, 504mg sodium

BEEF BURGUNDY

A hearty beef and mushroom stew flavored with dry red wine makes for a perfect midwinter supper.

ACTIVE TIME: 1 hour   **TOTAL TIME:** 2 hours, 30 minutes
MAKES: 10 servings

1	tablespoon olive oil
3	pounds boneless beef chuck, trimmed and cut into 1½-inch pieces
5	carrots, each peeled and cut into ½-inch pieces
3	garlic cloves, crushed with side of chef's knife
1	large (12-ounce) onion, cut into 1-inch pieces
2	tablespoons all-purpose flour
2	tablespoons low-sodium tomato paste
1	teaspoon salt
½	teaspoon coarsely ground black pepper
2	cups dry red wine
4	springs fresh thyme
1	(12-ounce) package mushrooms, each trimmed and cut into quarters
½	cup loosely packed fresh parsley leaves, chopped

1. In 5- to 6-quart Dutch oven, heat olive oil over medium heat.

2. Pat beef dry with paper towels. Add beef, in three batches, to olive oil and cook over medium-high heat until well browned on all sides, about 5 minutes per batch. With slotted spoon, transfer beef to medium bowl.

3. Preheat oven to 325°F. To drippings in Dutch oven, add carrots, garlic, and onion and cook, stirring occasionally, until vegetables are browned and tender, about 10 minutes. Stir in flour, tomato paste, salt, and pepper; cook, stirring, 2 minutes. Add wine and heat to boiling, stirring until browned bits are loosened from bottom of Dutch oven.

4. Return meat and meat juices to Dutch oven. Add thyme and mushrooms; heat to boiling. Cover Dutch oven and bake until meat is fork-tender, 1 hour 30 minutes to 2 hours, stirring once. Skim and discard fat from liquid; discard thyme sprigs. Sprinkle with parsley to serve.

Each serving: About 225 calories, 29g protein, 11g carbohydrate, 7g total fat (2g saturated), 2g fiber, 269mg sodium

CLASSIC BEEF STEW

Be sure to trim excess fat from the chuck to keep both calories and saturated fat in check.

ACTIVE TIME: 45 minutes   **TOTAL TIME:** 2 hours, 45 minutes

MAKES: 8 servings

2	pounds boneless beef chuck, trimmed of fat and cut into 1½-inch pieces
4	teaspoons olive oil
1	large (12-ounce) onion, chopped
2	garlic cloves, finely chopped
1	(14-ounce) can diced tomatoes
2	cups dry red wine
1	bay leaf
1	teaspoon salt
¼	teaspoon ground black pepper
¼	teaspoon dried thyme
1½	pounds potatoes, peeled and cut into 1½-inch pieces
6	carrots, peeled and cut into 1-inch pieces
1	cup frozen peas
2	tablespoons fresh parsley leaves, chopped

1. Preheat oven to 325°F. Pat beef dry with paper towels. In 6-quart Dutch oven, heat 2 teaspoons oil over medium-high heat until very hot. Add half of beef and cook 5 minutes or until well browned on all sides. Transfer beef to large bowl. Add remaining 2 teaspoons oil to Dutch oven and repeat with remaining beef.

2. Reduce heat to medium. Add onion to pot and cook, stirring occasionally, until tender, about 5 minutes. Add garlic and cook 30 seconds or until very fragrant. Stir in tomatoes with their juices. Add wine, bay leaf, salt, pepper, thyme, and beef with its accumulated juices. Heat to boiling over high heat. Cover and transfer to oven. Cook 1 hour. Add potatoes and carrots; cook 1 hour longer or until vegetables are fork-tender. Discard bay leaf.

3. With slotted spoon, transfer vegetables and beef to bowl and cover with foil to keep warm. Skim and discard fat from cooking liquid.

4. Raise heat to medium-high and cook liquid until slightly reduced, 5 to 7 minutes. Stir in frozen peas and cook 1 to 2 minutes longer or until heated through. Spoon liquid and peas over meat mixture. Sprinkle with parsley.

Each serving: About 290 calories, 27g protein, 2g carbohydrate, 7g total fat (2g saturated), 5g fiber, 450mg sodium

PORK AND PEPPERS RAGU

Serve this pepper-filled pork ragu over pureed cauliflower for a flat-tummy dinner.

ACTIVE TIME: 45 minutes   **TOTAL TIME:** 2 hours, 30 minutes
MAKES: 10 servings

3	tablespoons olive oil
1¼	teaspoons salt
½	teaspoon pepper
1	(3½-pound) boneless pork shoulder, trimmed and cut into 4-inch chunks
1	large red pepper, seeded and sliced
1	large green pepper, seeded and sliced
1	large onion, chopped
3	cloves garlic, chopped
3	tablespoons low-sodium tomato paste
¾	cup dry red wine
1	(28-ounce) can crushed tomatoes
2	bay leaves

1. Preheat oven to 325°F. In 6- to 8-quart Dutch oven or heavy saucepot, heat oil on medium-high until hot but not smoking. Season pork all over with ¾ teaspoon salt and pepper; add to pot. Cook 10 to 12 minutes or until browned on most sides; transfer to large plate.

2. To same pot, add peppers, onion, garlic, and ½ teaspoon salt. Cook 5 minutes or until beginning to soften, stirring occasionally. Add tomato paste; cook 1 minute, stirring. Add wine. Heat to boiling on high; boil 2 minutes or until reduced slightly. Add tomatoes and bay leaves; return pork to pot. Heat to boiling. Cover and cook 1½ to 2 hours or until pork is very tender. Transfer pork to cutting board; with 2 forks, pull pork into bite-size pieces. Discard bay leaves. Return pork and any juices to pot with tomato sauce, stirring to coat.

Each serving: About 260 calories, 25g protein, 11g carbohydrate, 13g total fat (4g saturated), 3g fiber, 450mg sodium

MOROCCAN-STYLE LAMB WITH WHOLE WHEAT COUSCOUS

This sweet but slightly spicy stew is served on a bed of couscous—grain-shaped semolina pasta.

ACTIVE TIME: 20 minutes **TOTAL TIME:** 2 hours, 5 minutes
MAKES: 8 servings

2	pounds boneless lamb shoulder, trimmed and cut into 1¼-inch pieces
2	tablespoons olive oil
2	garlic cloves, finely chopped
1½	teaspoons ground cumin
1½	teaspoons ground coriander
1	(12-ounce) large onion, cut into 8 wedges
1	(14½- to 16-ounce) can stewed tomatoes
1	(3-inch) cinnamon stick
1¼	teaspoons salt
¼	teaspoon cayenne pepper
1	cup water
2	pounds (3 large) sweet potatoes, peeled and cut into 2-inch pieces
2	cups whole wheat couscous
1	(15- to 19-ounce) can garbanzo beans, rinsed and drained
1	cup dark seedless raisins
¼	cup chopped fresh cilantro

1. Pat lamb dry with paper towels. In nonreactive 5-quart Dutch oven, heat 1 tablespoon oil over medium-high heat until very hot. Add half of lamb and cook until browned, using slotted spoon to transfer meat to bowl as it is browned. Repeat with remaining 1 tablespoon oil and remaining lamb.

2. To drippings in Dutch oven, add garlic, cumin, and coriander; cook 30 seconds. Return lamb to Dutch oven. Stir in onion, tomatoes, cinnamon stick, salt, cayenne, and water; heat to boiling over high heat. Reduce heat; cover and simmer, stirring occasionally, 45 minutes. Stir in sweet potatoes; cover and simmer 30 minutes longer.

3. Meanwhile, prepare couscous as label directs.

4. Add garbanzo beans and raisins to Dutch oven. Cover and cook, stirring once or twice, until lamb and vegetables are tender, about 5 minutes longer.

5. Just before serving, stir in cilantro. Serve lamb stew on couscous.

Each serving: About 520 calories, 29g protein, 80g carbohydrate, 12g total fat (3g saturated), 12g fiber, 595mg sodium

STEW SAVVY

A few simple steps are the keys to success when making stew.

- Always use a heavy pot, such as a Dutch oven, which promotes even cooking.

- When browning meat or vegetables, first pat them dry. Always add meat to the hot oil without crowding the pan, so that it browns rather than steams. Give meat or vegetables a chance to brown before turning, which will create browned bits on the bottom of the pan that will add rich flavor.

- Add enough liquid to cover or almost cover the ingredients.

- Cook stews slowly on top of the stove over low heat to tenderize the meat.

- Quicker-cooking ingredients, such as potatoes and peas, are usually added near the end of the cooking time, so they don't get overcooked.

LAMB NAVARIN

This classic vegetable-laden French ragout is perfect for spring.

ACTIVE TIME: 20 minutes   **TOTAL TIME:** 2 hours, 20 minutes
MAKES: 8 servings

3	pounds boneless lamb shoulder, trimmed and cut into 1-inch pieces
2	tablespoons butter
2	small onions, each cut into quarters, then crosswise into slices
1½	cups dry white wine
1½	cups low-sodium chicken broth
1	cup water
6	sprigs, plus 2 tablespoons chopped fresh parsley
2	thyme sprigs or ¼ teaspoon dried thyme
2	bay leaves
4	garlic cloves, finely chopped
½	teaspoon salt, plus more as needed
¼	teaspoon ground black pepper
1⅓	cup (8 ounces) peeled baby carrots
2	(4-ounce) small turnips, peeled and cut into ¾-inch pieces
1	cup (8 ounces) pearl onions, peeled
1½	pounds asparagus, trimmed and cut into 2-inch lengths
2	teaspoons sugar

1. Pat lamb dry with paper towels. In 5-quart Dutch oven, melt butter over medium heat. Cook lamb, in batches, until well browned, using slotted spoon to transfer cooked meat to bowl. Add onions to Dutch oven and cook, stirring, until tender, about 5 minutes. Add wine, broth, water, parsley sprigs, thyme sprigs, bay leaves, and lamb to pot; heat over high heat until boiling. Reduce heat; cover and simmer 15 minutes. Add garlic, salt, and pepper and simmer 30 minutes longer.

2. Add carrots, turnips, and pearl onions to Dutch oven; partially cover and cook until lamb is tender, about 30 minutes longer. Stir in asparagus and cook until vegetables are tender, 5 to 10 minutes longer.

3. With slotted spoon, transfer meat and vegetables to another dish to keep warm. Reduce stew liquid over medium-high heat until thickened, about 10 minutes.

4. Discard parsley, thyme sprigs, and bay leaves. Stir in sugar. Taste and add salt as needed. Spoon the stew liquid over meat and vegetables and sprinkle with parsley.

Each serving: About 310 calories, 39g protein, 14g carbohydrate, 11g total fat (5g saturated), 315mg sodium

VEAL AND MUSHROOM STEW

In this recipe, the veal is slowly simmered with mushrooms and a touch of sweet Marsala wine until tender. Peas are added for their subtle sweetness and color.

ACTIVE TIME: 30 minutes   **TOTAL TIME:** 1 hour, 30 minutes
MAKES: 6 servings

1½	pounds boneless veal shoulder, cut into 1½-inch pieces
¾	teaspoon salt
¼	teaspoon ground black pepper
3	tablespoons vegetable oil
1	pound white mushrooms, trimmed and cut in half
¼	pound shiitake mushrooms, stems removed
½	cup water
⅓	cup dry Marsala wine
1	(10-ounce) package frozen peas, thawed

1. Preheat oven to 350°F. Pat veal dry with paper towels. Sprinkle veal with salt and pepper. In nonreactive 5-quart Dutch oven, heat 2 tablespoons oil over medium-high heat until very hot. Add half of veal and cook until browned, using slotted spoon to transfer meat to bowl as it is browned. Repeat with remaining veal (without additional oil).

2. In Dutch oven, heat remaining 1 tablespoon oil over medium-high heat. Add white and shiitake mushrooms and cook, stirring occasionally, until lightly browned.

3. Return veal to Dutch oven; stir in water and Marsala, stirring until browned bits are loosened from bottom of pan. Heat veal mixture to boiling.

4. Cover Dutch oven and bake, stirring occasionally, until veal is tender, 1 hour to 1 hour 15 minutes. Stir in peas and heat through.

Each serving: About 250 calories, 26g protein, 12g carbohydrate, 11g total fat (2g saturated), 448mg sodium

Grilled Mexican Pizza (page 177)

4 | SANDWICHES & PIZZAS

Many diet plans would eliminate sandwiches, flatbreads, and pizzas from the menu since these foods are easy to stack with calorie-packed ingredients. But made with fresh ingredients, whole-grain breads, and lean proteins, these recipes are perfect for an on-the-go lunch or a quick and easy weeknight meal.

When building a sandwich, make sure to use spreads with heart-healthy fats. Add texture and flavors with crunchy seasonal vegetables. Expand your palette and consider Tofu Egg Salad Sandwiches (page 146). Not all sandwiches need meat like the veggie-forward Tomato-Eggplant Tartines (page 150). Turkey Burgers with Sweet Potato "Fries" (page 166) will also satisfy any craving.

Pizzas topped with veggies like Pizza Primavera (page 179) or Garden Pizza (page 180) are a great way to include a serving of vegetables in your meal. Or enjoy our fusion of cuisines with the Grilled Mexican Pizza (page 177). Served with a side salad or a piece of fruit, these delicious sandwiches and pizzas are a great meal option any time of day.

TOFU EGG SALAD SANDWICH

The familiar egg-salad seasonings lend themselves well to tofu. For a light lunch, serve with a mini whole wheat pita bread, lettuce, and tomato wedges.

TOTAL TIME: 15 minutes

MAKES: 4 servings

1	(15-ounce) package firm tofu, drained
1	stalk celery, chopped
½	small red pepper, finely chopped
1	green onion, chopped
¼	cup light mayonnaise
½	teaspoon salt
⅛	teaspoon turmeric
4	mini whole wheat pitas

1. In medium bowl, with fork, mash tofu until it resembles scrambled eggs; stir in celery, red pepper, green onion, mayonnaise, salt, and turmeric. Cover and refrigerate up to 1 day if not serving right away.

2. Cut each pita in half and stuff with tofu egg salad.

Each serving: About 220 calories, 13g protein, 21g carbohydrate, 10g total fat (1g saturated), 3g fiber, 501mg sodium

FLAT-TUMMY INGREDIENT: TOFU

You won't find it in the meat section, but tofu delivers plenty of protein. A Louisiana State University study found that tofu is a mighty diet food. Researchers served 42 overweight woman an appetizer. Half of the participants ate chicken and the other women tasted tofu. The participants who had tofu ate less food during their next meal. The outcome: Compared to chicken, tofu seemed to quash hunger.

EGG SALAD DELUXE SANDWICHES

Hard-cooked eggs are chopped and mixed with sautéed onions, mushrooms, and celery for a new take on classic egg salad. Serve on sweet, tender Boston lettuce leaves.

ACTIVE TIME: 20 minutes   **TOTAL TIME:** 40 minutes
MAKES: 6 servings

8	large eggs
3	tablespoons olive oil
1	onion, cut in half and thinly sliced
10	ounces mushrooms, sliced
2	stalks celery, finely chopped
¼	cup loosely packed fresh parsley leaves, chopped
½	teaspoon salt
¼	teaspoon coarsely ground black pepper
12	slices whole wheat bread

1. In 3-quart saucepan, place eggs and enough cold water to cover by at least 1 inch; heat to boiling on high heat. Immediately remove saucepan from heat and cover tightly; let stand 15 minutes. Cool eggs under cold running water until easy to handle.

2. Meanwhile, in nonstick 12-inch skillet, heat 1 tablespoon oil over medium heat until hot. Add onion and cook, stirring occasionally, until tender and golden, 10 to 12 minutes. Increase heat to medium-high; add mushrooms and cook until mushrooms are golden and all liquid evaporates, 8 minutes.

3. Remove shells from hard-cooked eggs. Finely chop eggs. In large bowl, toss eggs with mushroom mixture, celery, parsley, salt, pepper, and remaining 2 tablespoons oil.

4. Spread ⅙ of salad on top of each of six slices of bread. Top with remaining slices of bread and serve.

Each serving: About 320 calories, 16g protein, 28g carbohydrate, 16g total fat (4g saturated), 4g fiber, 515mg sodium

THE FLAT-TUMMY SANDWICH

A sandwich doesn't have to be loaded with fat and calories, especially when you're making it at home. Here's how to construct the perfect in-house sandwich in a snap.

BREAD: 200 CALORIES

Choose whole-grain bread for your sandwich—but watch the size. A big sub roll, for example, might have up to 500 calories. Instead, choose two slices of whole-grain or whole wheat sandwich bread or one small roll equal to about 200 calories.

CHEESE: 50 CALORIES

Add cheese to your sandwich without a worry but make sure to make a smart choice. One slice of reduced-fat Pepper Jack cheese, for example, is only 50 calories. Look for any variety of reduced-fat cheese with about 50 calories and no more than 3 or 4 fat grams per slice.

MEAT: 100 CALORIES

Many luncheon meats are high in calories and sodium. Sidestep cured meat or sausage and look for lower-calorie alternatives, such as chicken breast, roast beef, turkey breast, ham, and water-packed tuna. Aim for about 100 calories of lean protein, which is about 5 slices of meat (each deli slice is around 20 calories) or a 3-ounce can of tuna in water.

SPREADS: 50 CALORIES

Skip the full-fat mayonnaise and save a whole bunch of calories on your sandwich. Instead, combine reduced-fat mayonnaise with chopped fresh herbs for flavor. If you prefer to hold the mayo, spread your bread with naturally low-fat mustard. For a creamy mustard spread, we suggest combining Greek yogurt with a bit of mustard. Chutney or relish, delicious by itself or when blended with light mayonnaise or mustard, adds a delectable sweet-and-spicy dimension to a sandwich as well.

VEGGIES: NO LIMIT

Go wild—add spinach, lettuce, red pepper, onions, cucumber, jalapeños, mushrooms, tomato, or any other fresh vegetable to any sandwich for extra flavor, fiber, and virtually no calories. Avoid veggies packed or roasted in oil since they will add unwanted calories.

TOTAL CALORIE GOAL: AROUND 450

Now, to finish your meal, add a piece of fruit (a banana, pear, or nectarine for example). Voilà—the perfect lunch for a flat tummy!

THE SKINNY ON SANDWICH SPREADS (per tablespoon)

Hummus	1.5g fat	23 calories
Italian dressing	4g fat	43 calories
Ketchup	0g fat	15 calories
Light mayonnaise	4.5g fat	45 calories
Mustard	0.5g fat	9 calories

TOMATO-EGGPLANT TARTINES

Smoky eggplant, tart tomatoes, and crunchy rustic Italian bread make this recipe one irresistible lunch.

TOTAL TIME: 20 minutes
MAKES: 4 servings

8	thick slices rustic whole-grain Italian bread
1	large clove garlic, peeled
3	tablespoons extra-virgin olive oil
3	small eggplants, thinly sliced

Kosher salt

1	cup (4 ounces) shredded low-fat mozzarella
4	small tomatoes, thinly sliced
¼	cup grated Parmesan

Basil, for garnish

1. Heat grill to medium. Grill rustic Italian bread 5 minutes, or until well toasted, turning once. Transfer to large platter. Rub bread lightly with garlic; drizzle with 1 tablespoon olive oil.

2. Toss eggplants with remaining olive oil; sprinkle with salt. Grill 5 minutes; turn slices over and top with mozzarella. Grill 5 minutes or until cheese melts. Top bread with tomatoes and salt. Layer with eggplant. Sprinkle with Parmesan. Garnish with basil.

Each serving: About 320 calories, 15g protein, 32g carbohydrate, 15g total fat (3g saturated), 6g fiber, 572mg sodium

GRILLED PORTOBELLO AND TOMATO PANINI

To slim down the pesto, we've swapped in toasted almonds for the traditional pine nuts and skipped the Parmesan.

TOTAL TIME: 10 minutes
MAKES: 4 servings

Pesto

3	cups basil leaves
1/3	cup extra-virgin olive oil
1/4	cup almonds, toasted
2	small garlic cloves
1/4	teaspoon salt
1/4	teaspoon ground black pepper

Bread and fillings

1	loaf whole-grain bread (ciabatta, if possible)
4	large Portobello mushrooms, stems removed
3	tablespoons extra-virgin olive oil
2	ripe medium tomatoes, sliced 1/4 inch thick

1. Pulse basil, 1/3 cup olive oil, almonds, and garlic in food processor until very finely chopped. Sprinkle in salt and pepper and pulse to combine; pesto can be refrigerated in an airtight container up to 5 days.

2. Prepare outdoor grill for direct grilling over medium heat. Cut bread into four 4-inch-square pieces, then split each horizontally in half so you have 8 pieces.

3. Brush mushrooms and tomatoes with 3 tablespoons oil and place on grill. Grill 6 to 8 minutes, turning once. Transfer to plate.

4. Brush bread with oil and place on grill until slightly toasted, about 1 minute, flipping once. Transfer to plate.

5. Spread 1 tablespoon pesto on each piece of bread. On bottom half of each bread piece, layer 1 grilled mushroom and 3 slices tomato. Set top halves of bread on filling. Cut each sandwich in half and serve hot.

Each serving: About 330 calories, 9g protein, 36g carbohydrate, 19g total fat (3g saturated), 6g fiber, 361mg sodium

SPINACH AND HUMMUS WRAPS

A bag of prewashed spinach makes this dish a snap.

TOTAL TIME: 15 minutes
MAKES: 1 serving

Nonstick cooking spray
1   yellow pepper, sliced
1   cup mushrooms, sliced
1   cup spinach
1   multigrain flatbread
¼   cup hummus
¼   cup cucumber, sliced
¼   cup carrots, sliced or shredded
Crumbled feta

In nonstick skillet coated with cooking spray, sauté pepper with mushrooms until just tender. Add spinach and cook until wilted. Spread flatbread with hummus and top with cucumbers, carrots, and crumbled feta; add spinach mixture and roll up.

Each serving: About 300 calories, 16g protein, 48g carbohydrate, 8g total fat (4g saturated), 11g fiber, 599mg sodium

HEALTHY CLUB SANDWICHES

This carrot, sprout, and bean spread combo on whole-grain bread will delight your palate and satisfy your hunger.

TOTAL TIME: 25 minutes
MAKES: 4 servings

2	tablespoons olive oil
2	teaspoons, plus 1 tablespoon fresh lemon juice
1	teaspoon honey
1/8	teaspoon ground black pepper
1	cup (2 medium) carrots, shredded
2	cups alfalfa sprouts
1	garlic clove, finely chopped
1/2	teaspoon ground cumin

Pinch of cayenne pepper

1	(15- to 19-ounce) can sodium-free garbanzo beans, rinsed and drained
1	tablespoon water
12	slices multigrain bread, lightly toasted
1	large (10- to 12-ounce) ripe tomato, thinly sliced
1	(4-ounce) bunch watercress, tough stems trimmed

1. In medium bowl, whisk together 1 tablespoon oil, 2 teaspoons lemon juice, honey, and black pepper. Add carrots and alfalfa sprouts; toss until mixed and evenly coated with dressing.

2. In 2-quart saucepan, heat remaining 1 tablespoon oil over medium. Add garlic, cumin, and cayenne and cook until very fragrant. Stir in garbanzo beans and remove from heat. Add remaining 1 tablespoon lemon juice and water; mash to a coarse puree.

3. Spread garbanzo mixture on 8 toast slices. Place tomato slices and watercress over 4 slices of garbanzo-topped toast. Top remaining 4 garbanzo-topped slices with alfalfa-sprout mixture and place, topping side up, on watercress-topped bread. Cover with remaining toast slices. Cut sandwiches in half.

Each serving: About 380 calories, 14g protein, 57g carbohydrate, 12g total fat (2g saturated), 17g fiber, 270mg sodium

CURRIED CHICKEN PITAS

The addition of cantaloupe brings extra sweet flavor to these curry-spiced chicken salad sandwiches. They're the ideal choice for a light and casual summer meal.

TOTAL TIME: 20 minutes
MAKES: 4 servings

¼	cup packed fresh cilantro leaves, finely chopped
¼	cup plain, unsweetened Greek yogurt
2	tablespoons low-fat mayonnaise
1	tablespoon fresh lime juice
1	teaspoon peeled, grated fresh ginger
¼	teaspoon curry powder
¼	teaspoon ground coriander
2	cups chopped, cooked chicken breast meat
5	radishes, cut into ¼-inch-thick half-moons
1½	cups (8 ounces) cantaloupe, chopped
¼	small red onions, finely chopped
3	tablespoons roasted cashews, chopped
4	whole-grain pita breads, toasted, each cut into quarters

1. To make dressing, in small bowl, whisk cilantro, yogurt, mayonnaise, lime juice, ginger, curry powder, and coriander until well blended. In larger bowl, combine chicken, radishes, cantaloupe, and onion. If making ahead, cover bowls and refrigerate up to 1 day.

2. To serve, toss chicken mixture with half of dressing. Sprinkle with cashews. Spoon on top of pita pieces and serve with remaining dressing alongside.

Each serving: About 370 calories, 31g protein, 46g carbohydrate, 8g total fat (2g saturated), 5g fiber, 474mg sodium

CARIBBEAN WRAP

Pick up a rotisserie chicken at the grocery store and you're halfway finished making this wrap!

TOTAL TIME: 10 minutes
MAKES: 1 serving

½	cup chopped or shredded skinless, boneless white chicken breast meat (or ⅓ cup dark meat)
2	tablespoons chopped red onion
2	garlic cloves, chopped
½	cup cubed mango
¼	cup drained and rinsed low-sodium black beans

Pinch of red pepper flakes

2	teaspoons chopped cilantro
1	100% whole-grain corn tortilla
2	tablespoons roasted macadamia nuts
2	cups mixed greens

Spray dressing

Combine chicken with onion, garlic, mango, beans, red pepper, and cilantro. Spoon into tortilla and roll up. Serve with macadamia nuts and greens tossed with 10 to 15 pumps spray dressing.

Each serving: About 495 calories, 31g protein, 59g carbohydrate, 18g total fat (3g saturated), 13g fiber, 366mg sodium

OPEN-FACED CHICKEN QUESADILLA

If pressed for time, you can use a rotisserie chicken in this super-quick and delicious (and guilt-free) lunch!

TOTAL TIME: 10 minutes
MAKES: 1 serving

1	(8-inch) 100% whole-grain corn tortillas
Nonstick cooking spray	
½	cup shredded skinless white chicken breast meat
4	tablespoons shredded reduced-fat Cheddar cheese
2	tablespoons chopped green onions
¼	cup salsa
2	cups mixed salad greens
100-calorie dressing of your choice	

Place tortilla in a medium skillet coated with cooking spray. Top with chicken, cheese, and green onions. Cook until bottom of the tortilla browns and cheese melts, about 5 minutes. Serve with salsa and salad greens with dressing.

Each serving: About 375 calories, 28g protein, 23g carbohydrate, 16g total fat (5g saturated), 4g fiber, 265mg sodium

LETTUCE AND TOFU CHICKEN WRAPS

These fresh Thai-style wraps were our top pic in the family-friendly category at our first Cook Your Heart Out recipe contest.

ACTIVE TIME: 20 minutes   **TOTAL TIME:** 25 minutes
MAKES: 8 servings

6	cups water
4	ounces cellophane noodles (thin rice noodles)
12	ounces reduced-fat firm tofu, drained and cut into $1/2$-inch cubes
4	tablespoons fresh lime juice
2	tablespoons low-sodium soy sauce
1	tablespoon fish sauce
1	serrano pepper, seeded and minced
1	teaspoon sugar
$1^1/2$	teaspoons olive oil
1	red onion, finely chopped
1	pound ground chicken breast
2	garlic cloves, minced
1	cup packed fresh cilantro leaves, coarsely chopped
$1/2$	cup unsalted dry roasted peanuts, coarsely chopped
2	green onions, finely chopped
16	large Belgian lettuce leaves

Lime wedges for serving

1. Boil water in medium saucepan. Add noodles and remove pan from heat. Let stand 4 to 5 minutes or until noodles soften. Drain and rinse with cold water. With kitchen scissors, cut noodles into 1-inch pieces.

2. Pat tofu dry with paper towels. In small bowl, combine lime juice, soy sauce, fish sauce, pepper, and sugar. Set aside.

3. In large deep skillet, heat oil over medium-high. Add red onion and chicken. Sauté until softened, stirring frequently with a wooden spoon to break up chicken, until chicken is cooked through and begins to brown. Add tofu and cook for about 4 minutes, stirring frequently. Stir noodles and sauce into chicken mixture, and remove skillet from heat. Stir in cilantro, peanuts, and green onions. Serve chicken with lettuce leaves and lime wedges.

Each serving: About 210 calories, 18g protein, 19g carbohydrate, 7g total fat (1g saturated), 2g fiber, 405mg sodium

MANGO CHICKEN LETTUCE CUPS

Skip the bread and wrap these speedy, no-cook chicken wraps in crisp lettuce leaves instead. Mango, fresh mint, and jicama add Latin-style zing.

TOTAL TIME: 20 minutes

MAKES: 4 servings

1	large ripe mango, peeled, pitted, and chopped
1	cup finely chopped jicama
½	cup packed fresh mint leaves, finely chopped
¼	cup fresh lime juice
2	tablespoons extra-virgin olive oil
½	teaspoon Asian chili sauce (sriracha), plus more to taste
¼	teaspoon salt
3	cups coarsely shredded chicken meat (about ½ rotisserie chicken)
12	Boston lettuce leaves

1. In large bowl, combine mango, jicama, mint, lime juice, oil, chili sauce, and salt. Toss to combine. If making ahead, cover bowl and refrigerate mixture up to overnight.

2. To serve, add chicken to mango mixture; toss to combine. Place ⅓ cup chicken mixture in each lettuce leaf.

Each serving: About 325 calories, 32g protein, 17g carbohydrate, 15g total fat (3g saturated), 4g fiber, 400mg sodium

TURKEY-MEATBALL LETTUCE WRAPS

Wrap it up! These lean turkey meatballs served in lettuce wraps get their savory zest from garlic, mint, and Asian fish sauce. Carrots add crunch—and loads of vitamin A.

TOTAL TIME: 30 minutes
MAKES: 4 servings

3	limes
3	cups (about 6) carrots, shredded
1/2	cup packed fresh mint leaves, thinly sliced
2	garlic cloves, finely chopped
4	teaspoons low-sodium fish sauce
1¼	teaspoons sugar
3	teaspoons ground black pepper
1	pound lean (93% fat-free) ground turkey
12	Boston lettuce leaves

1. If using wooden skewers, presoak in cold water at least 30 minutes to prevent burning. Prepare outdoor grill for direct grilling on medium-high.

2. From 2 limes, squeeze ¼ cup juice into bowl. Cut remaining lime into wedges.

3. To lime juice, add carrots, half of mint, ¼ teaspoon garlic, 1 teaspoon fish sauce, ¼ teaspoon sugar, and ¼ teaspoon pepper. Stir; let stand.

4. In large bowl, with hands, combine turkey with remaining 1 tablespoon fish sauce, 1 teaspoon sugar, ½ teaspoon pepper, the remaining mint, and the remaining garlic. Shape mixture by tablespoonfuls into meatballs. Arrange on skewers, ½ inch apart; flatten slightly.

5. Grill, turning meatballs occasionally, 4 to 5 minutes or until grill marks appear and meat loses pink color.

6. Divide meatballs and carrot mixture among lettuce leaves. Serve with lime wedges.

Each serving (3 wraps): About 230 calories, 27g protein, 15g carbohydrate, 7g total fat (2g saturated), 4g fiber, 415mg sodium

GARDEN TURKEY SANDWICHES WITH LEMON MAYO

Turkey, tomato, and baby spinach on whole-grain bread make a satisfying lunch—or enjoy half a sandwich for a wholesome snack. Freshly grated lemon peel gives the low-fat mayonnaise spread a lift.

TOTAL TIME: 10 minutes
MAKES: 4 servings

1	teaspoon grated lemon peel
¼	cup low-fat mayonnaise
8	slices whole-grain bread
4	cups loosely packed baby spinach leaves
8	ounces turkey breast, sliced
2	tomatoes, sliced

1. In small bowl, stir grated lemon peel into mayonnaise; spread on one side of each bread slice.

2. On 4 slices bread, layer equal amounts spinach, turkey, and tomato, starting and ending with spinach. Top with remaining bread slices.

Each serving: About 300 calories, 26g protein, 33g carbohydrate, 7g total fat (2g saturated), 13g fiber, 320mg sodium

PULLED CRAN-TURKEY SANDWICHES

Use your leftover turkey and cranberry sauce to make some seriously delicious sweet-and-savory sliders.

TOTAL TIME: 20 minutes
MAKES: 4 servings

²/₃	cup leftover cranberry sauce
2	tablespoons ketchup
1	teaspoon Worcestershire sauce
½	teaspoon smoked paprika
3	cups shredded leftover cooked turkey meat
¼	cups low-sodium chicken broth
⅓	cup reduced-fat mayonnaise
4	whole-grain hamburger buns
1	cup shredded carrots

Dill pickle slices

1. In 2-quart saucepan, whisk cranberry sauce, ketchup, Worcestershire, and smoked paprika. Cook on medium 2 minutes or until hot.

2. Meanwhile, in microwave-safe baking dish or bowl, combine turkey and broth. Cover with vented plastic wrap and microwave on High 2 minutes or until hot.

3. Add cranberry mixture to turkey; stir until well coated. Spread mayonnaise on buns; top each with one-fourth of turkey mixture. Top turkey with carrots and pickle slices.

Each serving: About 400 calories, 35g protein, 47g carbohydrate, 9g total fat (2g saturated), 4g fiber, 630mg sodium

TURKEY BURGER WITH SWEET POTATO "FRIES"

Slimming down with a burger and fries sounds too good to be true—but it's not!

ACTIVE TIME: 30 minutes   **TOTAL TIME:** 35 minutes
MAKES: 4 servings

2	small (1 pound) sweet potatoes
2	tablespoons olive oil
2	teaspoons chili powder
¼	teaspoon salt
1	pound ground turkey breast
2	cloves garlic, pressed
½	cup chopped cilantro
½	avocado, plus more for serving
2	teaspoons lime juice
4	toasted whole-grain sandwich thins

Tomato, for serving

Cucumber, for serving

Lettuce, for serving

Sprouts, for serving

1. Cut sweet potatoes into ¼-inch-wide sticks; toss, on large rimmed baking sheet, with olive oil, 1 teaspoon chili powder and ¼ teaspoon salt. Roast at 450°F in oven, 20 to 25 minutes or until crisp, shaking once.

2. Mix ground turkey breast with garlic, cilantro, remaining chili powder, and remaining salt. Form into 4 patties. Grill on medium 12 to 15 minutes or until cooked through (165°F), turning once.

3. Mash avocado with lime juice. Place burgers on whole-grain sandwich thins; top with avocado and tomato, cucumber, lettuce, and sprouts as desired. Serve with fries.

Each serving: About 470 calories, 36g protein, 46g carbohydrate, 21g total fat (4g saturated), 11g fiber, 493mg sodium

TURKEY BURGERS WITH MINTED YOGURT SAUCE

Celebrate the flavors of Greece in this tasty, slimmed-down summer favorite.

ACTIVE TIME: 20 minutes **TOTAL TIME:** 35 minutes
MAKES: 4 servings

½	cup, plus 2 tablespoons plain, unsweetened Greek yogurt
2	green onions, green and white parts thinly sliced and kept separate
½	cup packed fresh mint leaves, finely chopped
1	pound lean ground turkey
1½	ounces feta cheese, finely crumbled
1½	teaspoons ground coriander
⅛	teaspoon salt
⅛	teaspoon ground black pepper
2	whole wheat pitas, cut in half
2	ripe tomatoes, thinly sliced

1. Prepare outdoor grill for covered direct grilling over medium.

2. In small bowl, combine ½ cup yogurt, white parts of onions, and half of chopped mint.

3. In large bowl, with hands, combine turkey, feta, coriander, salt, pepper, green parts of onions, remaining mint, and remaining 2 tablespoons yogurt. Mix well, then form into patties about 3½ inches in diameter and ¾ inch thick.

4. Place patties on hot grill grate; cover and cook 12 to 13 minutes or just until meat loses pink color throughout, turning once. (Instant-read thermometer inserted into center of burger should register 165°F.) During last 2 minutes of cooking, add pitas to grill. Cook 2 minutes or until warmed, turning once.

5. Open pitas. Divide burgers, tomato slices, and yogurt sauce among pitas.

Each serving: About 355 calories, 32g protein, 24g carbohydrate, 15g total fat (5g saturated), 4g fiber, 426mg sodium

TUNA SALAD SANDWICH

For even easier packaged fish, check out the no-fuss, no-draining-required variety in vacuum-packed pouches.

TOTAL TIME: 10 minutes
MAKES: 2 servings

6	ounces drained tuna packed in water
2	tablespoons dried cranberries
1	tablespoon chopped walnuts
¼	cup chopped celery
2	teaspoons reduced-fat mayonnaise
1	teaspoon Dijon mustard
1	whole-grain English muffin, toasted
2	lettuce leaves
2	cups mixed greens
½	cup grape tomatoes
½	cup sliced cucumbers

Spray dressing

Combine tuna with dried cranberries, walnuts, celery, mayonnaise, and mustard. Serve open-faced on an English muffin topped with lettuce leaves. Serve with mixed greens, grape tomatoes, and cucumbers tossed with 10 to 15 pumps spray dressing.

Each serving: About 265 calories, 25g protein, 27g carbohydrate, 7g total fat (1g saturated), 5g fiber, 542mg sodium

TUSCAN TUNA SALAD ON PITA

Here's a light new twist on an old favorite.

TOTAL TIME: 10 minutes
MAKES: 1 serving

¼	cup drained low-sodium cannellini beans
1	tablespoon chopped fresh basil leaves
1	teaspoon capers
2	teaspoons fresh lemon juice
1	teaspoon extra-virgin olive oil
3	ounces drained canned low-sodium tuna, packed in water
1	cup arugula

Salt and pepper to taste

1	(6-inch) whole wheat pita
1	cup grapes

Mash beans. Stir in basil, capers, lemon juice, olive oil, and tuna. Mix in arugula. Add salt and pepper to taste. Serve tuna in pita with grapes on the side.

Each serving: About 460 calories, 31g protein, 73g carbohydrate, 8g total fat (1g saturated), 8g fiber, 558mg sodium

ASIAN TUNA BURGERS

Serve these with pickled ginger, with or without a whole-grain bun.

ACTIVE TIME: 15 minutes   **TOTAL TIME:** 25 minutes
MAKES: 4 servings

1	(about 1 pound) tuna steak
1	green onion, thinly sliced
2	tablespoons low-sodium soy sauce
1	teaspoon peeled, grated fresh ginger
¼	teaspoon coarsely ground black pepper
¼	cup plain dried whole wheat bread crumbs
2	tablespoons sesame seeds

Nonstick cooking spray

1. Prepare outdoor grill for direct grilling over medium heat.

2. With large chef's knife, finely chop tuna and place in medium bowl. Add green onion, soy sauce, ginger, and pepper; mix until combined (mixture will be very soft and moist). Shape tuna mixture into four 3-inch patties.

3. On waxed paper, combine bread crumbs and sesame seeds. With hands, carefully press patties, one at a time, into bread-crumb mixture, turning to coat both sides. Spray both sides of tuna patties with cooking spray.

4. Place patties on hot grill rack over medium and grill, turning once, until browned outside and still slightly pink in center for medium-rare or until desired doneness, 6 to 7 minutes.

Each serving: About 215 calories, 29g protein, 5g carbohydrate, 8g total fat (2g saturated), 1g fiber, 340mg sodium

STEAK FAJITA WRAPS

Start with cooked flank steak (broil, bake, or sauté with nonstick cooking spray until done, about 10 minutes).

TOTAL TIME: 10 minutes
MAKES: 1 serving

1	(8-inch) 100% whole-grain corn tortilla
3	ounces cooked flank steak
¼	cup prepared salsa
¼	cup sliced avocado
2	tablespoons shredded reduced-fat Cheddar cheese

Apple or pear

Heat tortilla in the microwave for 10 seconds or until soft. Top with flank steak, salsa, sliced avocado, and cheese. Wrap the tortilla around the fillings. Heat in a nonstick skillet, toaster oven, or microwave, or serve cold. Enjoy with a medium apple or pear.

Each serving: About 450 calories, 30g protein, 46g carbohydrate, 17g total fat (6g saturated), 10g fiber, 617mg sodium

PULLED PORK SANDWICHES

The prep on this slow-cooked dish takes about ten minutes. For a stress-free morning, rub the pork and combine sauce ingredients the night before. Transfer any leftovers to airtight containers, then label and freeze them for up to three months.

Active time: 30 minutes   **Total time:** 8 hours, 30 minutes
Makes: 16 servings

2	tablespoons smoked paprika
1	tablespoon mustard powder
¼	cup, plus 1 tablespoon packed dark brown sugar
2	teaspoons salt
2	teaspoons ground black pepper
4	pounds boneless, untrimmed pork shoulder blade roast (Boston butt)
1	cup apple cider vinegar
½	cup ketchup
2	teaspoons crushed red pepper
1	cup water
2	tablespoons light mayonnaise
2	(14-ounce) bags coleslaw mix
16	whole wheat hamburger buns, lightly toasted

1. In 5- to 6-quart slow-cooker bowl, combine paprika, mustard powder, ¼ cup brown sugar, 1 teaspoon salt, and 1 teaspoon pepper. Add pork and rub mixture all over meat. Arrange pork in single layer in slow-cooker bowl, fat side up.

2. In medium bowl, whisk vinegar, ketchup, red pepper, remaining 1 teaspoon each salt and pepper, and remaining 1 tablespoon brown sugar. Pour ⅓ cup sauce into large bowl; cover and refrigerate. Pour water and remaining sauce into slow-cooker bowl. Cover slow cooker with lid, and cook as manufacturer directs on Low 8 to 10 hours, or until meat is fork-tender.

3. Carefully transfer meat to large bowl; remove fat and skin and discard. Using two forks, shred meat into small pieces. Carefully pour sauce from slow cooker into fat separator. Pour half of sauce over meat and pour remaining sauce into gravy boat. Discard fat.

4.When ready to serve, remove reserved sauce from refrigerator; with fork, whisk in mayonnaise. Add coleslaw mix, and toss until well combined. Divide meat among bottoms of buns; top with coleslaw, then tops of buns. Serve with reserved sauce alongside.

Each serving: About 280 calories, 18g protein, 33g carbohydrate, 9g total fat (3g saturated), 5g fiber, 607mg sodium

WHOLE WHEAT PIZZA DOUGH

This basic pizza dough can be made ahead and frozen, so it's ready whenever you want homemade pizza. If you're short on time, look for pre-made whole wheat dough at your local supermarket or pizzeria.

ACTIVE TIME: 20 minutes   **TOTAL TIME:** 30 minutes

MAKES: Enough dough for 1 (15-inch) crust

1¼	cups whole wheat flour
1½	cups all-purpose flour
1	package quick-rise yeast
1	teaspoon salt
1	cup very warm water (120°F to 130°F)
2	teaspoons cornmeal

1. In medium bowl, whisk together whole wheat and all-purpose flours. In large bowl, combine 2¼ cups flour blend, yeast, and salt. Stir in water until dough is blended and comes away from side of bowl.

2. Turn dough onto floured surface and knead until smooth and elastic, about 8 minutes, working in more flour (about ½ cup) while kneading. Shape dough into ball; cover with plastic wrap and let rest 10 minutes.

3. Grease 15-inch pizza pan; sprinkle with cornmeal. Pat dough onto bottom of pan, shaping dough into ½-inch-high rim at edge of pan.

Each serving: About 155 calories, 5g protein, 32g carbohydrate, 1g total fat (0g saturated), 3g fiber, 247mg sodium

GRILLED MEXICAN PIZZA

For an easy weeknight dinner or backyard barbecue, top a ready-made whole wheat pizza crust with black bean dip, reduced-fat cheese, and fresh vegetables, including avocado, which is loaded with healthy fat. (See photograph on page 144.)

ACTIVE TIME: 10 minutes   **TOTAL TIME:** 20 minutes
MAKES: 4 servings

⅓	cup prepared black bean dip
1	large (10-ounce) thin, baked whole wheat pizza crust (or see page 176)
2	slices reduced-fat Pepper Jack cheese, roughly chopped
1	ripe avocado, pitted, peeled, and cut into chunks
2	tablespoons fresh lime juice
2	cups shredded romaine lettuce
¼	teaspoon grated lime peel
1	ripe (6- to 8-ounce) medium tomato, chopped

1. Prepare outdoor grill for covered, direct grilling over medium.

2. Spread black bean dip evenly on crust, leaving ½-inch border; sprinkle with cheese. Place crust on hot grill rack; cover and cook until grill marks appear and cheese melts, 8 to 9 minutes.

3. Meanwhile, gently stir avocado with 1 tablespoon lime juice. Toss romaine with lime peel and remaining 1 tablespoon lime juice.

4. Top cooked pizza with romaine mixture and tomato, then with avocado. Cut into slices.

Each serving: About 350 calories, 11g protein, 44g carbohydrate, 15g total fat (3g saturated), 7g fiber, 481mg sodium

PIZZA PRIMAVERA

Preheat a baking sheet in a hot oven: This turns it into a baking stone for perfect pizza crust.

ACTIVE TIME: 15 minutes   **TOTAL TIME:** 40 minutes
MAKES: 4 servings

1	bunch asparagus, trimmed and thinly sliced on an angle
½	small red onion, thinly sliced
2	tablespoons olive oil
½	teaspoon pepper
	Whole Wheat Pizza Dough (page 176)
4	ounces low-fat cheese such as provolone

1. Place a large cookie sheet in a 475°F oven.

2. In a large bowl, toss asparagus, red onion, olive oil, and pepper.

3. Stretch and roll out pizza dough into a 12-inch circle on large sheet of parchment paper. Top dough with cheese, then the asparagus mixture.

4. Remove hot cookie sheet from oven. Carefully slide parchment with dough onto the baking sheet. Place in oven; bake 20 to 25 minutes or until bottom and edges are deep golden brown.

Each serving: About 415 calories, 17g protein, 54g carbohydrate, 15g total fat (4g saturated), 5g fiber, 675mg sodium

GARDEN PIZZA

Everyone's favorite takeout gets a low-fat, high-fiber makeover with a heap of fresh vegetables, a whole wheat crust, and a sprinkle of low-fat mozzarella.

ACTIVE TIME: 20 minutes, plus time to make dough **TOTAL TIME:** 40 minutes
MAKES: 8 servings

Whole Wheat Pizza Dough (page 176)

1	tablespoon vegetable oil
1	small (6-ounce) zucchini, cut into 1/4-inch pieces
1	small (6-ounce) yellow straight-neck squash, cut into 1/4-inch pieces
1	large tomato, seeded and cut into 1/4-inch pieces
1/2	teaspoon dried oregano
1/4	teaspoon ground black pepper
1/4	teaspoon salt
1	cup (4 ounces) shredded low-fat mozzarella cheese

1. Prepare pizza dough. Preheat oven to 450°F.

2. In 12-inch skillet, heat oil over medium high. Add zucchini and yellow squash and cook until tender. Stir in tomato, oregano, pepper, and salt.

3. Top pizza dough with squash mixture; sprinkle evenly with shredded mozzarella cheese. Bake pizza on bottom rack of oven until crust is golden and crisp, 20 to 25 minutes.

Each serving: About 215 calories, 9g protein, 34g carbohydrate, 5g total fat (2g saturated), 4g fiber, 455mg sodium

BISTRO PIZZA

This sophisticated pizza is topped with yellow pepper strips, asparagus, dollops of low-fat ricotta, and a sprinkling of Parmesan.

ACTIVE TIME: 20 minutes, plus time to make dough   **TOTAL TIME:** 40 minutes
MAKES: 8 servings

Whole Wheat Pizza Dough (page 176)

1	pound thin asparagus, trimmed and cut into 2-inch pieces
1	teaspoon olive oil
1/4	teaspoon salt
1	medium yellow pepper, cut into thin strips
1	cup low-fat ricotta cheese
2	tablespoons grated Parmesan cheese
1/4	teaspoon coarsely ground black pepper

1. Prepare pizza dough. Preheat oven to 450°F.

2. In small bowl, toss asparagus with oil and salt. Top pizza dough with pepper strips and asparagus. Dollop with teaspoons of ricotta; sprinkle with Parmesan and black pepper.

3. Bake pizza on bottom rack of oven until crust is browned, 20 to 25 minutes.

Each serving: About 215 calories, 10g protein, 35g carbohydrate, 4g total fat (2g saturated), 4g fiber, 405mg sodium

Gingery Shrimp Toasts (page 185)

5 | APPETIZERS & SNACKS

Eating healthful meals is one hurdle, but finding snacks that aren't filled with added sugar, white flour, and saturated fats can be harder. If following the recommended calorie intakes suggested in this book, we suggest two snacks throughout the day, totaling 400 calories. In this chapter, you'll find a whole buffet table of savory bites for noshing. Dips like Lemon Cilantro Eggplant Dip (page 190), The Perfect Homemade Hummus (page 189), and Tzatziki (page 192) are low in calories and delicious when scooped up with vegetable slices. If you crave something crunchy, snack on Kale Chips (page 207) or roasted garbanzo beans (page 208) which have more nutrients and less fat than potato chips.

These tasty recipes are great for parties as well. Along with savory dips, consider serving delicious finger foods like Cauliflower Popcorn (page 217) or Slimmed-Down Potato Skins (page 216) for predinner nibbles. Need a healthy and delicious appetizer for the sit-down meal? We have three recipes for steamed artichokes that we promise your guests will rave about.

GRILLED CHICKEN WITH CITRUS SAUCE

Entertaining is effortless with this easy-to-make hors d'oeuvre. Terrific substitutions include thin slices of beef or lamb, which grill on skewers as easily and quickly as chicken does.

TOTAL TIME: 30 minutes, plus marinating and chilling
MAKES: 20 servings

¼	cup extra-virgin olive oil
¼	cup lemon juice
3	tablespoons fresh oregano
¾	teaspoon salt
½	teaspoon fresh-ground pepper
1	pound boneless, skinless chicken breasts
1	cup plain, unsweetened Greek yogurt
2	teaspoons fresh orange juice
1	teaspoon orange zest
½	teaspoon garlic
½	teaspoon ground cumin

1. Marinate the chicken: Combine olive oil, 2 tablespoons lemon juice, 2 tablespoons oregano, ½ teaspoon salt, and pepper in a large bowl. Add the chicken and marinate for 20 minutes.

2. Make Citrus Sauce: Stir together the remaining ingredients in a medium bowl. Cover and refrigerate.

3. Cook the chicken: Heat grill to medium-high. Run skewers through chicken pieces and grill for about 4 minutes, turn over, and grill until cooked through—about 4 more minutes. Serve with Citrus Sauce.

Each serving: About 50 calories, 6g protein, 1g carbohydrate, 3g total fat (1g saturated), 0g fiber, 65mg sodium

GINGERY SHRIMP TOASTS

This savory update of our 1979 recipe features bold Asian flavors. (See photograph on page 182.)

ACTIVE TIME: 15 minutes   **TOTAL TIME:** 35 minutes
MAKES: 12 servings

1	large whole-grain baguette, sliced
4	tablespoons butter, melted
¼	cup packed fresh cilantro leaves, plus more for garnish
1	jalapeño chile, seeded and sliced
1	small shallot, sliced
4	thin coins peeled fresh ginger, coarsely chopped
¼	teaspoon sugar
¾	cup whole wheat panko (Japanese bread crumbs)
¼	teaspoon salt
1	pound shelled, deveined shrimp
2	tablespoons light mayonnaise

Sesame seeds, for garnish

1. Place oven rack 6 inches from broiler heat source. Arrange baguette slices in single layer on large foil-lined baking sheet. Broil 1 to 2 minutes or until tops are golden. Turn baguette slices over. Brush with some of the melted butter; set aside remaining butter and baguette slices.

2. In food processor, pulse cilantro, jalapeño, shallots, ginger, sugar, ¼ cup panko and salt until finely chopped. Add shrimp and mayonnaise; pulse until shrimp are just finely chopped, stopping and scraping side of bowl occasionally. Divide mixture among baguette slices.

3. In small bowl, combine remaining ½ cup panko and reserved melted butter. Top each toast with panko mixture, pressing to adhere. Broil 1 to 2 minutes or until browned and shrimp are cooked through. Serve topped with sesame seeds and cilantro leaves.

Each serving: About 160 calories, 9g protein, 19g carbohydrate, 6g total fat (3g saturated), 2g fiber, 446mg sodium

CAULIFLOWER TAPENADE

Swap in cauliflower for a creamier and sweeter version of tapenade.

ACTIVE TIME: 10 minutes   **TOTAL TIME:** 20 minutes, plus cooling
MAKES: 8 servings

3	cups (12 ounces) cauliflower florets
2	tablespoons water
1	cup extra-virgin olive oil
1	cup pitted green olives
2	green onions, sliced
2	tablespoons fresh lemon juice
½	teaspoon salt

Whole-grain baguette slices or crudités, for serving

1. In a bowl, combine cauliflower and water. Cover; microwave on High 7 minutes or until very soft. Let cool.

2. In blender, combine oil, olives, green onions, and lemon juice; blend until mostly smooth. Add cauliflower and salt; blend until smooth, stopping and stirring occasionally. Refrigerate until cool. Serve on baguette slices or with crudités for dipping.

Each serving: About 275 calories, 1g protein, 3g carbohydrate, 29g total fat (4g saturated), 1g fiber, 390mg sodium

THE PERFECT HOMEMADE HUMMUS

Look for tahini at health food stores and supermarkets.

TOTAL TIME: 15 minutes, plus chilling

MAKES: 16 servings

2	cups water, plus 2 tablespoons
4	cloves garlic cloves, peeled
1	large lemon
1	(15- to 19-ounce) can garbanzo beans, rinsed and drained
2	tablespoons tahini
3	tablespoons extra-virgin olive oil
1/2	teaspoon salt
1/8	teaspoon cayenne pepper
1/2	teaspoon paprika
2	tablespoons chopped fresh cilantro (optional)

Whole wheat pita bread wedges

Olives

1. In 1-quart saucepan, heat 2 cups water to boiling over high heat. Add garlic and cook 3 minutes to blanch; drain.

2. From lemon, grate 1 teaspoon peel and squeeze 3 tablespoons juice. In food processor with knife blade attached, combine beans, tahini, garlic, lemon peel and juice, oil, 2 tablespoons water, salt, and cayenne pepper. Puree until smooth. Transfer to platter; cover and refrigerate up to 4 hours. To serve, sprinkle with paprika and cilantro, if using. Serve with pita bread wedges and olives.

Each serving (1 tablespoon): About 28 calories, 1g protein, 2g carbohydrate, 2g total fat, (0g saturated), 0g fiber, 54mg sodium

LEMON CILANTRO EGGPLANT DIP

The light, nutty flavor of tahini, an essential ingredient in hummus, goes perfectly with rich roasted eggplant in this delicious dip.

ACTIVE TIME: 10 minutes
TOTAL TIME: 55 minutes, plus chilling
MAKES: About 2 cups

Nonstick cooking spray

2	(1-pound) eggplants, cut lengthwise in half
4	garlic cloves, not peeled
3	tablespoons tahini (sesame seed paste)
3	tablespoons fresh lemon juice
3/4	teaspoon salt
1/4	cup loosely packed fresh cilantro or mint leaves, chopped

1. Preheat oven to 450°F. Line 15 ½ x 10 ½-inch jelly-roll pan with foil and spray with nonstick cooking spray. Place eggplant halves, skin sides up, in foil-lined pan. Wrap garlic in foil and place in pan with eggplants. Roast 45 to 50 minutes or until eggplants are very tender and skin is shriveled and browned. Unwrap garlic. Cool eggplants and garlic until easy to handle.

2. When cool, scoop eggplant flesh into food processor with knife blade attached. Squeeze out garlic pulp from each clove and add to food processor with tahini, lemon juice, and salt; pulse to coarsely chop. Spoon dip into serving bowl; stir in cilantro. Cover and refrigerate at least 2 hours before serving. Refrigerate leftovers in an airtight container up to 3 days.

Each serving (2 tablespoons): About 20 calories, 0g protein, 4g carbohydrate, 0g total fat (0g saturated), 4g fiber, 220mg sodium

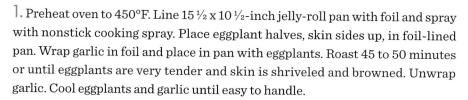

FLAT-TUMMY INGREDIENT: CILANTRO

Not only does cilantro add a bright burst of flavor with zero calories, but it's good for you, too! Fresh cilantro contains phytonutrients that provide antioxidant protection, as well as beta-carotene, vitamins A and K, iron, and dietary fiber.

SWEET AND SAVORY SNACK MIX

This hors d'oeuvre–worthy treat is also great for a brown-bag lunch.

ACTIVE TIME: 10 minutes
TOTAL TIME: 40 minutes
MAKES: 14 servings

4	tablespoons butter
3	tablespoons honey
3	tablespoons low-sodium soy sauce
2	teaspoons lime peel, grated
4	cups unsweetened 100% whole-grain shredded-wheat squares
2	cups whole-grain crackers, broken up
1	cup roasted salted edamame
1	cup roasted salted cashews

1. In small saucepan, melt butter, honey, soy sauce, and lime peel on medium. Combine unsweetened shredded wheat squares, whole-grain crackers, edamame, and cashews. Drizzle with butter mixture; toss well.

2. Transfer to 2 large rimmed baking sheets. Bake at 275°F in oven for 30 minutes, stirring and rotating pans halfway through. Cool completely. Can be stored in airtight container up to 3 weeks.

Each serving (½ cup): About 215 calories, 7g protein, 27g carbohydrate, 10g total fat (3g saturated), 4g fiber, 293mg sodium

TZATZIKI

In Greece, this is served as a dip with pita bread or as a cold sauce to accompany grilled fish or chicken.

TOTAL TIME: 20 minutes, plus overnight to drain, plus chilling
MAKES: 20 servings

2	cups (16 ounces) plain unsweetened Greek yogurt
1/2	English (seedless) cucumber, not peeled, finely chopped, plus a few very thin slices
1 1/2	teaspoons salt
1	to 2 garlic cloves, chopped
1	tablespoon chopped fresh mint or dill, plus additional sprigs
1	tablespoon extra-virgin olive oil
1/2	teaspoon red wine vinegar
1/4	teaspoon ground black pepper

1. Spoon yogurt into sieve lined with cheesecloth or coffee filter set over bowl; cover and refrigerate overnight. Transfer drained yogurt to medium bowl and discard liquid.

2. Meanwhile, in colander set over bowl, toss chopped cucumber with 1 teaspoon salt. Let drain at least 1 hour at room temperature, or cover and refrigerate up to 8 hours. In batches, wrap chopped cucumber in kitchen towel and squeeze to remove as much liquid as possible. Pat dry with paper towels, then add to bowl with yogurt.

3. With the side of chef's knife, mash garlic to a paste with remaining 1/2 teaspoon salt. Add garlic, chopped mint, oil, vinegar, and pepper to yogurt and stir to combine. Cover and refrigerate at least 2 or up to 4 hours. Serve chilled or at room temperature, topped with cucumber slices and mint sprigs. Makes about 1 1/4 cups.

Each serving (1 tablespoon): About 30 calories, 2g protein, 1g carbohydrate, 2g total fat (1g saturated), 0g fiber, 156mg sodium

HERBED YOGURT-CHEESE DIP

Here's an alternative to tzatziki without the cucumbers and vinegar that still delivers a garlicky, herbal tang.

TOTAL TIME: 20 minutes, plus overnight to drain

MAKES: 16 servings

2	cups (16 ounces) plain unsweetened Greek yogurt
1	garlic clove, crushed with garlic press
¼	cup chopped fresh basil
1	tablespoon extra-virgin olive oil
½	teaspoon salt

100% whole-grain crackers or cut-up vegetables

Prepare yogurt as in step 1 of Tzatziki recipe (page 192). Stir in garlic, basil, olive oil, and salt. Serve with crackers or cut-up vegetables.

Each serving (1 tablespoon): About 40 calories, 3g protein, 1g carbohydrate, 2g total fat (1g saturated), 0g fiber, 73mg sodium

SOUR CREAM AND ONION PARTY DIP

Store-bought tubs have more calories and fat than this slimmed-down version—and they don't taste nearly as good!

ACTIVE TIME: 10 minutes
TOTAL TIME: 35 minutes, plus chilling
MAKES: 16 servings

1½	cups plain unsweetened Greek yogurt
2	tablespoons extra-virgin olive oil
2	medium (6- to 8-ounce) yellow onions, finely chopped
¼	teaspoon sugar
¼	teaspoon salt
⅛	teaspoon ground black pepper
⅓	cup reduced-fat sour cream

Snipped chives, for garnish
Fresh veggie crudités, for serving

1. Line medium sieve set over deep bowl with basket-style coffee filter or paper towel. Spoon yogurt into filter; cover and refrigerate 25 minutes. Discard liquid in bowl.

2. Meanwhile, in 12-inch skillet, heat oil on medium until hot. Add onions, sugar, salt, and pepper. Cook 15 to 17 minutes or until dark golden brown, stirring onions occasionally.

3. Line plate with double thickness of paper towels. With slotted spoon, transfer onions to plate to drain further and cool. (Onions will crisp slightly as they cool, and a few pieces may stick to paper towels.)

4. In medium bowl, combine sour cream, strained yogurt, and onions. Stir well. Cover, and refrigerate at least 1 hour or up to 3 days. (Dip is best when refrigerated for a day; flavors develop more fully.) Garnish with chives and serve with fresh veggie crudités.

Each serving (2 tablespoons): About 50 calories, 3g protein, 3g carbohydrate, 3g total fat (1g saturated), 0g fiber, 44mg sodium

GUILTLESS GUACAMOLE

We combine creamy mashed white beans with a single avocado for a low-cal dip that's sure to satisfy.

TOTAL TIME: 15 minutes
MAKES: 12 servings

1	(15- to 19-ounce) can white kidney beans (cannellini), drained and rinsed
1	tablespoon lime juice, or more to taste
1	jalapeño chile, seeded
½	cup loosely packed cilantro leaves
¼	cup coarsely chopped sweet onion (such as Vidalia or Maui)
½	teaspoon salt
1	ripe avocado, halved and pitted
2	plum tomatoes

Sliced basil leaves, for garnish (optional)
Baked whole-grain tortilla chips or fresh-cut vegetables

1. In food processor with knife blade attached, puree beans and lime juice until smooth. Transfer to medium bowl.

2. In same processor, place jalapeño, cilantro, onion, and salt; pulse until juicy and thick.

3. With spoon, scoop avocado from peel into bowl with beans; mash with fork until mixture is blended, with some chunks remaining.

4. Cut each tomato crosswise in half. Squeeze halves to remove seeds and juice. Coarsely chop tomatoes. Stir onion mixture and tomatoes into avocado mixture until blended. If you prefer a little more zip, stir in additional lime juice to taste. Garnish with basil, if you like. Serve with chips or vegetables.

Each serving (¼ cup): About 65 calories, 2g protein, 8g carbohydrate, 3g total fat (0g saturated), 3g fiber, 155mg sodium

SPRING PEA DIP

This delicious dip has a luscious green color, fresh flavors, and a delicate texture. Serve it with assorted vegetables for dipping, such as cucumber strips, yellow and red pepper strips, and baby carrots, or with toasted whole wheat pita wedges.

ACTIVE TIME: 20 minutes   **TOTAL TIME:** 25 minutes
MAKES: 4 servings

1	pound fresh peas in the pod
¼	cup loosely packed fresh mint leaves, chopped
¼	teaspoon salt
¼	teaspoon ground black pepper
⅓	cup low-fat ricotta cheese
2	tablespoons freshly grated Parmesan cheese

1. Run thumb along length of seam to open pod and release peas.

2. In 1-quart saucepan, heat 1 inch water to boiling over high; add peas and bring to boiling. Reduce heat to medium; cover and cook 3 minutes or just until peas are tender. Drain peas and rinse under cold running water; drain well.

3. In food processor with knife blade attached, puree peas with mint, salt, and pepper. Transfer to small bowl; stir in ricotta and Parmesan. Serve dip right away, or cover and refrigerate to serve later.

Each serving (¼ cup): About 80 calories, 4g protein, 8g carbohydrate, 4g total fat (0g saturated), 4g fiber, 220mg sodium

> **TIP**
> To save a bit of time, or if it just isn't the right season, use 1 cup thawed frozen peas instead of the fresh, and skip straight to step 3.

BLACK BEAN DIP

This quick and convenient dip also makes a healthy, slimming filler for a whole wheat pita. You've got lunch!

TOTAL TIME: 10 minutes
MAKES: 4 servings

1	(14-ounce) can black beans, drained and rinsed
1	tablespoon fresh lime juice
1	teaspoon freshly grated lime peel
2	teaspoons chipotle pepper sauce
¼	cup chopped cilantro leaves
2	plum tomatoes, seeded and chopped

In food processor, puree beans with lime juice, lime peel, and chipotle pepper sauce. Transfer to small bowl and stir in chopped cilantro and chopped and seeded plum tomatoes.

Each serving (½ cup): About 85 calories, 6g protein, 17g carbohydrate, 1g total fat (0g saturated), 6g fiber, 224mg sodium

PEPPER DIP

A rich-tasting dip with a Middle Eastern accent. Serve it with vegetables and whole wheat pita chips, or spread it on a sandwich or burger.

TOTAL TIME: 45 minutes
MAKES: 8 servings

4	red peppers, roasted
1/2	teaspoon ground cumin
2	ounces walnuts (1/2 cup), toasted
2	slices firm whole wheat bread, torn into pieces
2	tablespoons balsamic or raspberry vinegar
1	tablespoon extra-virgin olive oil
1/2	teaspoon salt
1/8	teaspoon cayenne pepper

1. Cut roasted peppers into large pieces. In small skillet, toast cumin over low, stirring constantly, until very fragrant, 1 to 2 minutes.

2. In food processor with knife blade attached, process walnuts until ground. Add roasted peppers, cumin, bread, vinegar, oil, salt, and cayenne; puree until smooth. Transfer to bowl. If not serving right away, cover and refrigerate up to 4 hours.

Each serving (2 tablespoons): About 50 calories, 0g protein, 4g carbohydrate, 4g total fat (0g saturated), 0g fiber, 92mg sodium

PERFECT GUACAMOLE

While guacamole is usually served as a dip, it's also great as a condiment for tacos or burritos or on top of a veggie burger. However you serve it, it's full of vitamins and healthy fats.

TOTAL TIME: 15 minutes
MAKES: 14 servings

1	jalapeño chile, seeded and finely chopped
1/3	cup loosely packed fresh cilantro leaves, chopped
1/4	cup finely chopped sweet onion, such as Vidalia or Maui
1/2	teaspoon salt
2	ripe avocados
1	ripe plum tomato

1. In mortar, combine jalapeño, cilantro, onion, and salt; with pestle, grind until mixture becomes juicy and thick (onion can still be slightly chunky).

2. Cut each avocado lengthwise in half around seed. Twist halves in opposite directions to separate. Slip spoon between pit and fruit and work pit out. With spoon, scoop fruit from peel onto cutting board.

3. Cut tomato crosswise in half. Squeeze halves to remove seeds and juice. Coarsely chop tomato.

4. If mortar is large enough, add avocado and chopped tomato to onion mixture in mortar. If mortar is small, combine avocado, tomato, and onion mixture in bowl. Mash slightly with pestle or spoon until blended but still somewhat chunky.

5. Guacamole is best when served as soon as it's made. If you're not serving it right away, press plastic wrap directly onto surface of guacamole to prevent discoloration and refrigerate up to 1 hour.

Each serving (2 tablespoons): About 50 calories, 0g protein, 2g carbohydrate, 4g total fat (0g saturated), 6g fiber, 90mg sodium

FLAT-TUMMY INGREDIENT:
AVOCADOS

Avocados contain heart-healthy antioxidants that have been shown to reduce levels of bad (LDL) cholesterol, while elevating good (HDL) cholesterol. Enjoy them not only in guacamole, but as a topper for salads, sandwiches, or chilled soups.

HEALTHY MAKEOVER NACHOS SUPREME

Our Tex-Mex treat has fewer than half the calories (and 80% less fat) than your typical restaurant nachos. Our low-cal creamy sauce—a blend of low-fat milk and reduced-fat cheese—smothers homemade "baked" tortilla chips, slimmed-down refried beans, and fresh vitamin C–rich tomatoes.

ACTIVE TIME: 20 minutes   **TOTAL TIME:** 25 minutes
MAKES: 6 servings

8	100% whole-grain corn tortillas, cut into quarters
1/4	teaspoon salt
1/4	cup pickled sliced jalapeño chiles
1	(15-ounce) can no-salt-added black beans, rinsed and drained
1	cup low-fat (1%) milk
1	tablespoon cornstarch
1	tablespoon water
4	ounces reduced-fat (50%) extra-sharp Cheddar cheese, shredded
2	plum tomatoes, finely chopped
1	green onion, thinly sliced

1. Sprinkle one side of each tortilla with salt. In four batches, place tortillas between two paper towels on microwave-safe plate in single layer, spaced 1/2 inch apart. Microwave on High 2 minutes or until crisp.

2. Finely chop half of jalapeños; reserve remaining for serving. Reserve 1/4 cup beans; place remaining in medium bowl.

3. In 1½- to 2-quart saucepan, heat milk on medium until just bubbling around edges. In small bowl, stir cornstarch and water until cornstarch dissolves. With wire whisk, stir cornstarch mixture into hot milk. Heat to simmering, whisking constantly; simmer 2 minutes or until thickened, whisking constantly. Remove from heat. Add cheese and whisk until melted and smooth. Stir in chopped jalapeños.

4. Pour 1/4 cup cheese sauce over beans in bowl. With potato masher or fork, mash beans until almost smooth.

5. Place tortilla chips on serving plate. Spoon mashed beans over, then top with remaining sauce. Top with tomatoes, green onions, reserved beans, and reserved jalapeños.

Each serving: About 200 calories, 13g protein, 29g carbohydrate, 4g total fat (3g saturated), 6g fiber, 315mg sodium

PARSNIP CHIPS

Try this new twist on homemade potato chips!

ACTIVE TIME: 10 minutes   **TOTAL TIME:** 1 hour, 15 minutes
MAKES: 2 servings

8	ounces large parsnips
1	tablespoon olive oil
1/8	teaspoon salt
1/8	teaspoon pepper

Preheat oven to 275°F; line large baking sheet with foil. Using sharp mandolin, very thinly slice parsnips into rounds. Toss with olive oil, salt, and pepper. Arrange in single layer on baking sheet. Bake 50 to 55 minutes or until brown and curled. Let stand at least 10 minutes before serving.

Each serving: About 130 calories, 1g protein, 17g carbohydrate, 7g total fat (1g saturated), 5g fiber, 155mg sodium

PINEAPPLE AND TOASTED COCONUT SKEWERS

Spicy and sweet, this hors d'oeuvre is fun, healthy party fare.

TOTAL TIME: 10 minutes
MAKES: 1 serving

1/2	cup pineapple chunks
Pinch of cayenne pepper	
1	tablespoon toasted coconut chips
10	cashews

Thread pineapple onto skewers. Sprinkle with cayenne. Top with coconut chips and cashews.

Each serving: About 155 calories, 3 g protein, 18g carbohydrate, 9g total fat (3g saturated), 2g fiber, 30 mg sodium

SPICED APPLE WEDGES WITH YOGURT

This fragrant and low-fat snack can double as dessert.

ACTIVE TIME: 10 minutes **TOTAL TIME:** 30 minutes
MAKES: 2 servings

2	medium apples, thinly sliced
2	teaspoons grated peeled fresh ginger
1/2	teaspoon ground cinnamon

Vanilla Greek yogurt

Preheat oven to 375°F. On small rimmed baking sheet, toss apples with ginger and cinnamon. Roast 20 minutes or so until tender. Serve with a dollop of Greek yogurt.

Each serving: About 140 calories, 3g protein, 30g carbohydrate, 1g total fat (0g saturated), 2g fiber, 39mg sodium

KALE CHIPS

Our crisp kale chips are essentially fat free—perfect for guilt-free snacking.

ACTIVE TIME: 10 minutes
TOTAL TIME: 25 minutes
MAKES: 6 servings

1   (10-ounce) bunch kale, rinsed and dried well

Nonstick cooking spray

½   teaspoon kosher salt

Preheat oven to 350°F. From kale, remove and discard thick stems; tear leaves into large pieces. Spread leaves in single layer on 2 large baking sheets. Spray leaves with nonstick cooking spray to coat lightly; sprinkle with salt. Bake 12 to 15 minutes or just until crisp but not browned. Cool on baking sheets on wire racks.

Each serving (1 cup): About 15 calories, 1g protein, 3g carbohydrate, 0g total fat (0g saturated), 1g fiber, 175mg sodium

TIP

Kale chips are best when eaten the same day you make them. For longer storage, place uncooked dry rice in the bottom of an airtight container, then add the kale chips. The rice will absorb excess moisture so your kale chips stay crisp.

SPICED GARBANZO BEAN MUNCHIES

Instead of noshing on potato chips or pretzels, try these unassuming roasted snacks. The garbanzo beans boast a mild, nutty flavor that pairs well with cayenne and coriander—and are a flat-tummy-friendly treat to reach for when you get the urge to nibble.

ACTIVE TIME: 5 minutes   **TOTAL TIME:** 30 minutes
MAKES: 8 servings

1	(15-ounce) can garbanzo beans, rinsed and drained
2	tablespoons vegetable oil
1	teaspoon ground coriander
¼	teaspoon cayenne pepper
¼	teaspoon salt
1	tablespoon all-purpose flour

1. Preheat oven to 400°F. In jelly-roll pan, toss garbanzo beans with oil, coriander, cayenne, and salt. Sprinkle on flour and toss again to coat.

2. Roast 25 minutes or until golden and crisp, stirring once. Cool on paper towels. Store in an airtight container up to 1 day.

Each serving (2 tablespoons): About 50 calories, 3g protein, 10g carbohydrate, 4g total fat (0g saturated), 2g fiber, 85mg sodium

STEAMED ARTICHOKES WITH MUSTARD-SHALLOT VINAIGRETTE

A single artichoke per person makes an impressive appetizer.

ACTIVE TIME: 40 minutes   **TOTAL TIME:** 1 hour, plus cooling
MAKES: 4 servings

4	artichokes
5	lemons
¼	cup red wine vinegar
1	tablespoon Dijon mustard
¾	teaspoon salt
½	teaspoon coarsely ground black pepper
1	tablespoon minced shallot
½	cup extra-virgin olive oil

1. Rinse the artichokes. One artichoke at a time, bend back the outer green leaves from around the base and snap them off. With kitchen shears, trim the thorny tops from the remaining outer leaves, rubbing all the cut surfaces with a lemon half to prevent browning. Lay the artichoke on its side and cut off the stem level with the bottom of the artichoke. Cut 1 inch off the top, then place in bowl containing cold water and the juice of the remaining lemon half. Repeat with the remaining artichokes.

2. In a nonreactive 5-quart saucepot, heat 1 inch of water and 1 tablespoon lemon juice to boiling over high heat. Stand the artichokes in the boiling water. Reduce heat; cover and simmer 30 to 40 minutes until a knife inserted in bottom of an artichoke goes in easily. Drain and cool.

3. In medium bowl, with wire whisk, mix vinegar, mustard, salt, pepper, and shallots until blended. In thin, steady stream whisk in oil until blended. Serve artichokes with vinaigrette on the side.

Each serving: About 310 calories, 4g protein, 15g carbohydrate, 27g total fat (4g saturated), 7g fiber, 533mg sodium

VEGGIE ROLLS

These garden-fresh snacks are a party delight.

TOTAL TIME: 45 minutes, plus standing

MAKES: 16 to 20 servings

2	medium zucchini or yellow squash
1	(8-ounce) block low-fat cream cheese, softened
8	radishes, cut into matchsticks
2	carrots, cut into matchsticks
½	seedless cucumber, cut into matchsticks

Mint, parsley, or cilantro sprigs, for garnish

⅛	teaspoon salt

1. Peel and slice zucchini or yellow squash into wide ribbons.

2. Spread 1 tablespoon cream cheese on a ribbon and top with radishes, carrots, and cucumbers. Garnish with herbs.

3. Tightly roll up sushi-style—the cream cheese will act like "glue." Make up to 1 hour ahead; let stand at room temperature.

Each serving: About 35 calories, 1g protein, 3g carbohydrate, 2g total fat (1g saturated), 1g fiber, 65mg sodium

MORE DELICIOUS VARIATIONS

RED PEPPER-BASIL

Mix ½ cup finely chopped roasted red peppers into the cream-cheese spread. Fill roll with basil, bell peppers, and green apples.

Each serving: About 40 calories, 1g protein, 4g carbohydrate, 2g total fat (1g saturated), 1g fiber, 73mg sodium

ASIAN GARDEN

Mix 1 tablespoon low-sodium soy sauce and 2 teaspoons fresh lime juice into the cream-cheese spread. Fill roll with radishes, green onions, and carrots.

Each serving: About 35 calories, 1g protein, 3g carbohydrate, 2g total fat (1g saturated), 1g fiber, 84mg sodium

VEGGIE CHILI

Mix ½ cup shredded reduced-fat Cheddar cheese and 1 teaspoon chili powder into the cream-cheese spread. Fill roll with cilantro, cucumber, and jicama.

Each serving: About 40 calories, 2g protein, 3g carbohydrate, 3g total fat (2g saturated), 1g fiber, 88mg sodium

ZIPPY PEAR

Mix 1½ tablespoons horseradish and 1 tablespoon chives into the cream-cheese spread. Fill roll with parsley, pears, and celery.

Each serving: About 35 calories, 1g protein, 3g carbohydrate, 2g total fat (1g saturated), 1g fiber, 73mg sodium

BRAISED BABY ARTICHOKES WITH OLIVES

Cook baby artichokes the way Italians do—with garlic and olives.

ACTIVE TIME: 20 minutes   **TOTAL TIME:** 45 minutes
MAKES: 8 servings

2	pounds (about 16) baby artichokes
1	lemon, cut in half
¼	cup olive oil
3	garlic cloves, thinly sliced
1	cup water
½	teaspoon salt
½	teaspoon coarsely ground pepper
⅓	cup oil-cured olives, pitted and coarsely chopped

1. Trim artichokes: Bend back outer green leaves and snap them off at base until remaining leaves are green on top and yellow at bottom. Cut off stem, level with bottom of artichoke. Cut off top half of each artichoke and discard. Rub cut surfaces with 1 lemon half to prevent browning. Cut each artichoke lengthwise in half or into quarters if large, dropping them into bowl of cold water and juice of remaining lemon half.

2. In 12-inch skillet, heat 1 inch water to boiling over high heat. Drain artichokes and add to skillet; cook 5 minutes, then drain. Wipe skillet dry with paper towels.

3. In same skillet, heat oil over medium-high heat. Add garlic and cook, stirring, until golden. Add artichokes; cook, turning once, until lightly browned, about 2 minutes. Stir in water, salt, and pepper; cover and cook until knife inserted in bottom of artichoke goes in easily, about 5 minutes longer. Stir in olives and heat through.

Each serving: About 105 calories, 2g protein, 6g carbohydrate, 9g total fat (1g saturated), 383mg sodium

ROMAN-STYLE ARTICHOKES

Mint, garlic, and white wine are the hallmarks of this traditional dish.

ACTIVE TIME: 25 minutes   **TOTAL TIME:** 1 hour, 10 minutes
MAKES: 8 servings

8	medium artichokes
1/2	large lemon
1/4	cup olive oil
6	sprigs mint, plus additional chopped mint for garnish
3	cloves garlic
1/2	cup dry white wine
1/2	teaspoon salt
1/4	teaspoon ground black pepper
2	cups water

1. Trim artichokes: Lay each artichoke on its side and, with serrated knife, cut 1 inch off top of artichoke. Trim stem end, then cut off stem level with bottom of artichoke. Peel stem with vegetable peeler. Bend back dark outer leaves just from around base of artichoke; snap off and discard. With kitchen shears, trim thorny tips from remaining leaves. Rub lemon all over artichoke and stem to help prevent discoloring. Repeat with remaining artichokes.

2. In nonreactive 8-quart Dutch oven or saucepot, heat oil over medium heat until hot. Add mint sprigs and garlic and cook 3 minutes, stirring frequently. Add wine, salt, pepper, and water; heat to boiling over high heat.

3. Reduce heat to medium. Place artichokes, stem sides down, and stems in boiling liquid in Dutch oven. Cover and cook 30 to 40 minutes or until knife inserted in bottom of artichokes goes in easily.

4. Transfer artichokes with cooking liquid to 8 shallow soup bowls; serve warm or cool to room temperature. Sprinkle with remaining chopped mint.

5. To eat, starting at bottom of artichoke, pluck off leaves one by one. Dip leaves in broth and pull through your teeth, scraping off pulp. Discard leaves. When leaves are too small and thin to eat, pull them out to reveal fuzzy choke. With tip of spoon, scrape out choke and discard. Cut solid heart into chunks before eating.

Each serving: About 130 calories, 4g protein, 15g carbohydrate, 7g total fat (1g saturated), 7g fiber, 196mg sodium

MIXED BERRY CEVICHE

Juicy summer berries are an unexpected but delicious complement to sweet shrimp in this ceviche dish.

TOTAL TIME: 20 minutes, plus marinating
MAKES: 5 servings

5	tablespoons lime juice
1/4	cup finely chopped fresh mint leaves
1/4	cup extra-virgin olive oil
1	teaspoon red wine vinegar
1/2	teaspoon ground coriander
1/4	teaspoon crushed red pepper
1/8	teaspoon sugar
1/4	teaspoon salt
1¼	pound cooked, shelled, and deveined large shrimp
1	avocado
1/2	English (seedless) cucumber
4	ounces strawberries
6	ounces blueberries
1	cup red onion, finely chopped

Whole-grain tortilla chips

In large bowl, whisk together lime juice, mint, oil, vinegar, coriander, red pepper, sugar, and salt. Add shrimp, avocado, cucumber, strawberries, blueberries, and red onion; fold until well combined. Can be made up to 2 hours ahead; cover and refrigerate. Serve ceviche with whole-grain tortilla chips.

Each serving: About 350 calories, 30g protein, 16g carbohydrate, 19g total fat (2g saturated), 5g fiber, 429mg sodium

SLIMMED-DOWN POTATO SKINS

Our version of these tasty apps weighs in at just 120 calories per serving—versus the classic's 350—and has one-fifth the saturated fat. Our secret? Lighter ingredients (Greek yogurt, Pecorino cheese) that pack a lot of flavor.

ACTIVE TIME: 35 minutes

TOTAL TIME: 1 hour, 10 minutes

MAKES: 8 servings

4	large baking potatoes (12 ounces), well scrubbed
1	tablespoon extra-virgin olive oil, plus more to grease pan
⅛	teaspoon salt
⅛	teaspoon ground black pepper
⅓	cup plain, unsweetened Greek yogurt
1	ounce Pecorino Romano cheese, finely grated
1	large (10- to 12-ounce) ripe tomato, finely chopped
2	tablespoons snipped fresh chives

1. With fork, pierce each potato three times. Place potatoes on parchment paper. Microwave on High 8 minutes. Turn over; microwave on High 10 minutes longer or until tender. Cover with kitchen towel; let cool.

2. Preheat oven to 475°F. Cut each potato in quarters lengthwise. With spoon, scoop potato from skins, leaving about ¼ inch of potato with skin and being careful not to break through skin. Reserve cooked potato flesh for another use.

3. Grease 18 x 12-inch jelly-roll pan with olive oil and arrange skins, skin side up, in single layer. Brush with oil; sprinkle with salt and pepper.

4. Roast 13 to 15 minutes or until browned and crisp. Transfer, skin sides down, to serving plate.

5. To assemble, spread 1 teaspoon yogurt on each skin. Top with Pecorino, tomato, and chives.

Each serving: About 110 calories, 3g protein, 15g carbohydrate, 4g total fat (1g saturated), 3g fiber, 62mg sodium

CAULIFLOWER POPCORN

Here's a super-smart way to satisfy your cravings.

ACTIVE TIME: 5 minutes
TOTAL TIME: 35 minutes
MAKES: 6 servings

8	cups small cauliflower florets, stems trimmed
3	tablespoons olive oil
¼	cup grated Parmesan cheese
1	teaspoon garlic powder
½	teaspoon turmeric
½	teaspoon salt

1. On large rimmed baking sheet, toss cauliflower florets with olive oil, Parmesan cheese, garlic powder, turmeric and salt.

2. Roast in 475°F oven 25 to 30 minutes or until browned and tender. Serve immediately.

Each serving: About 110 calories, 4g protein, 8g carbohydrate, 8g total fat (2g saturated), 3g fiber, 267mg sodium

CAFÉ AU LAIT

No need to leave the house. You can make your own café au lait!

TOTAL TIME: 5 minutes
MAKES: 1 serving

1	cup brewed coffee
1	cup nonfat (0%) milk

Cinnamon or cocoa powder

Mix coffee with heated milk; add a sprinkle of cinnamon or cocoa powder for sweet flavor, if desired.

Each serving: About 85 calories, 9g protein, 12g carbohydrate, 0g total fat (0g saturated), 0g fiber, 108mg sodium

LOW-FAT LATTE

Making your own latte is just as easy as making café au lait!

ACTIVE TIME: 1 minute   **TOTAL TIME:** 2 minutes
MAKES: 1 serving

1	to 2 ounces powdered espresso
1	cup nonfat (0%) milk

Combine powdered espresso and milk; heat in the microwave for 1 minute.

Each serving: About 90 calories, 9g protein, 14g carbohydrate, 0g total fat (0g saturated), 0g fiber, 104mg sodium

BLENDER CAPPUCCINO

No cappuccino machine? No problem! Use your blender to make this frothy drink.

TOTAL TIME: 5 minutes
MAKES: 1 serving

½	cup double-strength coffee
¼	cup nonfat (0%) milk
4	ice cubes
1	packet calorie-free sweetener
⅛	teaspoon vanilla extract

Pinch of cinnamon

In blender, process coffee, milk, ice cubes, sweetener, vanilla extract, and cinnamon until pureed and frothy. Serve immediately.

Each serving: About 25 calories, 2g protein, 5g carbohydrate, 0g total fat (0g saturated), 0g fiber, 29mg sodium

FLAT-TUMMY TIPS:
10 REASONS YOU NEED TO DRINK
COFFEE EVERY SINGLE DAY

1. IT REALLY WAKES YOU UP.

So it's already your morning routine, but did you know that even just the scent of roasted beans could reduce the effects of sleep deprivation? Plus, it only takes 10 minutes for those first sips to start working—and they last up to four hours. That's a pretty good payoff.

2. IT MAKES YOUR POWER NAP SO MUCH BETTER.

Since it takes a brief while for the caffeine to enter your bloodstream, taking a 20-minute power nap after drinking your favorite caffeinated beverage is the ultimate energy boost. Goodbye, afternoon sluggishness. A "coffee nap" is the best way to beat heavy eyelids.

3. IT HELPS FIGHT BREAST CANCER.

Two or more cups a day can help stop breast cancer in its tracks, says a 2015 study. The brew's properties inhibit tumor growth and reduce the risk of recurrence. How? The caffeine and certain acids make affected cells more sensitive to treatment.

4. IT CAN BOOST YOUR METABOLISM.

It won't replace a trip to the gym, but the caffeine in your latte is a stimulant, which can get your metabolism going. Bonus: It also helps prevent adult-onset diabetes. In fact, one study found a 12% reduction, and there was a stronger link for women than men. So go ahead and order a refill.

5. IT CAN SLOW DOWN THE AGING PROCESS.

Bioactive compounds in your French Roast also make you stay sharp. Scientists found coffee minimized the decline of motor skills and memory associated with growing old. Even better, there are links between drinking coffee and reduced risks of dementia, Alzheimer's, and Parkinson's.

6. IT PROTECTS YOUR EYES.

Researchers discovered that a powerful antioxidant in coffee can help prevent vision loss, blindness, and glaucoma. The compound, chlorogenic acid, works by stemming retinal damage.

7. IT MAKES YOUR WORKOUT SEEM EASIER.

Some days the stationary bike is *not* your friend, but win it over with an espresso. Gym-goers who received caffeine from researchers beforehand rated their workouts as easier and more enjoyable than those without. Even better? Those test subjects ate an average of 72 fewer calories that same day.

8. IT CAN HELP PREVENT SKIN CANCER.

Avoiding the tanning booths is one easy step, but science shows java can also help fight against skin cancer. While it's no excuse to ignore sunscreen, an extra latte could reduce the risk of melanoma.

9. IT'S GREAT FOR YOUR HEART.

Your heart is hard at work all day long, beating over 4,000 times an hour. Keep it in tip-top shape by drinking three to five cups a day. You'll have a reduced risk for clogged arteries and heart attacks because it lowers your levels of coronary artery calcium.

10. IT HELPS WARD OFF DEPRESSION.

Here's something to smile about: A decade-long study that tested thousands of female coffee-drinkers saw a decreased risk of depression. Sure, a mug can make you feel more alert in a number of minutes, but isn't it nice to know your long-term happiness is also getting a boost?

"The 'magic' of coffee is in its potential to have both long-term and short-term benefits," agrees *Good Housekeeping*'s nutrition director Jaclyn London, RD. But she has one warning before you top up: "You still want to make sure you cap your daily intake of caffeine at around 300 to 400 milligrams per day (about 3 to 4 cups) and cut yourself off after 3 p.m. if you're super-sensitive." We'll drink another cup of coffee to that!

Minted Chicken with Asparagus (page 236)

6 | CHICKEN & TURKEY

Poultry is the most consumed meat in America. When consciously trying to eat leaner proteins, many people turn to white meat like chicken breasts as a weight-loss staple. Even the dark meat can be a healthy option once the skin is removed.

Poultry is also versatile and easy to prepare. The recipes in this chapter take you on a global tour: from Italian-inspired Chicken Parm Stacks (page 224) and Roman Chicken Sauté with Artichokes (page 242), to Asian-infused Chinese Five-Spice Grilled Chicken (page 227) and Hoisin-Sesame Chicken (page 230), to Mediterranean Chicken Sauté with Artichokes, Lemon, and Mint (page 234) and beyond. These recipes also offer a variety of preparations like sautéing, baking, grilling, and roasting. Roasted Lemon Chicken (page 231) cooked in the oven, Quick Chicken Kebabs (page 229) prepared on the grill, or Peanut Chicken Stir-Fry (page 240) made in a skillet—these meals are all weeknight champions. There's no better proof: With bold flavors and plenty of recipe variation, eating for a flat tummy does not have to be boring.

CHICKEN PARM STACKS

Chicken Parmesan goes healthy with grilled, rather than breaded, chicken and fresh veggies. A sprinkling of whole wheat bread crumbs adds crunch without a lot of carbs.

ACTIVE TIME: 20 minutes **TOTAL TIME:** 30 minutes
MAKES: 4 servings

1	slice whole wheat bread
4	teaspoons olive oil
1/4	cup packed fresh flat-leaf parsley leaves
1	clove garlic
3/8	teaspoon salt
3/8	teaspoon ground black pepper
1	pound chicken-breast cutlets
1	pound yellow squash, cut into 1/2-inch-thick slices
1	pound ripe tomatoes, cut into 1/2-inch-thick slices
1	ounce Parmesan cheese

Basil leaves for garnish

1. Arrange oven rack 6 inches from broiler heat source. Preheat broiler. Line 18 x by 12-inch jelly-roll pan with foil. Preheat large ridged grill pan or prepare outdoor grill for direct grilling over medium-high heat.

2. Tear bread into large chunks. In food processor with knife blade attached, pulse bread into fine crumbs. In small bowl, combine bread crumbs with 1 teaspoon oil.

3. In food processor, combine parsley, garlic, 1/4 teaspoon each salt and pepper, and remaining 3 teaspoons oil. Pulse until very finely chopped.

4. On large plate, rub half of parsley mixture all over chicken cutlets. Add chicken to hot grill pan or place on hot grill grate; cook 4 minutes. Turn chicken over and cook 3 to 4 minutes longer, until instant-read thermometer inserted into center of cutlet registers 165°F.

5. Meanwhile, arrange squash in prepared pan. Toss with remaining parsley mixture. Broil 7 to 9 minutes or until squash is tender and browned. Transfer squash to serving platter in single layer. Place chicken on top.

6. In same baking pan, arrange tomatoes in single layer. Divide crumb mixture evenly among tomatoes. Sprinkle with remaining ⅛ teaspoon each salt and pepper. Broil 30 seconds or until crumbs are golden brown.

7. Arrange tomato slices on top of chicken. With vegetable peeler, shave paper-thin slices of Parmesan over tomatoes. Garnish with basil.

Each serving: About 250 calories, 29g protein, 12g carbohydrate, 10g total fat (3g saturated), 415mg sodium

APRICOT-GLAZED CHICKEN

Quick-cooking and healthy spinach makes this scrumptious glazed chicken recipe an easy weeknight option.

TOTAL TIME: 30 minutes
MAKES: 4 servings

4	medium skinless, boneless chicken-breast halves (1 ½ pounds)
³/₈	teaspoon salt
¼	teaspoon ground black pepper
4	teaspoons olive oil
1	lemon
1	small onion, chopped
⅓	cup low-sugar apricot preserves
⅓	cup canned low-sodium chicken broth
1	tablespoon Dijon mustard
1	(9-ounce) package microwave-in-the-bag spinach

1. With meat mallet, pound chicken placed between two sheets waxed paper or plastic wrap to even ½-inch thickness; season with ¼ teaspoon salt and ⅛ teaspoon pepper.

2. In 12-inch skillet, heat 2 teaspoons oil on medium until hot. Add chicken and cook 6 to 8 minutes or until browned on both sides, turning over once. Transfer chicken to dish. Meanwhile, from lemon, grate ½ teaspoon peel and squeeze 1 tablespoon juice; set aside.

3. To same skillet, heat remaining 2 teaspoons oil on medium until hot. Add onion and cook 6 minutes or until tender. Add preserves, broth, mustard, and lemon peel; heat to boiling on medium-high. Boil 1 minute. Return chicken to skillet; reduce heat to medium-low and simmer 4 to 6 minutes, spooning preserve mixture over breasts frequently, until chicken is glazed and instant-read thermometer inserted sideways into center of cutlets registers 165°F.

4. Meanwhile, cook spinach as label directs. Transfer to serving bowl and toss with lemon juice and remaining ⅛ teaspoon each salt and pepper. Serve spinach with chicken; spoon any extra preserve mixture over chicken.

Each serving: About 305 calories, 41g protein, 13g carbohydrate, 9g total fat (2g saturated), 2g fiber, 408mg sodium

CHINESE FIVE-SPICE GRILLED CHICKEN

This quick and easy dish delivers lots of flavor from just a few ingredients. To keep the fat in check, remove the skin from the chicken before grilling. To make it a meal, serve with snow peas, fresh ginger, and garlic sautéed in light sesame oil, a flat-tummy all-star!

ACTIVE TIME: 10 minutes **TOTAL TIME:** 35 minutes, plus marinating

MAKES: 4 servings

¼	cup dry sherry
1	tablespoon Asian sesame oil
1	teaspoon Chinese five-spice powder
¼	teaspoon cayenne pepper
1	(3½ pound) chicken, cut into 8 pieces, skin removed from all but wings
⅓	cup low-sodium hoisin sauce
1	tablespoon low-sodium soy sauce
1	teaspoon sesame seeds for garnish

1. In large bowl, whisk together sherry, sesame oil, five-spice powder, and cayenne pepper.

2. Add chicken to spice mixture and toss until evenly coated. Cover bowl and let stand 15 minutes at room temperature, turning chicken occasionally.

3. Prepare outdoor grill for direct grilling over medium heat.

4. Place chicken on hot grill rack. Cover grill and cook chicken, turning pieces once, until juices run clear when chicken is pierced with knife, 20 to 25 minutes. (Instant-read thermometer inserted into center of chicken pieces should register 165°F.) Remove chicken to platter as pieces are done.

5. In small bowl, mix hoisin and soy sauces. Brush sauce mixture all over chicken and return to grill. Cook until glazed, 4 to 5 minutes longer, turning once. Place chicken on same platter; sprinkle with sesame seeds.

Each serving (without skin): About 310 calories, 38g protein, 9g carbohydrate, 12g total fat (3g saturated), 0g fiber, 557mg sodium

QUICK CHICKEN KEBABS

Three ingredients pack a ton of flavor in this fruity kebab recipe.

TOTAL TIME: 25 minutes

MAKES: 4 servings

1	pound skinless, boneless chicken thighs, cubed
¼	teaspoon kosher salt
3	large nectarines, pitted and cubed
1	bunch green onions, cut into 1-inch pieces

1. Season chicken thighs with salt; thread onto skewers along with nectarines and green onions.

2. Grill on medium-high for 10 minutes, turning once, until chicken is cooked through (165°F).

Each serving: About 200calories, 21g protein, 15g carbohydrate, 7g total fat (2g saturated), 3g fiber, 208mg sodium

FLAT-TUMMY INGREDIENT: NECTARINES

Nectarines are a stone fruit available during the summer months, from May through the end of August. They tend to be smaller, firmer, and more aromatic than peaches, plus they are smooth to the touch. When picking nectarines, look at the background color, particularly around the stem. Avoid fruits with any green tints. To store, leave at room temperature. Nectarines have a variety of vitamins and minerals like beta-carotene, vitamin A, vitamin C, and potassium. They are also a good source of fiber.

HOISIN-SESAME CHICKEN

These chicken thighs are brushed with hoisin sauce and sprinkled with sesame seeds before baking. A luscious hoisin and chili dipping sauce is served on the side.

ACTIVE TIME: 10 minutes   **TOTAL TIME:** 30 minutes
MAKES: 4 servings

8	small bone-in chicken thighs (2 pounds), skin and fat removed
1/4	cup low-sodium hoisin sauce, plus 2 tablespoons
2	tablespoons sesame seeds
2	tablespoons chili sauce
1 1/2	teaspoons chopped, peeled fresh ginger
1 1/2	teaspoons rice vinegar
1/4	teaspoon Chinese five-spice powder

1. Preheat oven to 475°F.

2. Arrange chicken thighs in 15½ x 10½-inch jelly-roll pan. Into cup, pour ¼ cup hoisin sauce; use to brush both sides of thighs. Sprinkle with sesame seeds. Bake 20 to 25 minutes, until instant-read thermometer inserted into thickest part of thigh registers 165°F.

3. Meanwhile, prepare dipping sauce: In microwave-safe cup, combine chili sauce, ginger, vinegar, five-spice powder, and remaining 2 tablespoons hoisin sauce. Just before serving, heat mixture in microwave oven on High 45 seconds, stirring once. Serve chicken with dipping sauce.

Each serving: About 305 calories, 29g protein, 14g carbohydrate, 14g total fat (4g saturated), 660mg sodium

TIP

When removing the chicken skin, you'll get a good grip with less mess by holding the skin with a paper towel while peeling it away from the meat.

ROASTED LEMON CHICKEN

Lemons and herbs infuse this roasted chicken. Be sure to serve it with the flavorful pan juices.

ACTIVE TIME: 10 minutes   **TOTAL TIME:** 1 hour, 10 minutes, plus standing

MAKES: 4 servings

1	(3½ pound) chicken
3	lemons
2	tablespoons chopped fresh chives
1	tablespoon chopped fresh tarragon leaves
1	tablespoon olive oil
½	teaspoon kosher salt
¼	teaspoon ground black pepper

1. Preheat oven to 450°F. Remove bag with giblets and neck from chicken cavity; discard or reserve for another use. Place chicken, breast side up, on rack in small 13 x 9-inch roasting pan.

2. From 1 lemon, grate 1 teaspoon peel. Place peel in small bowl; stir in chives, tarragon, and oil. With fingertips, gently separate skin from meat on chicken breast, then rub herb mixture on meat under skin. Cut all lemons into quarters. Place quarters from grated lemon inside chicken cavity; reserve remaining lemon quarters. Tie chicken legs together with string.

3. Sprinkle chicken with salt and pepper.

4. Roast chicken 30 minutes. Add reserved lemon quarters to pan, tossing with juices. Roast chicken 30 minutes longer, until instant-read thermometer inserted in thickest part of thigh registers 165°F.

5. When chicken is done, lift from roasting pan and tilt slightly to allow juices inside cavity to run into roasting pan.

6. Place chicken on platter. With slotted spoon, transfer roasted lemon quarters to platter with chicken. Let chicken stand 10 minutes to allow juices to set for easier carving. Skim and discard fat from pan juices. Serve chicken with roasted lemon wedges and pan juices.

Each serving: About 360 calories, 37g protein, 6g carbohydrate, 22g total fat (6g saturated), 3g fiber, 350mg sodium

LEMON-OREGANO CHICKEN

Try other citrus-herb combinations, such as lime-cilantro, lemon-basil, or orange-sage using this same preparation method.

ACTIVE TIME: 15 minutes **TOTAL TIME:** 45 minutes
MAKES: 4 servings

Nonstick cooking spray

3	lemons
¼	cup loosely packed fresh oregano leaves, chopped
¼	cup loosely packed fresh parsley leaves, chopped
1	tablespoon olive oil
¾	teaspoon salt
¼	teaspoon ground black pepper
1	chicken (about 3½ pounds), cut into 8 pieces and skin removed from all but wings

1. Preheat oven to 450°F. Line jelly-roll pan with nonstick foil or foil coated with nonstick cooking spray. From 2 lemons, grate 1 tablespoon peel and squeeze 3 tablespoons juice. Cut remaining lemon into wedges; set aside.

2. In large bowl, combine lemon peel and juice, oregano, parsley, olive oil, salt, and pepper. Add chicken pieces; toss to coat. Arrange chicken pieces in prepared pan.

3. Roast chicken, without turning, 30 to 35 minutes or until juices run clear when thickest part of chicken is pierced with tip of knife. Transfer to warm platter. Serve with lemon wedges to squeeze over chicken.

Each serving: About 300 calories, 40g protein, 3g carbohydrate, 14g total fat (3g saturated), 0g fiber, 553mg sodium

LEMON-MINT CHICKEN CUTLETS ON WATERCRESS

The tang of lemon and the peppery punch of watercress make this a refreshing choice on a hot summer night. Another plus is that these thin cutlets will cook up in just a few minutes.

ACTIVE TIME: 15 minutes   **TOTAL TIME:** 20 minutes
MAKES: 4 servings

1¼	pounds thinly sliced skinless, boneless chicken breasts
2	lemons
2	tablespoons extra-virgin olive oil
2	tablespoons chopped fresh mint, plus more for garnish
½	teaspoon salt
½	teaspoon coarsely ground black pepper
1	(4-ounce) bag baby watercress

1. Heat large ridged grill pan over medium-high heat until hot, or prepare outdoor grill for direct grilling over medium-high heat.

2. Pound chicken to uniform ¼-inch thickness, if necessary.

3. From lemons, grate 1 tablespoon plus 1½ teaspoons peel and squeeze 3 tablespoons juice. In large bowl, mix lemon peel and juice, oil, 2 tablespoons mint, salt, and pepper until dressing is blended.

4. Reserve ¼ cup dressing. In large bowl, toss chicken with remaining dressing. Place chicken on hot grill pan or rack and cook until juices run clear when breast is pierced with tip of knife, 4 to 5 minutes, turning over once.

5. To serve, toss watercress with reserved dressing and top with chicken. Sprinkle with additional mint for garnish.

Each serving: About 225 calories, 34g protein, 2g carbohydrate, 9g total fat (1g saturated), 1g fiber, 375mg sodium

CHICKEN SAUTÉ WITH ARTICHOKES, LEMON, AND MINT

One skillet and 30 minutes is all it takes to bring this Greek-inspired sauté to the table.

ACTIVE TIME: 10 minutes   **TOTAL TIME:** 20 minutes
MAKES: 4 servings

4	medium skinless, boneless chicken breast halves (1½ pounds)
¼	teaspoon salt
⅛	teaspoon ground black pepper
4	teaspoons olive oil
1	(8- to 10-ounce) package frozen artichoke hearts, thawed
¾	cup low-sodium chicken broth
¼	cup loosely packed fresh mint leaves, chopped, plus additional for garnish
1	tablespoon fresh lemon juice
¼	cup crumbled feta cheese

1. Place chicken between 2 sheets plastic wrap. With meat mallet or bottom of skillet, pound chicken to even ½-inch thickness; sprinkle with salt and pepper to season both sides.

2. In 12-inch skillet, heat 2 teaspoons olive oil on medium. Add chicken and cook 12 to 14 minutes or until browned on both sides and chicken has lost its pink color throughout, turning over once. Transfer chicken to shallow serving bowl; cover with foil to keep warm.

3. To same skillet, add remaining 2 teaspoons oil and heat on medium until hot. Add artichokes and cook 3 minutes or until browned, stirring occasionally. Stir in broth and heat to boiling on medium-high; boil 2 to 3 minutes or until liquid is reduced by half. Remove skillet from heat; stir in mint and lemon juice.

4. To serve, spoon artichoke sauce over chicken; top with feta. Garnish with additional chopped mint leaves.

Each serving: About 285 calories, 43g protein, 7g carbohydrate, 9g total fat (3g saturated), 3g fiber, 350mg sodium

MINTED CHICKEN WITH ASPARAGUS

This easy, weeknight-friendly chicken dish is delicately flavored with a blend of mint, coriander, and lime. If you don't have chicken on hand, you can use pork chops instead. (See photograph on page 222.)

ACTIVE TIME: 25 minutes   **TOTAL TIME:** 30 minutes
MAKES: 4 servings

½	teaspoon grated lime peel
2	tablespoons fresh lime juice
½	cups fresh mint leaves
1	clove garlic
2	teaspoons brown sugar
½	teaspoon ground coriander or cumin
3	tablespoons canola oil
¼	teaspoon pepper
1¼	pounds thin chicken cutlets
1	bunch thin asparagus
4	slices multigrain bread
¼	teaspoon salt
8	cups mixed baby greens

1. Prepare outdoor grill for covered direct grilling on medium.

2. From lime, grate peel and squeeze juice.

3. In food processor, pulse mint, grated lime peel, garlic, sugar, coriander, and 2 teaspoons oil until smooth, occasionally scraping down side of bowl. Transfer to small bowl.

4. Rub chicken with 2 tablespoons mint mixture; sprinkle with pepper. Grill, covered, 6 to 8 minutes or until cooked through (165°F), turning over once.

5. Meanwhile, toss asparagus with 1 teaspoon oil. Grill, covered, 5 to 6 minutes, turning occasionally. Grill bread 1 to 2 minutes per side.

6. To bowl with reserved mint mixture, add lime juice, remaining 2 tablespoons oil, and salt, whisking to combine. Thinly slice chicken. Divide greens among 4 serving plates; top with chicken and asparagus. Drizzle with mint dressing and serve with grilled bread.

Each serving: About 460 calories, 38g protein, 40g carbohydrate, 16g total fat (2g saturated), 8g fiber, 360mg sodium

TIP

Amp up the vitamins with steamed spinach instead of mixed greens.

ASPARAGUS-CHICKEN ROULADES

When food is "butterflied," it is cut horizontally almost in half, then opened flat, resembling a butterfly.

ACTIVE TIME: 18 minutes   **TOTAL TIME:** 28 minutes
MAKES: 4 servings

4	medium skinless, boneless chicken breast halves (1¼ pounds)
1	lemon
3	ounces low-fat goat cheese, softened
½	cup loosely packed fresh mint leaves, chopped
¾	pound thin asparagus, trimmed
¼	teaspoon ground black pepper
¼	teaspoon salt
1	tablespoon olive oil
½	cup low-sodium chicken broth

1. Holding knife parallel to work surface and against a long side of chicken-breast half, cut chicken almost in half, making sure not to cut all the way through. Open breast half and spread out like a book. Repeat with remaining chicken breasts.

2. From lemon, grate ½ teaspoon peel and squeeze 1 tablespoon juice; set aside juice. In small bowl, stir goat cheese, mint, and lemon peel until mixed.

3. Spread goat-cheese mixture evenly on cut sides of breast halves. Place one-fourth of uncooked asparagus on a long side of each breast half. Roll up each breast half to enclose asparagus, allowing ends of stalks to stick out if necessary; secure with toothpicks. Sprinkle chicken roulades with pepper and salt.

4. In 12-inch skillet, heat oil over medium-high heat until hot. Add roulades and cook, covered, 9 to 11 minutes or until chicken loses its pink color throughout, turning roulades to brown all sides.

5. Transfer roulades to cutting board; keep warm. To same skillet, add broth and reserved lemon juice; heat to boiling, scraping up any browned bits. Remove skillet from heat.

6. To serve, discard toothpicks from roulades. Cut roulades crosswise into 1-inch-thick slices. Place each sliced roulade on a dinner plate; drizzle with pan sauce.

Each serving: About 250 calories, 37g protein, 4g carbohydrate, 10g total fat (2g saturated), 1g fiber, 274mg sodium

SUMMER SQUASH AND CHICKEN

Toss these wholesome ingredients on the grill for a simple, satisfying summer meal.

ACTIVE TIME: 15 minutes   **TOTAL TIME:** 25 minutes, plus marinating

MAKES: 4 servings

1	lemon
1	tablespoon extra-virgin olive oil
½	teaspoon salt
¼	teaspoon coarsely ground black pepper
4	skinless, boneless chicken thighs (1¼ pounds)
4	medium (8-ounce) yellow summer squash and/or zucchini, each cut lengthwise into 4 wedges
¼	cup snipped fresh chives for garnish

1. From lemon, grate 1 tablespoon peel and squeeze 3 tablespoons juice. In medium bowl, with wire whisk, whisk together lemon peel and juice, oil, salt, and pepper; transfer 2 tablespoons to cup and set aside.

2. Add chicken to bowl with lemon marinade; cover and let stand 15 minutes at room temperature or 30 minutes in the refrigerator.

3. Meanwhile, prepare grill for direct grilling over medium heat.

4. Discard chicken marinade. Place chicken and squash on hot grill rack. Cover and grill until chicken loses pink color throughout and squash is tender and browned, 10 to 12 minutes, turning each piece over once and removing pieces as they are done. (Instant-read thermometer inserted into thickest part of thighs should register 165°F.)

5. Transfer chicken and squash to cutting board. Cut chicken into 1-inch-wide strips; cut each squash wedge crosswise in half.

6. To serve, on large platter, toss squash with reserved lemon-juice marinade, then toss with chicken and sprinkle with chives.

Each serving: About 255 calories, 29g protein, 8g carbohydrate, 8g total fat (3g saturated), 3g fiber, 240mg sodium

PEANUT CHICKEN STIR-FRY

Delight your family by preparing this popular Chinese restaurant dish at home. Using instant rice, chicken tenders, and prepackaged broccoli florets, you'll have it on the table in a flash.

ACTIVE TIME: 10 minutes **TOTAL TIME:** 20 minutes
MAKES: 4 servings

1	cup instant brown rice
1	cup low-sodium chicken broth
2	tablespoons low-sodium soy sauce
1	tablespoon cornstarch
2	teaspoons vegetable oil
1	pound chicken-breast tenders, each cut lengthwise in half
1	(12-ounce) package broccoli florets
1	small red pepper, cut into 1-inch pieces
1	small onion, cut in half and sliced
1	teaspoon grated, peeled fresh ginger
½	cup unsalted roasted peanuts
1	teaspoon Asian sesame oil

1. Prepare rice as label directs.

2. Meanwhile, in small bowl, whisk together broth, soy sauce, and cornstarch until smooth.

3. In nonstick 12-inch skillet, heat oil over medium. Add chicken and cook, stirring frequently (stir-frying), until it just loses pink color throughout, 4 to 5 minutes. Transfer chicken to bowl.

4. To same skillet, add broccoli, red pepper, onion, ginger, and ¼ cup broth mixture. Cover skillet and cook, stirring occasionally, until vegetables are tender-crisp, about 3 minutes. Stir in remaining broth mixture and add chicken with any juices to skillet; heat to boiling over medium-high. Boil until mixture has thickened slightly, about 1 minute. Remove skillet from heat; stir in peanuts and sesame oil.

5. To serve, spoon rice onto four dinner plates; top with chicken mixture.

Each serving: About 425 calories, 37g protein, 34g carbohydrate, 17g total fat (3g saturated), 5g fiber, 383mg sodium

CHICKEN WITH PEARS AND MARSALA

Fresh pears and a wine sauce spiked with sage transform basic chicken breasts into an elegant main course. Serve with steamed broccoli florets for a complete flat-tummy dinner.

ACTIVE TIME: 10 minutes   **TOTAL TIME:** 25 minutes
MAKES: 4 servings

1	teaspoon vegetable oil
4	small skinless, boneless chicken-breast halves (1 pound)
1/4	teaspoon salt
1/8	teaspoon ground black pepper
2	Bosc or Anjou pears, each peeled, cored, and quartered
3/4	cup low-sodium chicken broth
1/2	cup dry Marsala wine
1	tablespoon cornstarch
2	teaspoons chopped fresh sage leaves

1. In nonstick 10-inch skillet, heat oil over medium heat. Add chicken; sprinkle with salt and pepper. Cook, turning once, until chicken loses pink color throughout, 10 to 12 minutes. (Instant-read thermometer inserted horizontally into center of breast should register 165°F.) Transfer to plate; keep warm.

2. To skillet, add pears and cook until browned on all sides, 3 to 5 minutes. Meanwhile, in cup, whisk broth, wine, cornstarch, and sage until blended.

3. Carefully add broth mixture to skillet; boil 1 minute to thicken slightly. Return chicken with any juices to skillet; heat through.

Each serving: About 195 calories, 27g protein, 12g carbohydrate, 3g total fat (1g saturated), 1g fiber, 190mg sodium

ROMAN CHICKEN SAUTÉ WITH ARTICHOKES

A quick, colorful, and light dish that comes together in minutes, this is a great antidote to same-old, same-old chicken.

ACTIVE TIME: 15 minutes   **TOTAL TIME:** 30 minutes
MAKES: 6 servings

1¼	pounds chicken-breast tenders, each cut crosswise in half, then cut lengthwise in half
¼	teaspoon salt
¼	teaspoon ground black pepper
3	teaspoons olive oil
2	cloves garlic, thinly sliced
1	(13¾- to 14-ounce) can artichoke hearts, drained and each cut into quarters
½	cup dry white wine
½	cup low-sodium chicken broth
1	pint grape tomatoes
1	teaspoon grated fresh lemon peel, plus additional for garnish
1	(5- to 6-ounce) bag baby arugula

1. Sprinkle chicken with salt and pepper to season all sides. In 12-inch skillet, heat 2 teaspoons oil on medium-high until very hot. Add chicken and cook 8 minutes or until browned on the outside and no longer pink inside, stirring occasionally. With slotted spoon, transfer chicken to bowl.

2. To same skillet, add remaining 1 teaspoon oil. Reduce heat to medium and add garlic; cook 30 seconds or until golden. Stir in artichokes, and cook 3 to 4 minutes or until browned. Stir in wine, and cook 1 minute on medium-high heat.

3. Add chicken broth and tomatoes; cover and cook 2 to 3 minutes or until most tomatoes burst. Remove skillet from heat. Return chicken to skillet; stir in lemon peel until combined. Arrange arugula on platter; top with sautéed chicken mixture. Garnish chicken with lemon peel.

Each serving: About 165 calories, 25g protein, 7g carbohydrate, 4g total fat (1g saturated), 1g fiber, 255mg sodium

HONEY-MUSTARD CHICKEN

Everything for this meal cooks in the oven at the same time—the red potatoes, onion, and the chicken breasts.

ACTIVE TIME: 10 minutes
TOTAL TIME: 1 hour, 35 minutes
MAKES: 4 servings

1½	pounds small red potatoes, each cut into quarters
1	jumbo onion (1 pound), cut into 8 wedges
6	teaspoons olive oil
½	teaspoon salt
¼	teaspoon coarsely ground black pepper
4	medium chicken-breast halves, skin removed
2	tablespoons honey mustard

1. Preheat oven to 450°F. In small roasting pan (13 x 9 inches), toss potatoes and onion with 4 teaspoons oil, salt, and pepper. Place pan on rack positioned in middle of oven and roast 25 minutes.

2. Meanwhile, place chicken-breast halves in second small roasting pan (13 x 9 inches); coat chicken with 1 teaspoon oil. In cup, mix remaining 1 teaspoon oil with honey mustard; set aside.

3. After potatoes and onions have baked 25 minutes, remove pan from oven and carefully turn pieces with metal spatula. Return to oven, placing pan on rack positioned in lower third of oven. Place chicken on rack positioned in upper third of oven.

4. After chicken has baked 10 minutes, brush with honey mustard mixture. Continue baking chicken, along with potatoes and onions, 12 to 15 minutes longer, until instant-read thermometer inserted horizontally into center of breast registers 165°F; potatoes and onions should be golden and tender. Serve hot.

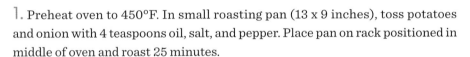

Each serving: About 380 calories, 31g protein, 44g carbohydrate, 10g total fat (1g saturated), 5g fiber, 505mg sodium

CHICKEN BREASTS SIX EASY WAYS!

TOTAL TIME: 30 minutes

MAKES: 4 servings

Skinless, boneless chicken breasts are the darling of cooks looking to cut fat and calories. This recipe scores, thanks to a choice of easy sauces. In a nonstick 12-inch skillet, heat **1 teaspoon vegetable oil** over medium heat until very hot. Add **4 small skinless, boneless chicken breast halves** (4 to 5 ounces each). Cook until chicken is golden brown and loses its pink color throughout or for 4 to 5 minutes per side. Remove chicken from pan and reduce heat to medium, then make one of the following sauces.

Apple-Curry Sauce

Place **2 teaspoons vegetable oil** in skillet. Add **1 Golden Delicious apple**, peeled, cored, and sliced, and **1 small onion**, sliced. Cook, stirring, until tender. Stir in **1¹/₂ teaspoons curry powder** and ¹/₄ **teaspoon salt**; cook 1 minute. Stir in ¹/₂ **cup mango chutney** and ¹/₂ **cup water**. Heat to boiling; boil 1 minute. Spoon equally over chicken breasts.

Each serving: About 315 calories, 29g protein, 31g carbohydrate, 7g total fat (1g saturated), 1g fiber, 521mg sodium

Chinese Ginger Sauce

Add **1 teaspoon vegetable oil** to skillet. Add **1 red bell pepper**, thinly sliced, and cook until tender-crisp. Add ¹/₂ **cup water, 2 tablespoons low-sodium soy sauce, 2 tablespoons seasoned rice vinegar**, and **1 tablespoon peeled and grated fresh ginger**. Heat to boiling; boil 1 minute. Sprinkle with **2 chopped green onions**. Spoon equally over chicken breasts.

Each serving: About 215 calories, 30g protein, 6g carbohydrate, 7g total fat (1g saturated), 1g fiber, 558mg sodium

Black Bean Salsa

Add **1 can (15 to 19 ounces) low-sodium black beans**, rinsed and drained; **1 jar (10 ounces) low-sodium thick-and-chunky salsa; 1 can (8³/₄ ounces) whole-**

kernel corn, drained; **2 tablespoons chopped fresh cilantro**; and ¹/₄ **cup water** to skillet. Cook, stirring, until heated through, about 1 minute. Spoon equally over chicken breasts.

Each serving: About 330 calories, 36g protein, 30g carbohydrate, 6g total fat (1g saturated), 6g fiber, 416mg sodium

Provençal Sauce

Place **1 teaspoon olive oil** in skillet. Add **1 medium onion**, chopped, and cook, stirring, until tender. Stir in **1 can (14¹/₂ ounces) Italian-style stewed tomatoes**, ¹/₂ **cup pitted ripe olives** (each cut in half), **1 tablespoon drained capers**, and ¹/₄ **cup water**. Cook, stirring, until heated through, about 1 minute. Spoon equally over chicken breasts.

Each serving: About 240 calories, 30g protein, 11g carbohydrate, 8g total fat (1g saturated), 2g fiber, 563mg sodium

TWO GREAT TOPPINGS!

Prepare chicken breasts as directed (page 244), then serve with these sauces.

CUCUMBER RAITA

Peel, seed, and coarsely shred **1 medium cucumber**. Squeeze out as much liquid as possible. In a small bowl, combine the cucumber with **1 cup (8 ounces) plain Greek yogurt**. Season with **salt and pepper**. Add a **tablespoon of chopped fresh mint**, if you like.

Each serving (3 ounces): About 65 calories, 6g protein, 4g carbohydrate, 3g total fat (2g saturated), 0g fiber, 85mg sodium

SPICY STRAWBERRY SALSA

Mix ³/₄ **cups finely chopped strawberries**, ¹/₂ **cup finely chopped bell peppers**, ¹/₄ **cup finely chopped red onion**, ¹/₈ **cup lime juice**, 1 **tablespoons minced jalapeño**, and ¹/₄ **teaspoon salt**.

Each serving (3 ounces): About 25 calories, 1g protein, 6g carbohydrate, 0g total fat (0g saturated), 2g fiber, 153mg sodium

PANKO-MUSTARD CHICKEN

This recipe for oven-baked chicken couldn't be simpler—or more delicious. The breasts are brushed with a zippy mustard mixture and then coated in Japanese-style bread crumbs, which become brown and crispy in the oven. Serve with asparagus stir-fried in light sesame oil and garlic and finished with a sprinkle of soy sauce and sesame seeds.

ACTIVE TIME: 15 minutes   **TOTAL TIME:** 30 minutes
MAKES: 4 servings

1	shallot, minced
2	tablespoons butter
2	tablespoons Dijon mustard with seeds
2	teaspoons chopped fresh tarragon
½	cup whole wheat panko (Japanese-style bread crumbs)
4	medium skinless, boneless chicken-breast halves (1¼ pounds)
¼	teaspoon salt

1. Preheat oven to 475°F.

2. In small microwave-safe bowl, place shallots and 2 teaspoons butter. Heat in microwave oven on High 1 minute to cook shallots slightly. Stir in mustard and tarragon.

3. In another small microwave-safe bowl, place remaining 4 teaspoons butter. Heat in microwave oven on High until melted, 15 to 20 seconds. Stir in panko until mixed.

4. Arrange chicken breasts in 15½ x 10½-inch jelly-roll pan; sprinkle with salt. Spread mustard mixture evenly over breasts; top with panko mixture, patting on gently. Bake in top third of oven until chicken loses pink color throughout, 12 to 15 minutes. (Instant-read thermometer inserted horizontally into center of breasts should register 165°F.)

Each serving: About 250 calories, 30g protein, 8g carbohydrate, 9g total fat (5g saturated), 1g fiber, 429mg sodium

CHICKEN ADOBO OVER GINGERY RICE

Flat tummy, Filipino-style! A blend of garlic, soy, vinegar, and spices makes this dish super-tasty without any oil.

ACTIVE TIME: 15 minutes
TOTAL TIME: 1 hour, 15 minutes
MAKES: 4 servings

Chicken

1	cup low-sodium soy sauce
¾	cup rice wine vinegar
1	medium onion, chopped
¼	cup brown sugar
2	tablespoons lime juice
1	tablespoon fresh ginger, peeled and grated
3	garlic cloves, smashed
3	bay leaves
2	teaspoons pepper
2	pounds skinless, boneless chicken thighs

Rice

1	cup long-grain brown rice
1	tablespoon grated ginger
1	bay leaf
Pinch of salt	
½	teaspoon pepper

Green Beans

1	pound green beans
1	tablespoon garlic, minced
Lime juice	

1. In a 5-quart saucepot, mix soy sauce, rice wine vinegar, onion, brown sugar, lime juice, ginger, garlic, bay leaves, and pepper. Add chicken thighs. Cover; heat to simmering on high. Reduce heat; simmer 1 hour.

2. Serve with long-grain brown rice (cooked as label directs, with ginger, bay leaf, salt, and pepper) and green beans (steamed with garlic and lime juice).

Each serving: About 370 calories, 32g protein, 33g carbohydrate, 12g total fat (3g saturated), 4g fiber, 305mg sodium

RUSTIC SMOKY GLAZED CHICKEN AND VEGGIE BAKE

Roast spice-rubbed chicken and veggies for an easy and hearty meal.

ACTIVE TIME: 15 minutes **TOTAL TIME:** 45 minutes
MAKES: 6 servings

2	teaspoons smoked paprika
2	teaspoons ground cumin
1/2	teaspoon pepper
2	tablespoons, plus 2 teaspoons extra-virgin olive oil
1	teaspoon kosher salt
1	pound potatoes
1/2	pound carrots
1/4	pound Brussels sprouts
1/4	pound onion
1/4	pound halved mushrooms
1/4	pound asparagus, cut up
1/4	pound whole green beans
1 1/2	pound chicken pieces

Chopped parsley, for serving
Lemon wedges, for serving

1. Preheat oven to 450°F. Make rub: Combine paprika, cumin, and pepper.

2. On a large rimmed baking sheet, toss 2 tablespoons olive oil, one-third of rub, and ½ teaspoon salt with potatoes, carrots, Brussels sprouts, and onion. Roast 10 minutes.

3. On another baking sheet, toss 2 teaspoons olive oil and one-third of rub with mushrooms, asparagus, and green beans. Push to one side of pan. On other side, arrange chicken pieces. Sprinkle with remaining rub. Season veggies and chicken with ½ teaspoon salt. Roast both pans 20 to 35 minutes or until chicken is cooked and all veggies are softened (transfer chicken from pan to platter if cooked before veggies are tender). To serve, garnish with parsley and squeeze of lemon.

Each serving: About 270 calories, 18g protein, 23g carbohydrate, 13g total fat (3g saturated), 5g fiber, 440mg sodium

MOROCCAN-SPICED CHICKEN AND COUSCOUS

Pair this spicy chicken dinner with a glass of Beaujolais-Villages.

ACTIVE TIME: 10 minutes   **TOTAL TIME:** 45 minutes
MAKES: 6 servings

12	chicken thighs and drumsticks (about 3½ pounds)
Nonstick cooking spray	
1	teaspoon cumin
½	teaspoon cardamom
½	teaspoon cinnamon
1	teaspoon salt
½	teaspoon pepper
3½	cups whole wheat couscous, cooked
½	cup roasted peppers, chopped
½	cup sliced almonds
⅓	cup golden raisins
2	green onions, finely chopped

1. Arrange chicken on large rimmed baking sheet; spray with cooking spray. Sprinkle with mixture of cumin, cardamom, cinnamon, salt, and pepper.

2. Roast in 475°F oven for 35 minutes or until chicken is cooked (165°F).

3. Toss couscous with roasted peppers, almonds, raisins, and green onions. Serve chicken on couscous.

Each serving (without skin): About 405 calories, 35g protein, 36g carbohydrate, 14g total fat (3g saturated), 7g fiber, 491mg sodium

MOROCCAN OLIVE AND ORANGE CHICKEN

For perfectly golden cutlets, set a timer and sear each one at least 2 minutes before turning.

TOTAL TIME: 20 minutes
MAKES: 4 servings

3	tablespoons olive oil
1	pound thin chicken-breast cutlets
¼	teaspoon salt
¼	teaspoon pepper
¼	cup all-purpose flour
1	small red onion, sliced
2	large navel oranges
¼	cup pitted green olives, halved
¼	cup water
Parsley	
2	cups cooked brown rice pilaf

1. In 12-inch skillet, heat olive oil on medium-high.

2. Sprinkle chicken with salt and pepper; dredge in flour. Cook 3 or 4 minutes or until browned, turning once. Transfer to plate.

3. Reduce heat to medium. Add red onion. Cook 2 minutes or until browned, stirring once. Squeeze juice of 1½ navel oranges into skillet. Thinly slice remaining ½ orange; add to skillet along with green olives and water.

4. Return chicken to skillet. Cook 3 minutes. Scraping browned bits off bottom of pan.

5. Garnish with parsley. Serve over rice pilaf.

Each serving: About 390 calories, 30g protein, 36g carbohydrate, 15g total fat (2g saturated), 3g fiber, 627mg sodium

TURKEY BREAST WITH VEGETABLE GRAVY

We slimmed down this holiday centerpiece by serving a turkey breast without its skin, degreasing the drippings, and thickening the gravy with roasted vegetables—but your guests will never know it. Now holiday dinners don't have to be flat-tummy fails!

ACTIVE TIME: 40 minutes **TOTAL TIME:** 2 hours, 40 minutes, plus standing
MAKES: 8 servings

1	(6-pound) bone-in turkey breast
½	teaspoon salt
¼	teaspoon ground black pepper
2	medium onions, each cut into quarters
2	stalked celery, each cut into 3-inch pieces
2	carrots, peeled and cut into 3-inch pieces
3	garlic cloves, peeled
½	teaspoon dried thyme
1	(14½-ounce) can low-sodium chicken broth
1	cup water

1. Preheat oven to 350°F. Rinse turkey breast inside and out with cold running water and drain well. Pat dry with paper towels. Rub outside of turkey with salt and pepper.

2. Place turkey, skin side up, on rack in medium roasting pan (14 x 10 inches).

3. Scatter onions, celery, carrots, garlic, and thyme around turkey in roasting pan. Cover turkey with loose tent of foil. Roast turkey 1 hour. Remove foil and roast 1 hour to 1 hour and 15 minutes longer, checking for doneness during last 30 minutes. Turkey breast is done when instant-read thermometer inserted in thickest part of breast (not touching bone) registers 165°F. Internal temperature of meat will rise to 170°F upon standing.

4. Transfer turkey to warm platter. Let stand 15 minutes for easier carving.

5. Meanwhile, prepare gravy: Remove rack from roasting pan. Pour vegetables and pan drippings into sieve set over 4-cup liquid measure or medium bowl; transfer solids to blender. Let juices stand until fat rises to top, about 1 minute. Skim and discard fat from drippings.

6. Add broth to hot roasting pan and heat to boiling, stirring until browned bits are loosened from bottom of pan. Pour broth mixture through sieve into pan juices in measuring cup.

7. In blender, puree reserved solids with pan juices and water until smooth. Pour puree into 2-quart saucepan; heat to boiling over high heat. Makes about 4 cups gravy.

8. To serve, remove skin from turkey. Serve sliced turkey with gravy.

Each serving (without skin): About 310 calories, 64g protein, 0g carbohydrate, 4g total fat (1g saturated), 0g fiber, 333mg sodium

Each serving gravy (½ cup): About 30 calories, 2g protein, 5g carbohydrate, 0g total fat (0g saturated), 1g fiber, 39mg sodium

TURKEY MEATBALL LETTUCE WRAPS

Lean turkey meatballs in lettuce cups get their savory zing from garlic, mint, and Asian fish sauce, while carrots add crunch. No grill? To cook the meatballs on a stovetop, use a grill pan and increase the cooking time to eight minutes.

ACTIVE TIME: 25 minutes   **TOTAL TIME:** 30 minutes, plus soaking skewers
MAKES: 4 servings

4	metal or bamboo skewers
3	limes
3	cups shredded carrots
1/2	cup packed fresh mint leaves, thinly sliced
2	garlic cloves, finely chopped
4	teaspoons sugar-free Asian fish sauce
3/4	teaspoon ground black pepper
1	pound lean (93%) ground turkey
12	Boston lettuce leaves

1. If using bamboo skewers, soak them in hot water for at least 30 minutes. Prepare outdoor grill for direct grilling over medium-high heat.

2. From 2 limes, squeeze 1/4 cup juice into small bowl. Cut remaining lime into wedges.

3. To lime juice, add carrots, 1/4 cup mint, 1/4 teaspoon garlic, 1 teaspoon fish sauce, and 1/4 teaspoon pepper. Stir; let stand.

4. In large bowl, with hands, combine turkey with remaining 1 tablespoon fish sauce, 1/2 teaspoon pepper, 1/4 cup mint, and garlic. Shape 1 tablespoon of mixture into meatball. Repeat with remaining mixture. Arrange on skewers, 1/2 inch apart; flatten slightly.

5. Grill meatballs 4 to 5 minutes or until grill marks appear and meat loses pink color throughout, turning occasionally.

6. Divide meatballs and carrot mixture among lettuce leaves. Serve with lime wedges.

Each serving: About 230 calories, 27g protein, 15g carbohydrate, 7g total fat (2g saturated), 4g fiber, 415mg sodium

HEALTHY MAKEOVER TURKEY MEAT LOAF

In the kingdom of comfort food, meat loaf is royalty. To get the comfort without the calories, try this version, made with 93 percent lean ground turkey.

ACTIVE TIME: 15 minutes   **TOTAL TIME:** 1 hour, 10 minutes, plus standing
MAKES: 8 servings

1	tablespoon olive oil
2	medium stalks celery, finely chopped
1	small onion, finely chopped
1	clove garlic, crushed with press
2	pounds lean ground turkey
3/4	cup (from 1½ slices bread) fresh whole wheat bread crumbs
1/3	cup nonfat (0%) milk
1	tablespoon Worcestershire sauce
2	large egg whites
1/2	cup ketchup
1/2	teaspoon salt
1/4	teaspoon coarsely ground black pepper
1	tablespoon Dijon mustard

1. Preheat oven to 350°F. In 12-inch nonstick skillet, heat oil on medium and cook celery and onion 10 minutes or until tender, stirring occasionally. Add garlic and cook 1 minute. Transfer vegetables to large bowl; cool slightly.

2. To bowl with vegetables, add turkey, bread crumbs, milk, Worcestershire sauce, egg whites, ¼ cup ketchup, salt, and pepper; mix with hands until well combined but not overmixed. In cup, combine Dijon and remaining ¼ cup ketchup.

3. In 13 x 9-inch metal baking pan, shape meat mixture into 9 x 5-inch loaf. (This will allow meat loaf to brown all over, not just on top.) Spread ketchup mixture on top of loaf.

4. Bake meat loaf 55 to 60 minutes or until meat thermometer inserted in center reaches 160°F. (Temperature will rise to 165°F upon standing.)

5. Let meat loaf stand 10 minutes before removing from pan to set juices for easier slicing. Transfer meat loaf to platter and serve.

Each serving: About 230 calories, 25g protein, 11g carbohydrate, 11g total fat (3g saturated), 1g fiber, 500mg sodium

SWEET POTATO SHEPHERD'S PIE

Shepherd's pie Louisiana style—with collard greens, sweet potatoes, and Cajun spices.

ACTIVE TIME: 30 minutes **TOTAL TIME:** 1 hour, 10 minutes
MAKES: 6 servings

2½	pounds sweet potatoes, washed
½	cups water
½	cup low-fat (1%) milk
½	teaspoon salt
¼	teaspoon ground black pepper
1	tablespoon canola oil, plus 1 teaspoon
1	large (12-ounce) onion, finely chopped
1	(12-ounce) bunch collard greens, stems discarded, leaves very thinly sliced
2	garlic cloves, chopped
1	pound lean (93%) ground turkey
2	teaspoons salt-free Cajun seasoning
2	tablespoons low-sodium tomato paste
2	tablespoons finely chopped fresh flat-leaf parsley leaves, for garnish

1. Preheat oven to 400°F.

2. In large microwave-safe bowl, combine sweet potatoes and ¼ cup water. Cover with vented plastic wrap and microwave on High 15 minutes or until tender. When cool enough to handle, discard peels. In large bowl, mash potatoes with milk and ⅛ teaspoon each salt and pepper.

3. Meanwhile, in 12-inch skillet, heat 1 tablespoon oil on medium-high. Add onion and cook 5 minutes or until browned, stirring occasionally. Add collard greens and ⅛ teaspoon each salt and pepper. Cook 1 minute or until just wilted, stirring. Transfer to medium bowl.

4. In same skillet, heat remaining 1 teaspoon oil. Add garlic and cook 15 seconds. Add turkey and remaining ¼ teaspoon salt. Cook 3 minutes or until browned, breaking meat into small pieces and stirring. Reduce heat to medium and add Cajun seasoning. Cook 1 minute, stirring. Add tomato paste and remaining ¼ cup water. Cook 2 minutes, stirring.

5. In 8-inch square shallow baking dish, spread half of mashed sweet potatoes. Top with turkey mixture, then collard greens mixture. Spread remaining sweet potato mixture on top. Bake 30 minutes or until golden on top. Garnish with parsley.

Each serving: About 290 calories, 19g protein, 33g carbohydrate, 10g total fat (2g saturated), 6g fiber, 278mg sodium

Pork with Crispy Kale (page 297)

7 | BEEF, PORK & LAMB

A source of filling protein, meats are a great addition to any meal on a flat-tummy plan. When shopping, make sure to look for lean cuts of beef, pork, and lamb. That being said, if a recipe requires a fatty cut, you can always trim the meat before cooking to minimize the saturated fat in your diet.

A great piece of meat can be elevated by a delicious sauce, too. Although prepared sauces add flavor and are a huge time-saver, it is important to check the ingredients on the label since many have sneaky sources of sodium and sugar. Plus, it is easy to whip up a homemade sauce! In this chapter, many recipes include a simple, delicious sauce like Skirt Steak with Chimichurri Sauce (page 263) and Pork and Snow Pea Stir-Fry (page 281).

Other dishes like Beef and Barley with Carrots and Mushrooms (page 272), Sheperd's Pie (page 276), and Lean Lemony Veal with Baby Artichokes (page 278) incorporate plenty of vegetables, whether on the side or as part of the main dish, making for a nutrient-rich meal. Vegetables also add heft to a dish without many additional calories.

In this chapter you will also learn how to determine the doneness of meat while cooking, ensuring perfect results and food safety, too. Whether you crave a hearty steak, a slender BBQ pulled pork, an Italian bracciole, an Asian-inspired stir-fry, or a Mediterranean-style lamb dish, there are dozens of great recipes to choose from. Dig in!

STRIP STEAK WITH RED PEPPER VINAIGRETTE

A colorful, flavorful vinaigrette dresses up succulent grilled steak. Pair each serving with 1 cup sliced steamed zucchini tossed with olive oil, lemon juice, and fresh parsley—all flat-tummy all-stars.

ACTIVE TIME: 10 minutes **TOTAL TIME:** 20 minutes
MAKES: 4 servings

1	large garlic clove
1/4	cup loosely packed fresh parsley leaves
1	tablespoon fresh oregano leaves
1/2	cup red wine vinegar
1	teaspoon paprika
1	teaspoon chili powder
3/4	teaspoon salt
1/4	cup extra-virgin olive oil
1/2	small red pepper, cut into 1/4-inch chunks
1	plum tomato, seeded and chopped
2	(10-ounce) boneless beef top loin (strip) or rib-eye steaks, 3/4 inch thick
1/4	teaspoon coarsely ground black pepper

1. In blender, pulse garlic, parsley, and oregano until coarsely chopped. Add vinegar, paprika, chili powder, and 1/4 teaspoon salt; blend until well combined. With blender running, add oil through hole in cover in slow, steady stream until mixture thickens. Transfer to small bowl; stir in red pepper and tomato. If not serving right away, cover and refrigerate up to 2 days. Makes about 1 cup vinaigrette.

2. Heat nonstick 10-inch skillet over medium heat until very hot. Sprinkle steaks with pepper and remaining 1/2 teaspoon salt. Place steaks in skillet; cook 3 to 5 minutes per side for medium-rare or to desired doneness. (Instant-read thermometer inserted horizontally into center of steak should register 145°F.) Serve with vinaigrette.

Each serving (1/2 steak with 2 tablespoons vinaigrette): About 295 calories, 30g protein, 2g carbohydrate, 19g total fat (6g saturated), 0g fiber, 440mg sodium

SKIRT STEAK WITH CHIMICHURRI SAUCE

This fresh and flavorful garlic and herb sauce hails from Argentina, where it's paired with various grilled meats. Wrap the steak in romaine leaves to add a bit of crunch.

ACTIVE TIME: 15 minutes   **TOTAL TIME:** 25 minutes, plus standing
MAKES: 4 servings

Chimichurri Sauce

1	garlic clove, crushed with garlic press
1/4	teaspoon salt
1	cup loosely packed fresh Italian parsley leaves, chopped
1	cup loosely packed fresh cilantro leaves, chopped
2	tablespoons extra-virgin olive oil
1	tablespoon red wine vinegar
1/4	teaspoon crushed red pepper

Steak

1	beef skirt steak or flank steak (1¼ pounds)
1/4	teaspoon salt
1/8	teaspoon coarsely ground black pepper

1. Prepare chimichurri sauce: In small bowl, stir together garlic, salt, parsley, cilantro, oil, vinegar, and crushed red pepper until mixed. (Alternatively, pulse ingredients in mini food processor or blender just until mixed.) Makes about ¼ cup. Sauce can be refrigerated up to 2 days; bring it to room temperature before serving.

2. Prepare outdoor grill for direct grilling over medium heat.

3. Sprinkle steak with salt and pepper; place on hot grill rack. Cover and grill 3 minutes per side for medium-rare or to desired doneness. (Instant-read thermometer inserted horizontally into center should register 145°F.)

4. Transfer steak to cutting board; let stand 10 minutes to set juices for easier slicing. Thinly slice steak crosswise against the grain. Serve with chimichurri sauce.

Each serving (½ steak with 1 tablespoons sauce): About 300 calories, 40g protein, 1g carbohydrate, 14g total fat (5g saturated), 1g fiber, 380mg sodium

ASIAN BEEF KABOOM KEBABS

Simple skewers deliver a fun, pro-flat-tummy dinner.

TOTAL TIME: 15 minutes, plus marinating
MAKES: 16 servings

½	cup packed fresh cilantro leaves
¼	cup low-sodium soy sauce
2	tablespoons honey
2	tablespoons vegetable oil
1	tablespoon coriander seeds
1	clove garlic
2	teaspoons rice vinegar
1½	pound beef top sirloin, trimmed and thinly sliced into 2-inch-long pieces

1. In blender or food processor, blend cilantro, soy sauce, honey, vegetable oil, coriander seeds, garlic, and rice vinegar until mostly smooth; transfer half to large bowl along with beef. Toss beef to coat. Reserve remaining marinade for basting. Marinate beef at least 30 minutes or up to 1 day, covered and refrigerated.

2. Thread beef onto skewers. Grill on medium-high 6 to 7 minutes or until cooked through and charred in spots, turning and brushing with reserved marinade occasionally.

Each serving: About 75 calories, 9g protein, 1g carbohydrate, 4g total fat (1g saturated), 0g fiber, 55mg sodium

TIP
You can pair your beef kebabs with grilled veggies such as ribboned summer squash, green onions, and radishes threaded on skewers. To keep them from drying out, brush them with a bit of olive oil mixed with grated lemon and chopped mint before grilling.

STEAK WITH OVEN FRIES

While the potatoes are in the oven, you can pan-fry the steak, make the red-wine-and-shallot sauce, and even whip up a salad and dressing.

ACTIVE TIME: 15 minutes   **TOTAL TIME:** 40 minutes
MAKES: 4 servings

Oven Fries (page 424)

1	beef flank steak (1 pound)
1/4	teaspoon coarsely ground black pepper
2	teaspoons olive oil
1	large shallot, finely chopped
1/2	cup dry red wine
1/2	cup low-sodium chicken broth
2	tablespoons chopped fresh parsley

1. Prepare Oven Fries.

2. Meanwhile, pat steak dry with paper towels; sprinkle pepper on both sides. Heat nonstick 12-inch skillet over medium heat until hot. Add steak and cook 7 to 8 minutes per side, turning once, for medium-rare, or until desired doneness. (Instant-read thermometer inserted horizontally into center of steak should register 145°F.) Transfer steak to cutting board; keep warm.

3. To drippings in skillet, add oil; heat over medium heat. Add shallots and cook, stirring occasionally, until golden, about 2 minutes. Increase heat to medium-high. Add wine and broth; heat to boiling. Cook 3 to 4 minutes. Stir in parsley.

4. To serve, holding knife almost parallel to cutting surface, slice steak crosswise into thin slices. Spoon red-wine sauce over steak slices and serve with Oven Fries.

Each serving (with oven fries): About 350 calories, 28g protein, 32g carbohydrate, 11g total fat (4g saturated), 3g fiber, 334mg sodium

PEPPERCORN-CRUSTED FILET MIGNON

Time to fire up the barbecue! The grilled sweet peppers are a nice foil to the pepper-studded steak.

ACTIVE TIME: 15 minutes **TOTAL TIME:** 35 minutes, plus standing
MAKES: 4 servings

1	tablespoon whole black peppercorns
1	teaspoon whole fennel seeds
4	(4-ounce) beef tenderloin steaks (filet mignon), 1 inch thick
3	peppers (red, yellow, and/or orange)
1	tablespoon minced fresh parsley leaves
1	teaspoon extra-virgin olive oil
3/4	teaspoon salt

1. Prepare outdoor grill for direct grilling over medium-high heat.

2. Meanwhile, on cutting board, with rolling pin, crush peppercorns and fennel seeds. With hands, pat spice mixture around edges of steaks. Cover and refrigerate steaks up to 24 hours, until ready to cook.

3. Cut each pepper lengthwise in half; discard stems and seeds. With hand, flatten each pepper half.

4. Place peppers, skin side down, on hot grill rack. Cover and grill until skins are charred and blistered, 8 to 10 minutes. Transfer peppers to bowl; cover with plate and let steam at room temperature about 15 minutes, until cool enough to handle. Adjust grill temperature to medium.

5. Remove peppers from bowl. Peel off skins and discard. Cut peppers lengthwise into ¼-inch-wide strips. Return to same bowl and toss with parsley, oil, and ¼ teaspoon salt.

6. Sprinkle steaks with remaining ½ teaspoon salt. Place on hot grill rack. Cover and grill 4 to 5 minutes per side for medium-rare or to desired doneness. (Instant-read thermometer inserted horizontally into center of steak should register 145°F.) Serve steaks topped with grilled peppers.

Each serving: About 230 calories, 26g protein, 9g carbohydrate, 10g total fat (3g saturated), 2g fiber, 495mg sodium

LONDON BROIL WITH GARLIC AND HERBS

Round steak, not the most tender of cuts, benefits from a quick marinade of vinegar, garlic, and oregano. For a tasty side dish, grill tomato halves brushed with olive oil and sprinkled with Parmesan alongside the steak.

ACTIVE TIME: 10 minutes **TOTAL TIME:** 25 minutes, plus marinating
MAKES: 6 servings

2	tablespoons red wine vinegar
1	tablespoon olive oil
2	garlic cloves, crushed with garlic press
3/4	teaspoon dried oregano
3/4	teaspoon salt
1/2	teaspoon ground black pepper
1	(1½-pound) beef top round steak, 1 inch thick

1. Prepare outdoor grill for direct grilling over medium heat. In large resealable plastic bag, mix vinegar, oil, garlic, oregano, salt, and pepper. Add steak, turning to coat. Seal bag, pressing out excess air. Place bag on plate and marinate 15 minutes at room temperature.

2. Remove steak from marinade; discard marinade. Place steak on hot grill rack. Grill 7 to 8 minutes per side for medium-rare or to desired doneness. (Instant-read thermometer inserted horizontally into center of steak should register 145°F.)

3. Transfer steak to platter. Let stand 10 minutes to set juices for easier slicing. To serve, thinly slice steak across the grain.

Each serving: About 200 calories, 26g protein, 1g carbohydrate, 10g total fat (3g saturated), 0g fiber, 340mg sodium

IS THAT STEAK DONE YET?

You've got three options when it comes to determining the doneness of a steak.

1. Using an instant-read meat thermometer, check the steak's internal temperature. Insert the thermometer horizontally into the center of the steak, taking care to avoid any bone or gristle to ensure an accurate reading of the meat's temperature.

2. Cut a small slit in the meat near the bone or near the center of a boneless steak. Rare steak will be bright red in the center and pinkish toward the surface; medium-rare, very pink in the center and slightly brown toward the surface; medium, light pink in the center with a brown outer portion; and well-done, uniformly brown throughout. (Unlike hamburgers, steak can safely be eaten rare or medium-rare.)

3. To test doneness without cutting, try the chef's method: Compare the feel of the meat in the top center of the steak to the skin between the thumb and index finger when your hand is relaxed (hanging loosely), lightly fisted, and tightly clenched. A rare steak feels soft and spongy and offers very little resistance when pressed, similar to a relaxed hand. A medium-rare steak is springy to the touch, as on a loosely fisted hand. Medium steak feels firm, with minimal give, like a tight fist.

TANGERINE STIR-FRY

A mélange of broccoli, tangerines, and red pepper ensures that this stir-fry is as colorful as it is delicious.

ACTIVE TIME: 20 minutes   **TOTAL TIME:** 35 minutes
MAKES: 4 servings

3	tangerines (1½ pounds)
½	cup dry sherry
2	tablespoons low-sodium hoisin sauce
2	tablespoons cornstarch
2	tablespoons low-sodium soy sauce
1	(1-pound) beef flank steak, cut crosswise into ⅛-inch-thick slices
5	teaspoons vegetable oil
1	(12-ounce) bag broccoli florets
1	red pepper, thinly sliced
1	tablespoon peeled, grated fresh ginger

1. With vegetable peeler, remove peel from 1 tangerine. With small knife, remove any white pith from peel; slice peel very thinly and set aside. Squeeze ½ cup juice from tangerines; stir in sherry and hoisin sauce and set aside. In medium bowl, combine cornstarch, soy sauce, and steak; set aside.

2. In nonstick 12-inch skillet, heat 1 teaspoon oil over medium heat until very hot. Add broccoli, red pepper, ginger, and tangerine peel to skillet and cook 3 to 4 minutes, stirring, or until vegetables are tender-crisp. Transfer to large bowl.

3. In same skillet, heat 2 teaspoons oil over medium heat; add half of beef and cook 2 to 3 minutes, stirring, or until lightly browned. Transfer to bowl with broccoli mixture. Repeat with remaining 2 teaspoons oil and beef.

4. Add juice mixture to skillet and heat to boiling; boil 1 minute. Return vegetables and beef to skillet; heat through.

Each serving: About 315 calories, 28g protein, 17g carbohydrate, 14g total fat (4g saturated), 3g fiber, 466mg sodium

BRACCIOLE WITH GRAPE TOMATOES

This Italian stuffed and rolled beef specialty is traditionally simmered slowly in tomato sauce. We offer a quicker method: roasting the beef at high heat and pairing it with tiny sweet grape tomatoes. Serve with a side of broccoli rabe sautéed with garlic and sprinkled with Parmesan cheese.

ACTIVE TIME: 15 minutes **TOTAL TIME:** 40 minutes
MAKES: 8 servings

1/2	cup Italian-style bread crumbs
1	garlic clove, crushed with garlic press
1/4	cup finely grated Pecorino Romano cheese
1/2	cup packed fresh flat-leaf parsley leaves, finely chopped
4	teaspoons olive oil
1/2	teaspoon ground black pepper
1	(1¾- to 2-pound) beef flank steak
1/4	teaspoon salt
2	pints grape tomatoes

1. Preheat oven to 475°F. In small bowl, combine bread crumbs, garlic, Pecorino, parsley, 1 tablespoon oil, and ¼ teaspoon pepper.

2. On large sheet of waxed paper, with flat side of meat mallet or heavy skillet, pound steak to even ½-inch thickness. Spread crumb mixture over steak in even layer; press into meat. Starting at one long side, roll steak into cylinder (about 3 inches in diameter) to enclose filling completely. (Some bread crumbs may spill out.) With butcher's twine or kitchen string, tie roll tightly at 1-inch intervals. Place roll in center of 18 x 12-inch jelly-roll pan. Rub salt and remaining 1 teaspoon oil and ¼ teaspoon pepper all over steak. Scatter tomatoes around steak.

3. Roast 25 to 27 minutes or until temperature on instant-read thermometer, inserted into thickest part of roll, registers 135°F. Let steak stand in pan 10 minutes to set juices for easier slicing. Remove and discard twine; cut roll crosswise into ½-inch-thick slices. Transfer meat and tomatoes with their juices to serving platter.

Each serving: About 225 calories, 22g protein, 10g carbohydrate, 14g total fat (5g saturated), 1g fiber, 290mg sodium

BEEF AND BARLEY WITH CARROTS AND MUSHROOMS

This is a hearty dinner of sautéed beef tossed with a rich barley-and-mushroom pilaf. Because top round steak is a very lean cut, it must be thinly sliced across the grain—otherwise, it may be tough.

ACTIVE TIME: 30 minutes **TOTAL TIME:** 1 hour, 10 minutes
MAKES: 6 servings

3	cups boiling water
1	(1/2-ounce) package dried porcini mushrooms
1	pound beef top round steak, 3/4 inch thick
1	teaspoon olive oil
1	tablespoon low-sodium soy sauce
1	(8-ounce) package sliced white mushrooms
2	medium carrots, peeled, cut lengthwise in half, then crosswise into 1/4-inch-thick slices
1	medium onion, finely chopped
1/2	teaspoon salt
1/4	teaspoon ground black pepper
1/4	teaspoon dried thyme
1 1/2	cups pearl barley
1	(14 1/2-ounce) can low-sodium chicken broth
1/2	cup loosely packed fresh parsley leaves

1. Into medium bowl, pour boiling water over porcini; let stand 10 minutes.

2. Meanwhile, cut steak lengthwise in half. With knife held in slanted position, almost parallel to cutting surface, slice each half of steak crosswise into 1/8-inch-thick slices.

3. In deep nonstick 12-inch skillet, heat oil over medium-high heat until very hot. Add half of steak slices and cook until they just lose their pink color, about 2 minutes, stirring constantly. Transfer steak to medium bowl, repeat with remaining steak. Toss steak with soy sauce; set aside.

4. To same skillet, add white mushrooms, carrots, onion, salt, pepper, and thyme, and cook over medium-high heat until vegetables are tender-crisp, about 10 minutes, stirring occasionally.

5. While vegetables are cooking, with slotted spoon, remove porcini from soaking water, reserving liquid. Rinse porcini to remove any sand; coarsely chop. Strain soaking water through sieve lined with paper towel into medium bowl and set aside.

6. Add barley, broth, porcini, and mushroom-soaking water to vegetables in skillet; heat mixture to boiling over medium-high heat. Reduce heat to medium-low; cover and simmer until barley and vegetables are tender and most of the liquid has evaporated, 35 to 40 minutes, stirring occasionally. Stir in steak mixture and parsley; heat through.

Each serving: About 325 calories, 27g protein, 46g carbohydrate, 5g total fat (1g saturated), 10g fiber, 346mg sodium

GLAZED MEAT LOAF

Adding ground turkey meat and oats to the traditional ground beef base makes this meat loaf lighter and healthier—but it's just as hearty and comforting as any old-fashioned recipe.

ACTIVE TIME: 35 minutes   **TOTAL TIME**: 1 hour, 35 minutes
MAKES: 8 servings

Nonstick cooking spray

1	cup quick-cooking oats
1/2	cup nonfat (0%) milk
1	medium onion, finely chopped
2	pinches salt
1	large red pepper, finely chopped
3	garlic cloves, crushed with garlic press
2	teaspoons low-sodium soy sauce
1/4	cup ketchup, plus 2 tablespoons
1	pound lean (93%) ground beef sirloin
1	pound ground turkey breast
3	medium carrots, grated
2	tablespoons spicy brown mustard
1/4	teaspoon ground black pepper

1. Preheat oven to 400°F. Line jelly-roll pan with foil; lightly coat with nonstick cooking spray. In medium bowl, stir together oats and milk.

2. Coat bottom of 12-inch skillet with nonstick cooking spray; heat over medium. Add onion and a pinch of salt; cook 2 to 4 minutes or until onion softens, stirring occasionally. Add red pepper and garlic; cook 4 to 6 minutes or until pepper softens, stirring often. Transfer to medium bowl; refrigerate to cool.

3. Meanwhile, in small bowl, whisk together soy sauce and 1/4 cup ketchup.

4. In large bowl, with hands, combine beef, turkey, carrots, oat mixture, cooled vegetable mixture, mustard, remaining 2 tablespoons ketchup, remaining pinch of salt, and black pepper until mixed.

5. Form mixture into 8 x 4-inch loaf on prepared pan. Brush top and sides with soy ketchup. Bake 45 to 50 minutes, until instant-read thermometer inserted in center registers 165°F.

Each serving: 240 calories, 25g protein, 17g carbohydrate, 8g total fat (3g saturated), 3g fiber, 360mg sodium

SHEPHERD'S PIE

This slender redo of the classic recipe—rich in protein, fiber, and six types of vegetables—trims the calories by more than 50 percent per serving.

ACTIVE TIME: 50 minutes   **TOTAL TIME:** 1 hour, 15 minutes
MAKES: 6 servings

2	pounds all-purpose potatoes, peeled and cut into quarters
½	cup low-fat (1%) milk
2	tablespoons reduced-fat or Neufchâtel cream cheese
¾	teaspoon salt
¾	teaspoon ground black pepper
1	pound extra-lean (97%) ground beef
2	(10- to 12-ounce) large onions, finely chopped
2	large carrots, finely chopped
2	large celery stalks, finely chopped
½	cup dry white wine
1½	teaspoons fresh thyme leaves, chopped
1	(10-ounce) package frozen peas, thawed
1	(10-ounce) package frozen corn, thawed

1. In covered 4-quart saucepan, place potatoes and enough cold water to cover; heat to boiling on high. Reduce heat to medium; uncover and simmer 18 minutes or until tender. Drain well; return to saucepan. Add milk, cream cheese, and ¼ teaspoon each salt and pepper; mash until smooth.

2. Preheat oven to 425°F. Heat 12-inch skillet on medium-high until hot. Add beef and ¼ teaspoon each salt and pepper; cook 3 to 5 minutes or until browned and cooked through, stirring. With slotted spoon, transfer beef to large bowl.

3. To same skillet on medium-high, add onions, carrots, celery, and ¼ teaspoon each salt and freshly ground black pepper. Cook 8 minutes or until tender, stirring. Add wine to skillet; cook 2 minutes, stirring to incorporate browned bits from pan, or until reduced by half. Stir in thyme and beef, along with any juices.

4. In 3-quart shallow baking dish, spread half of potatoes in an even layer. Top with beef mixture, peas, and corn. Spoon remaining potatoes evenly on top; spread to cover filling. Bake 25 minutes or until top is golden brown.

Each serving: About 350 calories, 25g protein, 55g carbohydrate, 5g total fat (2g saturated), 8g fiber, 360mg sodium

LEAN LEMONY VEAL AND BABY ARTICHOKES

Once baby artichokes are trimmed, they're completely edible because they're so young and the choke hasn't developed yet. They pair perfectly with tender veal cutlets in this brothy sauce lightly flecked with tarragon.

TOTAL TIME: 50 minutes
MAKES: 4 serving

8	baby artichokes
½	teaspoon, plus a pinch of salt
1	pound veal cutlets
1	lemon
2	teaspoons olive oil
¼	teaspoon ground black pepper
2	medium shallots
½	cup water
1	cup low-sodium chicken broth
1	tablespoon all-purpose flour
1	teaspoon minced fresh tarragon leaves

1. Trim baby artichokes: Bend back green outer leaves and snap them off at base until remaining leaves are half green (at the top) and half yellow (at the bottom). Trim stem ends and cut across top of each artichoke at point where yellow meets green (about ½ inch from top).

2. In nonstick 12-inch skillet, heat ½ inch water salted with a pinch of salt to boiling over medium-high heat. Add artichokes; reduce heat to medium-low and cook, covered, 12 minutes or until artichokes are fork-tender. Drain artichokes in colander; cool until easy to handle. Cut each baby artichoke lengthwise into quarters. Do not discard center portion.

3. Meanwhile, if veal cutlets are large, cut each crosswise in half. If necessary, with meat mallet, pound cutlets to even ⅛-inch thickness. From lemon, grate 2 teaspoons peel and squeeze 1 tablespoon juice.

4. In same skillet, heat 1 teaspoon oil over medium-high heat until hot but not smoking. Add half of cutlets; sprinkle with ¼ teaspoon salt and ⅛ teaspoon pepper, and cook 2 minutes or until they just lose their pink color throughout, turning over once. Transfer cutlets to platter and keep warm. Repeat with

remaining cutlets, 1 teaspoon oil, ¼ teaspoon salt, and ⅛ teaspoon pepper (reduce heat to medium if cutlets are browning too quickly).

5. To same skillet, add shallots and water, and cook over medium heat 1 minute. In cup, mix broth and flour. Increase heat to medium-high; add broth mixture and lemon peel, and boil 1 minute or until slightly thickened. Add artichokes, tarragon, and lemon juice, and cook 1 minute to heat through, stirring gently.

6. To serve, spoon artichokes with sauce over veal on platter.

Each serving: About 195 calories, 28g protein, 10g carbohydrate, 5g total fat (1g saturated), 3g fiber, 428mg sodium

TIP

If using medium artichokes, with serrated knife, cut 1 inch straight across top of each artichoke. Cut off stem; peel. Pull dark outer leaves from artichoke bottom. With kitchen shears, trim thorny tips of remaining leaves. Cut artichoke lengthwise into sixths. Scrape out choke, removing center petals and fuzzy center portion; discard. Repeat with remaining artichoke. Rinse artichokes well. Cook as in step 2.

ORANGE PORK AND ASPARAGUS STIR-FRY

Slices of lean pork tenderloin are quickly cooked with fresh asparagus and juicy orange pieces to create a light, flavorful meal.

ACTIVE TIME: 20 minutes **TOTAL TIME:** 25 minutes
MAKES: 4 servings

2	navel oranges
1	teaspoon olive oil
1	(12-ounce) pork tenderloin, trimmed, thinly sliced diagonally
3/4	teaspoon salt
1/4	teaspoon ground black pepper
1 1/2	pounds thin asparagus, trimmed, each stalk cut in half
1	garlic clove, crushed with garlic press
1/4	cup water

1. From 1 orange, grate 1 teaspoon peel and squeeze 1/4 cup juice. Cut off peel and white pith from remaining orange. Cut orange into 1/4-inch slices; cut each slice into quarters.

2. In nonstick 12-inch skillet, heat 1/2 teaspoon oil on medium until hot but not smoking. Add half of pork and sprinkle with 1/4 teaspoon salt and 1/8 teaspoon pepper. Cook, stirring frequently, until pork just loses pink color, 2 to 3 minutes. Transfer pork to plate. Repeat with remaining 1/2 teaspoon oil, remaining half of pork, 1/4 teaspoon salt, and remaining 1/8 teaspoon pepper. Transfer pork to same plate.

3. To same skillet, add asparagus, garlic, orange peel, water, and remaining 1/4 teaspoon salt; cover and cook, stirring occasionally, until asparagus is tender-crisp, 2 to 3 minutes. Return pork to skillet. Add orange juice and orange pieces; heat through, stirring often.

Each serving: About 165 calories, 24g protein, 8g carbohydrate, 4g total fat (1g saturated), 2g fiber, 495mg sodium

PORK AND SNOW PEA STIR-FRY

Frozen snow peas are the secret behind this easy, flat-tummy, single-serving dish.

TOTAL TIME: 10 minutes
MAKES: 1 serving

3	ounces pork tenderloin
2	teaspoons peanut oil
2	teaspoons minced garlic
2	teaspoons minced ginger
1	cup thawed frozen snow peas
½	teaspoon low-sodium soy sauce
1	to 2 teaspoons lime juice
1	cup cooked brown rice

1. Cut pork into bite-sized pieces. Heat a wok over high heat, add 1 teaspoon peanut oil, then add pork. Cook until pork browns, then remove from wok.

2. Add remaining peanut oil to wok and cook garlic, ginger, and snow peas until peas soften and begin to brown.

3. Add pork back to wok with soy sauce and lime juice. Serve over brown rice.

Each serving: About 455 calories, 25g protein, 56g carbohydrate, 14g total fat (3g saturated), 3g fiber, 144mg sodium

GINGERED PORK AND VEGETABLE STIR-FRY

Serve each person ¾ cup brown cooked rice on the side. To make 4 servings, use 1 cup uncooked rice and follow package instructions for cooking.

ACTIVE TIME: 15 minutes   **TOTAL TIME:** 30 minutes
MAKES: 4 servings

1	pork tenderloin (12 ounces), trimmed and thinly sliced
2	tablespoons peeled, grated fresh ginger
1	cup low-sodium chicken broth

Sugar to taste

2	teaspoons cornstarch
2	teaspoons canola oil
8	ounces snow peas, strings removed
1	(8-ounce) medium zucchini, cut lengthwise in half and thinly sliced crosswise
3	green onions, cut into 3-inch pieces

1. In medium bowl, toss pork and ginger. In cup, whisk broth, sugar, and cornstarch until smooth; set aside.

2. In nonstick 12-inch skillet, heat 1 teaspoon oil over medium heat until hot. Add snow peas, zucchini, and green onions and cook, stirring frequently (stir-frying), until lightly browned and tender-crisp, about 5 minutes. Transfer vegetables to large bowl.

3. In same skillet, heat remaining 1 teaspoon oil; add pork and stir-fry until pork just loses its pink color, about 3 minutes. Transfer to bowl with vegetables.

4. Stir cornstarch mixture; add to skillet and heat to boiling. Boil, stirring constantly, until sauce thickens slightly, about 1 minute. Return pork and vegetables to skillet and stir until coated with sauce; heat through.

Each serving: About 170 calories, 21g protein, 10g carbohydrate, 5g total fat (1g saturated), 2g fiber, 72mg sodium

FLAT-TUMMY FACT

If you've always believed that frozen fruits and vegetables are less nutritious than fresh ones, it's time to think again. Produce picked at the peak of ripeness does have more vitamins and minerals, but nutrient levels drop during shipping and storage. And they sink even further if you add the days that the produce lingers in your crisper. Frozen veggies and fruit, on the other hand, are usually picked ripe and immediately flash-frozen, so they retain most of their nutrients. For calorie control, be sure to select frozen produce without added sugar, syrup, sauce, or cheese.

TOMATILLO PORK

Tomatillos, also called Mexican green tomatoes, are the main ingredient in salsa verde. They bring a bright hint of lemon to this set-and-forget dish.

ACTIVE TIME: 10 minutes   **TOTAL TIME:** 8 hours on low or 5 hours on high
MAKES: 8 servings

1	large bunch cilantro
3	garlic cloves, sliced
2	pounds (8 small) red potatoes, cut into quarters
1	(3-pound) bone-in pork-shoulder roast, well trimmed
1	(16- to 18-ounce) jar salsa verde (green salsa)

1. From bunch of cilantro, remove and set aside 15 large sprigs. Remove enough leaves from remaining cilantro to equal ½ cup, loosely packed. Refrigerate leaves to sprinkle over pork after cooking.

2. In 4½- to 6-quart slow-cooker pot, combine cilantro sprigs, garlic, and potatoes. Place pork on top of potato mixture. Pour salsa over and around pork. Cover slow cooker with lid and cook as manufacturer directs on low setting 8 to 10 hours (or on high setting 5 to 5½ hours).

3. Transfer pork to cutting board and slice. Transfer pork and potatoes to warm deep platter. Skim and discard fat and cilantro from cooking liquid. Spoon cooking liquid over pork and potatoes. Sprinkle reserved cilantro leaves over pork.

Each serving: About 300 calories, 25g protein, 27g carbohydrate, 9g total fat (3g saturated), 2g fiber, 295mg sodium

TEN HELPFUL HINTS
FOR THE SLOW COOKER

1. Tougher cuts of meat and poultry—such as pork and lamb shoulder, chuck roast, beef brisket, and poultry legs—are best suited for slow cooking. Skim and discard fat from cooking liquid when done.

2. When cooking with fish and other seafood in the slow cooker, add these ingredients during the last hour of cooking.

3. Avoid using ground meat; long, slow cooking compromises its texture, giving it a mealy, sandy quality.

4. Slow cooking tends to intensify flavorful spices and seasonings such as chili powder and garlic, so use them conservatively. Dried herbs may lose flavor, so adjust seasonings at the end of cooking. If you're using fresh herbs, save some to toss in at the last minute for best flavor.

5. For richer flavor in stews, sprinkle meat and poultry with flour and brown in skillet before slow cooking. Scrape up browned bits in skillet and add to the pot to help thicken sauce and enhance taste.

6. To make cleanup easier, use slow-cooker pot liners.

7. For even cooking, fill slow-cooker pot at least halfway—but never to the brim. For soups and stews, leave about 2 inches of space between the food and lid.

8. Resist stirring the pot because meat and vegetables may break up.

9. If your recipe produces more liquid than you want, remove solids with a slotted spoon to a serving dish and keep warm. Turn slow-cooker temperature to high; cook remaining liquid, uncovered, to reduce to desired thickness.

10. Most recipes can be prepped the night before—all you have to do in the morning is toss in ingredients and flip the switch on the slow cooker! Premeasure ingredients, precut vegetables, trim meats, and mix liquids and seasonings. Refrigerate components separately in bowls or zip-tight plastic bags.

CRISPY SESAME PORK

For perfectly crisp meat, test the oil temperature before frying. Drop in a bread crumb; if it sizzles, it's hot enough.

TOTAL TIME: 30 minutes
MAKES: 4 servings

3	tablespoons low-sodium soy sauce
2	tablespoons brown sugar
⅓	cup panko bread crumbs
2	tablespoons sesame seeds
1	egg
4	thin boneless pork chops (about 1 pound)
3	tablespoons canola oil
5	ounces salad greens
1	cup grape tomatoes, halved
1	cup shredded carrots

1. In a small saucepan, whisk together soy sauce and brown sugar. Heat to simmering on medium. Simmer for 2 minutes; cool.

2. On a medium plate, combine panko and sesame seeds. In a shallow bowl, beat 1 egg. Dip pork chops in egg, then coat in panko mixture.

3. In a 12-inch skillet, heat canola oil on medium-high until hot. Fry chops 3 minutes per side or until cooked (145°F.). Drain on paper towels; cut into cubes.

4. In a large bowl, toss salad greens with grape tomatoes, carrots, and pork with soy reduction.

Each serving: About 375 calories, 24g protein, 19g carbohydrate, 22g total fat (4g saturated), 2g fiber, 520mg sodium

CHINESE RED-COOKED PORK SHOULDER

Pork cooked in a slow cooker becomes so tender it almost melts in your mouth. This fragrant, Asian-style stew is simmered for hours in a combination of soy sauce, dry sherry, fresh ginger, and orange peel. Baby carrots and broccoli florets make it a complete one-pot meal.

ACTIVE TIME: 10 minutes **TOTAL TIME:** 8 hours, 10 minutes
MAKES: 10 servings

1/4	cup dry sherry
1/4	cup rice vinegar
4	tablespoons low-sodium soy sauce
1	onion, chopped
1	(2-inch) piece fresh ginger, peeled and thinly sliced into rounds
2	garlic cloves, crushed with garlic press
2	strips (3 x 3/4 inches each) fresh orange peel
1	(3-inch) cinnamon stick
1	whole star anise
1	(1-pound) bag peeled baby carrots
4	pounds well-trimmed boneless pork shoulder, cut into 1 1/2-inch chunks
2	(10-ounce) packages frozen broccoli florets, thawed

1. In 6- to 6½-quart slow-cooker bowl, combine sherry, rice vinegar, and 3 tablespoons soy sauce. Stir in onion, ginger, garlic, orange peel, cinnamon, star anise, and carrots. Top with pork; do not stir. Cover slow cooker with lid and cook as manufacturer directs on Low 8 hours.

2. When pork has cooked 8 hours, open lid and stir in thawed broccoli. Cover and continue to cook until broccoli is heated through, about 10 minutes.

3. Discard cinnamon stick and star anise. Skim and discard fat from cooking liquid. Stir in remaining 1 tablespoon soy sauce.

Each serving: About 320 calories, 38g protein, 12g carbohydrate, 13g total fat (4g saturated), 2g fiber, 590mg sodium

> **TIP**
> You want 4 pounds of solid meat. If the pork is not well trimmed when you buy it, purchase 4½ or 5 pounds so you'll have enough meat after you cut away the excess fat and skin.

PORK CHOPS WITH PEPPERS AND ONION

Boneless chops are smothered in green onions and red peppers for this fast and easy skillet dinner. Add a side of steamed spinach or zucchini, if you like.

ACTIVE TIME: 10 minutes   **TOTAL TIME:** 30 minutes
MAKES: 4 servings

4	(4-ounce) boneless pork loin chops, ½ inch thick and trimmed
½	teaspoon salt
¼	teaspoon ground black pepper
2	teaspoons olive oil
1	bunch green onions, green tops cut diagonally into 3-inch pieces, white bottoms thinly sliced crosswise
2	red peppers, cut into 1½-inch pieces
1	garlic clove, crushed with garlic press
⅛	teaspoon crushed red pepper
½	cup low-sodium chicken broth

1. Heat nonstick 12-inch skillet over medium heat until hot but not smoking. Add pork chops to skillet and sprinkle with salt and pepper. Cook until lightly browned outside and still slightly pink inside, about 8 minutes, turning over once; reduce heat to medium if chops are browning too quickly. (Instant-read thermometer inserted horizontally into center of chops should register 145°F.) Transfer chops to plate; keep warm.

2. To same skillet over medium heat, add oil and green-onion tops; cook 4 minutes. With slotted spoon, transfer green-onion tops to small bowl. In same skillet, cook red peppers and green-onion bottoms, stirring occasionally, 8 to 10 minutes. Add garlic and crushed red pepper, and cook, stirring, 1 minute. Stir in broth and half of green-onion tops; heat through. Spoon pepper mixture onto platter; arrange pork and remaining green-onion tops on peppers.

Each serving: About 280 calories, 26g protein, 7g carbohydrate, 17g total fat (5g saturated), 2g fiber, 355mg sodium

PORK AND SAUERKRAUT

Slow-cooking boneless pork loin creates a fork-tender meat that's impossible to resist—especially when it's also simmered with apples, potatoes, sauerkraut, brown sugar, and caraway seeds.

ACTIVE TIME: 8 minutes   **TOTAL TIME:** 8 hours, 8 minutes
MAKES: 6 servings

4	large red-skinned potatoes
3	cups sauerkraut
1	large onion
1	large Granny Smith or other tart apple
2	tablespoons packed brown sugar
1	teaspoon caraway seeds
1	teaspoon minced garlic
½	teaspoon ground black pepper
1	(1¼-pound) boneless-pork loin roast

1. Put potatoes in a 4-quart or larger slow cooker.

2. Mix remaining ingredients except pork. Put half the mixture on potatoes. Add pork, top with remaining sauerkraut mixture.

3. Cover and cook on high 8 hours or until pork is tender. Slice pork; serve sauerkraut mixture on the side.

Each serving: About 365 calories, 25g protein, 55g carbohydrate, 6g total fat (2g saturated), 8g fiber, 559mg sodium

SAUERKRAUT RELISH

Fermented foods like sauerkraut are flat-tummy-friendly. Serve this tangy relish with roast beef, pork, poultry, or frankfurters. If you like, store in decorative jars in the refrigerator.

TOTAL TIME: 15 minutes, plus chilling overnight
MAKES: 28 servings

3	(2-pound) bags sauerkraut	1	(1-pound) package light brown sugar
1	medium green pepper		
1	medium red pepper	2	teaspoons caraway seeds
1	(16-ounce) bottle apple cider vinegar		

1. Rinse sauerkraut under cold running water; drain well. Dice green and red peppers.

2. In large bowl, stir sauerkraut, peppers, cider vinegar, brown sugar, and caraway seeds until mixed. Cover with plastic wrap and refrigerate overnight to allow flavors to develop.

Each serving (¼ cup): About 30 calories, 0g protein, 7g carbohydrate, 0g total fat (0g saturated), 1g fiber, 202mg sodium

SURPRISING GOOD-FOR-YOUR-WAIST PICKS

BEEF TENDERLOIN STEAKS: Ounce for ounce, this melt-in-your-mouth cut has about the same calorie and fat content as skinless chicken thighs.

CHICKEN THIGHS: They are higher in fat and calories than breasts, but as long as you remove the skin and any excess fat, economical thighs fit into a good-for-you diet. They also provide 25 percent more iron and more than twice as much zinc as the same amount of breast meat.

PORK: Tenderloin and boneless loin chops compare favorably, calorie-wise, with skinless chicken. So, if your family is crying "fowl," vary the menu with these lean, healthy cuts of pork.

SPICE-BRINED PORK LOIN

Brining pork in a blend of kosher salt, sugar, and spices infuses it with flavor and keeps it tender and juicy. Allow the pork to soak in the brine for 18 to 24 hours before roasting. Serve with a side of sautéed garlicky greens or broccoli.

ACTIVE TIME: 20 minutes **TOTAL TIME:** 1 hour, 20 minutes, plus brining and standing
MAKES: 12 servings

2	cups cold water
¼	cup kosher salt
2	tablespoons coriander seeds
2	tablespoons cracked black pepper
2	tablespoons fennel seeds
2	tablespoons cumin seeds

Peel from 1 navel orange, white pith removed

3	cups ice
1	(3-pound) boneless pork loin roast, trimmed
4	garlic cloves, crushed with side of chef's knife

1. In 2-quart saucepan, heat 1 cup water, salt, coriander, pepper, fennel, cumin, and orange peel to boiling over high heat. Reduce heat to low; simmer 2 minutes. Remove saucepan from heat; stir in ice until almost melted. Stir in remaining 1 cup water.

2. Place pork with garlic in large resealable plastic bag with brine. Seal bag, pressing out excess air. Place bag in bowl or small roasting pan and refrigerate 18 to 24 hours.

3. Preheat oven to 400°F. Remove pork from bag; discard brine (it's okay if some spices stick to pork). Place pork on rack in medium roasting pan (14 x 10 inches). Roast until thermometer inserted into thickest part of meat reaches 145°F, 1 hour to 1 hour 15 minutes (temperature will rise 5°F to 10°F upon standing). Transfer pork to cutting board and let stand 10 minutes to set juices for easier slicing.

Each serving: About 175 calories, 24g protein, 1g carbohydrate, 8g total fat (3g saturated), 0g fiber, 445mg sodium

CURRIED PORK AND APPLES

A simple skillet dinner: Tender slices of pork and tart apples are flavored with curry, then tossed with baby carrots.

ACTIVE TIME: 5 minutes **TOTAL TIME:** 15 minutes
MAKES: 4 servings

1	(16-ounce) bag peeled baby carrots
1/4	cup water
1	tablespoon olive oil
1	Gala or Golden Delicious apple, unpeeled, cored, and cut into 1/2-inch cubes
2	teaspoons curry powder
1	garlic clove, crushed with garlic press
1	(1-pound) pork tenderloin, trimmed and cut into 3/4-inch-thick slices
1/2	teaspoon salt
1/4	cup apple cider or apple juice

1. Place carrots in covered microwavable dish with water. Cook in microwave oven on High until carrots are tender, about 6 minutes.

2. Meanwhile, in nonstick 12-inch skillet, heat oil over medium heat. Add apple, curry powder, and garlic; cook, stirring, 1 minute.

3. Add pork and salt, and cook until pork is still slightly pink in center, 6 to 8 minutes. (An instant-read thermometer inserted horizontally into pork slices should register 145°F.) Add cider and cooked carrots with any liquid, and heat to boiling; cook 1 minute.

Each serving: About 250 calories, 25g protein, 17g carbohydrate, 9g total fat (2g saturated), 3g fiber, 390mg sodium

TIP

Serve with 4 cups shredded cabbage sautéed in olive oil and garnished with a splash of apple cider vinegar and 1 tablespoon toasted, chopped pecans.

PORK MEDALLIONS WITH ASPARAGUS SALAD

Herbed tenderloin is served atop a fiber-rich salad of crunchy carrots, asparagus, and greens.

ACTIVE TIME: 20 minutes   **TOTAL TIME:** 40 minutes
MAKES: 4 servings

½	cup packed fresh flat-leaf parsley leaves
1	tablespoon fresh rosemary, finely chopped
1	(12-ounce) pork tenderloin
2	large carrots
1	pound asparagus, ends trimmed
¼	teaspoon salt
¼	teaspoon freshly ground black pepper
1	teaspoon extra-virgin olive oil, plus 1 tablespoon
1	bunch radishes, trimmed and cut into thin wedges
1	green onion, thinly sliced
1	(5-ounce) package baby greens and herbs mix
¼	cup balsamic vinegar

1. Preheat oven to 400°F. Heat large saucepot of water to boiling on high.

2. Finely chop one-third of parsley. Rub chopped parsley and rosemary all over tenderloin and let stand while oven heats.

3. Fill large bowl with ice and water. Add carrots to boiling water. Cook 5 minutes. With tongs, transfer to ice water. When cool, remove with tongs to cutting board. Add asparagus to boiling water. Cook 3 minutes or until bright green and tender-crisp. Transfer to ice water. When cool, drain well.

4. Sprinkle ⅛ teaspoon each salt and pepper all over pork. In ovenproof 12-inch skillet, heat 1 teaspoon oil on medium-high heat. Add pork; cook 6 to 8 minutes or until evenly browned, turning. Transfer to oven. Roast 8 to 10 minutes or until instant-read thermometer inserted in thickest part of pork registers 145°F; let rest 5 minutes.

5. While pork cooks, cut carrots into 2-inch-long matchsticks. Cut asparagus into 2-inch-long pieces. In large bowl, toss carrots, asparagus, radishes, green onion, baby greens, and remaining parsley with remaining ⅛ teaspoon each salt and pepper as well as remaining 1 tablespoon oil. Add balsamic vinegar; toss to combine. Divide salad among serving plates. Slice pork; arrange on top of salads.

Each serving: About 235 calories, 26g protein, 14g carbohydrate, 8g total fat (2g saturated), 5g fiber, 255mg sodium

PORK TENDERLOIN WITH MELON SALSA

This fruity and earthy dish is just a quick pop in the oven away.

ACTIVE TIME: 10 minutes
TOTAL TIME: 25 minutes
MAKES: 4 servings

1	(1¼-pound) pork tenderloin
1	tablespoon olive oil
½	teaspoon salt
2	cups finely chopped cantaloupe
¼	cup fresh cilantro, finely chopped
¼	cup orange segments
2	tablespoons lime juice
½	teaspoon chili powder

1. On baking sheet, brush pork tenderloin with butter; season with ¼ teaspoon salt. Roast at 450°F for 20 minutes or until cooked.

2. Combine cantaloupe, cilantro, orange segments, lime juice, chili powder, and ¼ teaspoon salt.

3. Slice pork and serve over mixed greens, topped with melon salsa.

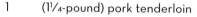

Each serving: About 220 calories, 28g protein, 10g carbohydrate, 7g total fat (2g saturated), 1g fiber, 410mg sodium

PORK WITH CRISPY KALE

Incredibly quick and easy, this nutritious meal is a delicious way to serve up the classic combo of pork and greens. (See photograph on page 260.)

ACTIVE TIME: 10 minutes   **TOTAL TIME:** 25 minutes
MAKES: 4 servings

2	cloves garlic
4	sprigs rosemary
¼	cup prepared horseradish sauce
1	(1¼ pound) pork tenderloin
½	teaspoon salt
¼	teaspoon ground black pepper
12	cups kale leaves
2	tablespoons olive oil

1. In food processor, pulse garlic cloves with leaves from the rosemary sprigs until finely chopped; stir into prepared horseradish sauce. Season pork tenderloin with ¼ teaspoon each salt and pepper; coat with horseradish mixture. On foil-lined rimmed baking sheet, roast pork at 450°F for 10 minutes.

2. Meanwhile, toss kale, olive oil, and ¼ teaspoon salt. Remove sheet from oven; sprinkle kale around pork on sheet and roast 15 to 17 minutes, or until kale is crispy and pork is cooked through.

Each serving: About 340 calories, 36g protein, 21g carbohydrate, 15g total fat (3g saturated), 8g fiber, 490mg sodium

BBQ PORK WITH SWEET POTATO SALAD

Lean tenderloin pairs well with a colorful salad.

ACTIVE TIME: 25 minutes   **TOTAL TIME:** 35 minutes
MAKES: 4 servings

2	tablespoons low-sodium tomato paste
1	tablespoon honey
3	cloves garlic, crushed with a press
1	teaspoon chili powder
2	tablespoons vegetable oil
1/4	teaspoon ground black pepper
1	(1¼-pound) pork tenderloin
1¼	pound sweet potatoes, peeled and cut into ½-inch chunks
1	pound Brussels sprouts, trimmed and cut into halves
1/4	teaspoon salt
5	stalks celery, thinly sliced
2	medium shallots, thinly sliced
1/4	cup low-fat mayonnaise
1	tablespoon red wine vinegar
1/4	cup fresh flat-leaf parsley leaves, chopped

1. Preheat oven to 450°F. Line a large rimmed baking sheet with foil.

2. In a medium bowl, whisk tomato paste, honey, garlic, chili powder, 1 tablespoon vegetable oil, and pepper; add pork and turn to coat. Place pork on prepared backing sheet. Roast for 5 minutes.

3. Meanwhile, in a medium saucepot, cover sweet potatoes with cold water by 1 inch. Heat to boiling on high, partially covered. Reduce heat to a simmer; simmer for 12 minutes or until very tender.

4. In another large bowl, toss the Brussels sprouts with remaining 1 tablespoon oil and ⅛ teaspoon salt. Arrange on same baking sheet as pork. Roast together 20 to 25 minutes or until sprouts are tender and pork is cooked through (145°F).

5. When the sweet potatoes are cooked, drain well; transfer to a large bowl along with celery, shallots, mayonnaise, vinegar, parsley, and ⅛ teaspoon salt. Gently fold to combine. Serve alongside sliced pork and sprouts.

Each serving: About 425 calories, 35g protein, 42g carbohydrate, 14g total fat (3g saturated fat), 9g fiber, 439mg sodium

BUTTERFLIED LAMB WITH MOROCCAN FLAVORS

This grilled leg of lamb features fabulous exotic flavor and requires very little work.

ACTIVE TIME: 15 minutes **TOTAL TIME:** 30 minutes, plus marinating
MAKES: 12 servings

⅓	cup loosely packed fresh cilantro leaves, chopped
¼	cup olive oil
2	tablespoons dried mint
2	teaspoons ground coriander
1	teaspoon ground ginger
1	teaspoon salt
½	teaspoon coarsely ground black pepper
½	teaspoon chili powder
3½	pounds butterflied boneless lamb leg, trimmed

1. In small bowl, stir together cilantro, oil, mint, coriander, ginger, salt, pepper, and chili powder.

2. Place lamb in 13 x 9-inch baking dish. Rub with cilantro mixture to coat completely. Cover and refrigerate at least 1 hour or up to 4 hours.

3. Prepare outdoor grill for direct grilling over medium-low heat.

4. Place lamb on hot grill rack. Cover and grill lamb 15 to 25 minutes for medium-rare or to desired doneness, turning lamb over occasionally. (Instant-read thermometer should register 145°F.) Thickness of butterflied lamb will vary throughout; cut off sections as meat is cooked through and transfer to cutting board.

5. Let lamb stand 10 minutes to allow juices to set for easier slicing. Thinly slice lamb to serve.

Each serving: About 225 calories, 28g protein, 1g carbohydrate, 12g total fat (3g saturated), 0g fiber, 270mg sodium

TIP You can ask your butcher to debone a 4½-pound half lamb leg shank and slit the meat lengthwise so that it opens like a thick steak.

MIDDLE EASTERN LAMB STEAKS

Aromatic spices—thyme, coriander, cumin, and allspice—in a quick tomato relish add zip to pan-seared lamb steaks. See "Meze in Minutes" (page 302), for easy, flat-tummy-conscious ideas to round out the meal.

ACTIVE TIME: 15 minutes   **TOTAL TIME:** 35 minutes
MAKES: 4 servings

1	teaspoon dried thyme
1	teaspoon ground coriander
1	teaspoon ground cumin
1/2	teaspoon ground allspice
1/2	teaspoon salt
1/4	teaspoon ground black pepper
1	(28-ounce) can whole tomatoes
1	teaspoon vegetable oil
1	red onion, chopped
1/4	cup dried currants
2	tablespoons chopped fresh parsley leaves
2	(8-ounce) center-cut lamb leg steaks, 3/4 inch thick, trimmed

1. In small bowl, stir together thyme, coriander, cumin, allspice, salt, and pepper. Drain tomatoes, reserving 1/2 cup juice; chop tomatoes.

2. In nonstick 12-inch skillet, heat oil over medium heat until hot. Add onions and 2 teaspoons thyme mixture. Cook, stirring occasionally, until onion is slightly softened, 5 minutes. Add chopped tomatoes, reserved juice, and currants. Cook, stirring occasionally, until slightly thickened, 6 minutes. Transfer tomato mixture to bowl; stir in 1 tablespoon chopped parsley.

3. Coat lamb steaks with remaining thyme mixture. In same skillet, cook lamb over medium heat 4 to 5 minutes per side for medium-rare or to desired doneness. (Instant-read thermometer inserted horizontally into center of steaks should register 145°F.) Cut each steak in half.

4. To serve, spoon tomato relish into deep platter; top with lamb and sprinkle with remaining 1 tablespoon parsley.

Each serving: About 255 calories, 26g protein, 17g carbohydrate, 9g total fat (3g saturated), 3g fiber, 555mg sodium

MEZE IN MINUTES

A tradition in the Middle East, Greece, and Turkey, meze are little savory dishes to be nibbled before a meal with drinks. Choose from the following options paired with sliced cucumbers, radishes, or ripe tomato wedges, if you like.

- Olives tossed with chopped fresh oregano, garlic, and lemon zest.
- Hummus drizzled with extra-virgin olive oil and sprinkled with cayenne pepper.
- Babaganoush or seasoned roasted eggplant dip.
- Roasted red peppers, available jarred or homemade.

ROASTED RED PEPPERS

You can purchase these peppers readymade, but it's easy enough to roast them, too. If you're not using them right away, refrigerate in an airtight container up to 3 days or freeze up to 3 months.

1. Preheat broiler and line broiling pan with foil. Cut each pepper lengthwise in half; remove and discard stems and seeds. Arrange peppers, cut side down, in prepared broiling pan. Place pan in broiler, 5 to 6 inches from heat source. Broil, without turning, until skin is charred and blistered, 8 to 10 minutes.

2. Wrap peppers in foil and allow to steam at room temperature 15 minutes or until cool enough to handle.

3. Remove peppers from foil. Peel skin and discard. Slice or chop as recipe directs.

GRILLED LAMB CHOPS

Greek yogurt is great solo, but even better in our simple grilled lamb chops recipe, so pick up a big tub—you'll finish it in a flash.

ACTIVE TIME: 10 minutes   **TOTAL TIME:** 22 minutes
MAKES: 4 servings

1½	cups Greek yogurt
2	tablespoons chopped fresh mint
2	teaspoons grated peeled fresh ginger
1	teaspoon garam masala spice blend
¾	teaspoon salt
¾	teaspoon pepper
1¼	pound shoulder blade lamb chops

1. In large dish, combine yogurt, mint, ginger, garam masala, and ¼ teaspoon each salt and pepper. Add lamb chops. Turn to coat; let stand.

2. Preheat outdoor grill on medium. Remove lamb from marinade; sprinkle with ½ teaspoon each salt and pepper. Grill, covered, 10 to 12 minutes for medium-rare, turning once.

Each serving: About 230 calories, 20g protein, 1g carbohydrate, 16g total fat (6g saturated), 0g fiber, 348mg sodium

Mussels with Tomatoes and White Wine (page 342)

8 | FISH & SHELLFISH

Freshwater and saltwater fish are an excellent source of lean protein and are a great addition to a flat-tummy-focused diet. Unlike other proteins, fish is low in saturated fat and cold-water fish like tuna and salmon are a good source of heart-healthy omega-3 fatty acids. The American Heart Association recommends 2 servings of omega-3-rich fish each week. Each serving should be 3.5 ounces. To meet these requirements, we have selected delicious fish recipes like "BBQ" Salmon and Brussels Bake (page 328) and Pan-Seared Tuna (page 335). Include these delicious and healthy fish in your weeknight meal roundup. Since fish cooks quickly, these dishes will be on the table in a snap!

Fish and shellfish also pair nicely with a variety of flat-tummy all-stars like fruits and vegetables for balanced meals. Halibut with Corn Salsa (page 315) offers a flavor boost with a garnish of corn, tomatoes, and olives. Tarragon-Rubbed Salmon with Nectarine Salsa (page 321) is a great combination of flavorful fish, sweet and juicy stone fruit, and fragrant spice. Scallop and Asparagus Stir-Fry (page 339) features delicate shellfish in a light, Asian-inspired sauce. Dive into delicious dishes that will leave you guilt-free *and* satisfied.

THAI SNAPPER IN FOIL PACKETS

Tender fillets seasoned with lime and ginger are easily cooked in a foil packet, which helps to seal in the juice. Pair the fish with ½ cup steamed edamame beans.

ACTIVE TIME: 20 minutes   **TOTAL TIME:** 30 minutes
MAKES: 4 servings

3	tablespoons fresh lime juice
1	tablespoon sugar-free Asian fish sauce
1	tablespoon olive oil
1	teaspoon grated, peeled fresh ginger
½	teaspoon minced garlic
4	(6-ounce) red snapper fillets
1	large carrot, peeled and cut into 2¼-inch-long matchstick-thin strips
1	green onion, thinly sliced
¼	cup packed fresh cilantro leaves

1. Prepare outdoor grill for direct grilling over medium heat.

2. In small bowl, mix lime juice, fish sauce, olive oil, ginger, and garlic.

3. From roll of foil, cut four 16 x 12-inch sheets. Fold each sheet crosswise in half and open up again.

4. Place 1 red snapper fillet, skin side down, on half of each piece of foil. Top with carrot strips, green onion slices, then cilantro leaves. Spoon lime-juice mixture over snapper and vegetables. Fold other half of foil over fish. Fold and crimp foil edges all around to create sealed packets.

5. Place packets on hot grill rack; grill 8 minutes, until fish flakes easily when tested with fork.

6. To serve, with kitchen shears, cut an X in top of each packet so steam can escape, then transfer each fillet to plate.

Each serving: About 220 calories, 36g protein, 5g carbohydrate, 6g total fat (1g saturated), 1g fiber, 445mg sodium

SNAPPER LIVORNESE

Vibrant with olives, capers, and basil, this preparation works beautifully with any lean white fish.

ACTIVE TIME: 10 minutes
TOTAL TIME: 35 minutes
MAKES: 4 servings

1	tablespoon olive oil
1	garlic clove, finely chopped
1	(14- to 16-ounce) can crushed tomatoes
⅛	teaspoon salt
⅛	teaspoon ground black pepper
4	(6-ounce) red snapper fillets
¼	cup chopped fresh basil
¼	cup Kalamata or Gaeta olives, pitted and chopped
1	teaspoon capers, drained

1. In nonstick 10-inch skillet, heat oil over medium heat. Add garlic and cook just until very fragrant, about 30 seconds. Stir in tomatoes with their juice, salt, and pepper, breaking up tomatoes with spoon. Heat to boiling; reduce heat and simmer 10 minutes.

2. With tweezers, remove any bones from snapper fillets. Place fillets, skin side down, in skillet. Cover and simmer until fish is just opaque throughout, about 10 minutes. With wide-slotted spatula, transfer fish to warm platter. Stir basil, olives, and capers into tomato sauce and spoon over snapper.

Each serving: About 250 calories, 36g protein, 6g carbohydrate, 8g total fat (1g saturated), 554mg sodium

COD WITH MUSHROOM RAGOUT

The rich earthiness of mushrooms meets mild cod to deliver a delicious low-calorie entrée.

ACTIVE TIME: 10 minutes **TOTAL TIME:** 30 minutes
MAKES: 4 servings

1	large sweet potato, peeled and cut into 1/2-inch chunks
2	tablespoons extra-virgin olive oil
2	large shallots, thinly sliced
1/2	teaspoon salt
1/2	teaspoon ground black pepper
2	(10-ounce) packages sliced mushrooms
2	tablespoons water
4	(6-ounce) skinless cod filets
1/4	cup packed fresh flat-leaf parsley leaves, finely chopped
1/2	cup dry white wine

1. Preheat oven to 450°F.

2. On 18 x 12-inch jelly-roll pan, combine sweet potato, 1 tablespoon oil, half of shallots, and 1/8 teaspoon each salt and pepper. Arrange in single layer on one side of pan. Roast 15 minutes.

3. Meanwhile, in 12-inch skillet, heat remaining 1 tablespoon oil over medium-high. Add remaining shallot and cook 2 to 3 minutes or until tender and golden brown, stirring occasionally. Add mushrooms and water; cook 8 minutes or until liquid evaporates, stirring occasionally.

4. Arrange cod on other side of roasting pan. Sprinkle with 1/8 teaspoon each salt and pepper. Roast alongside sweet potatoes 8 to 10 minutes or until fish is just opaque throughout. (Instant-read thermometer inserted horizontally into fish should register 145°F.)

5. Stir parsley, wine, and remaining 1/4 teaspoon each salt and pepper into mushroom mixture. Cook 1 minute or until wine is reduced by half.

6. Divide sweet potatoes and cod among serving plates. Spoon mushroom ragout over cod.

Each serving: 295 calories, 33g protein, 22g carbohydrate, 09g total fat (1g saturated), 4g fiber, 420mg sodium

GINGER-SHALLOT COD ON WATERCRESS

The tangy sauce for this low-fat roasted cod features fresh ginger, soy sauce, vinegar, shallot, and hot sauce. Sweet summer squash and spicy watercress round out the meal.

ACTIVE TIME: 25 minutes   **TOTAL TIME:** 35 minutes
MAKES: 4 servings

1	large shallot, finely chopped
2	teaspoons minced, peeled fresh ginger
1	tablespoon sherry vinegar
4	drops hot-pepper sauce, such as Tabasco
2½	tablespoons low-sodium soy sauce
1	tablespoon butter
4	(4-ounce) skinless cod fillets
⅛	teaspoon salt
⅛	teaspoon finely ground black pepper
1	teaspoon vegetable oil
2	medium yellow summer squash, thinly sliced
12	ounces watercress
¼	cup packed fresh flat-leaf parsley leaves, plus more for garnish

1. Preheat oven to 450°F. Line jelly-roll pan with foil.

2. In 1-quart saucepan, heat shallots, ginger, vinegar, hot sauce, and 2 tablespoons soy sauce to boiling on high heat. Reduce heat to maintain steady simmer; cook 3 to 4 minutes or until liquid is almost evaporated, stirring. Stir in butter; keep sauce warm on low heat.

3. Meanwhile, place cod in prepared pan; sprinkle with salt and pepper. Roast 8 to 10 minutes or until fish just turns opaque throughout. (Instant-read thermometer inserted horizontally into center should register 145°F.)

4. While cod cooks, in 12-inch skillet, heat oil on medium-high heat. Add squash; cook 2 to 3 minutes or until just browned, stirring. Add half of watercress; gently turn to wilt, then add parsley and remaining watercress and 1 tablespoon soy sauce. Cook 1 to 2 minutes or until greens wilt, stirring. Transfer to four plates.

5. Arrange cod on top of greens; spoon sauce over fish. Garnish with parsley.

Each serving: About 160 calories, 22g protein, 7g carbohydrate, 5g total fat (1g saturated), 2g fiber, 591mg sodium

FISH 'N' CHIPS

Avoid a mess and crush chips for the coating right in the bag. Make a small hole in the top to release excess air and then go to town with a rolling pin.

TOTAL TIME: 20 minutes
MAKES: 4 servings

Nonstick cooking spray
1½   pounds cod fillets, cut into strips
3   large egg whites, beaten
4   ounces salt-and-vinegar potato chips, finely crushed
⅛   teaspoon, plus ¼ teaspoon salt
1   pound frozen peas
2½   tablespoons butter
1   tablespoon lemon juice
½   teaspoon black pepper
Lemon wedges, for serving
Chives, for serving

1. Line large baking sheet with foil; spray generously with nonstick spray. Dip cod fillets into egg whites, then potato chips; arrange on prepared pan. Spray fish with nonstick spray.

2. Bake at 450°F for 12 minutes. Sprinkle with ⅛ teaspoon salt.

3. Microwave frozen peas, butter, lemon juice, remaining salt, and pepper on High for 5 minutes; puree in food processor.

4. Serve fish with peas, lemon wedges, and chives.

Each serving: About 425 calories, 36g protein, 17g carbohydrate, 9g total fat (6g saturated), 5g fiber, 549mg sodium

FLOUNDER PESTO ROLL-UPS

Fresh fish fillets are spread with store-bought pesto and baked with white wine with plum tomatoes for a simple yet satisfying meal. Serve roast broccoli florets tossed with pine nuts and grated Parmesan alongside the fish.

ACTIVE TIME: 15 minutes **TOTAL TIME:** 35 minutes
MAKES: 4 servings

4	(6-ounce) flounder fillets
8	teaspoons prepared basil pesto
¼	teaspoon salt
¼	cup dry white wine
4	plum tomatoes, chopped
¼	cup loosely packed fresh parsley leaves, chopped, for garnish

1. Preheat oven to 400°F. Place fillets, skin sides down, on work surface. Spread 2 teaspoons pesto on each fillet; sprinkle with salt. Starting at narrow end of each fillet, roll up jelly-roll fashion. Place rolls, seam sides down, in 8-inch-square glass baking dish.

2. Pour wine over fillets and top with tomatoes. Cover dish and bake 20 minutes or until fish flakes easily when tested with fork. (Instant-read thermometer inserted horizontally into center of fillet should register 145°F.) Sprinkle with parsley to serve.

Each serving: About 205 calories, 31g protein, 5g carbohydrate, 6g total fat (1g saturated), 1g fiber, 335mg sodium

COD VERACRUZ

This is fish, Mexican-style. Chile aficionados may want to add a little more cayenne pepper or hot chili powder.

ACTIVE TIME: 15 minutes   **TOTAL TIME:** 50 minutes
MAKES: 4 servings

4	tablespoons vegetable oil
1	yellow pepper, cut into thin strips
1	medium onion, thinly sliced
1	jalapeño chile, seeded and finely chopped
1	garlic clove, thinly sliced
3/4	teaspoon chili powder
1/2	teaspoon salt
1	(14½- to 16-ounce) can tomatoes in puree
1/2	teaspoon ground coriander
1/4	teaspoon ground cumin
1/8	teaspoon cayenne pepper
4	(4-ounce) cod steaks, ¾ inch thick

1. In nonstick 12-inch skillet, heat 2 tablespoons oil over medium heat. Add yellow pepper and onion and cook, stirring, until tender and golden, 15 minutes. Add jalapeño, garlic, ½ teaspoon chili powder, and ¼ teaspoon salt and cook, stirring, 3 minutes.

2. Add tomatoes with their puree and cook, breaking up tomatoes with side of spoon, until mixture has slightly reduced, about 10 minutes.

3. Meanwhile, in cup, combine coriander, cumin, remaining ¼ teaspoon each chili powder and salt, and cayenne. Sprinkle both sides of cod steaks with spice mixture.

4. In 10-inch skillet, heat remaining 2 tablespoons oil over medium-high heat until hot. Add cod and cook until steaks are just opaque throughout and nicely browned, 3 to 4 minutes per side. To serve, arrange fish on platter and top with warm tomato sauce.

Each serving: About 254 calories, 19g protein, 12g carbohydrate, 14g total fat (2g saturated), 3g fiber, 508mg sodium

HALIBUT WITH CORN SALSA

Mild and satisfyingly meaty, halibut gets instant oomph from a garden-ripe garnish of briny green olives, corn, and tomatoes.

ACTIVE TIME: 20 minutes   **TOTAL TIME:** 30 minutes
MAKES: 4 servings

4	(6-ounce) skinless halibut or cod fillets
Pinch of cayenne pepper	
½	teaspoon salt
1	pound plum tomatoes, chopped
¼	cup pitted green olives, thinly sliced
1	tablespoon champagne vinegar
1	tablespoon fresh lemon juice
2	tablespoons extra-virgin olive oil
1	small shallot, finely chopped
1½	cups fresh corn kernels
2	tablespoons snipped fresh chives, plus additional for garnish
1	tablespoon finely chopped fresh mint leaves, plus additional for garnish

1. Fill 5-quart saucepot with 1 inch water. Fit a steamer insert or basket into saucepot. (Water should not touch bottom of steamer.) Cover and heat to boiling, then reduce heat to low to maintain very gentle simmer.

2. Season both sides of fish with cayenne and ¼ teaspoon salt; place in single layer in steamer. Cover and steam 20 minutes or until opaque throughout.

3. Meanwhile, in large bowl, combine tomatoes, olives, vinegar, lemon juice, 1 tablespoon oil, and remaining ¼ teaspoon salt. Set tomato mixture aside.

4. In 12-inch skillet, heat remaining 1 tablespoon oil on medium-high. Add shallots and cook 1 minute or until browned, stirring. Add corn and cook 2 to 3 minutes or until browned, stirring occasionally. Transfer to bowl with tomato mixture. Add herbs and stir until well mixed.

5. Divide tomato mixture among serving plates. Remove steamer from saucepot. Carefully remove fish from steamer and place on top of tomato mixture on each plate. Garnish with chives and mint; serve immediately.

Each serving: About 340 calories, 40g protein, 16g carbohydrate, 12g total fat (1g saturated), 3g fiber, 474mg sodium

ALMOND-CRUSTED TILAPIA

Appealingly lean and with no fishy taste, mild-mannered tilapia still has plenty of heart-healthy omega-3 fats. (Bonus: It is also one of the least mercury-laden fish and low in sodium.) Green beans and mushrooms deliver fiber and potassium, while crunchy almonds boast antioxidants.

ACTIVE TIME: 15 minutes   **TOTAL TIME:** 30 minutes
MAKES: 4 servings

2	lemons
2	tablespoons olive oil
½	teaspoon salt
¼	teaspoon coarsely ground pepper
	Nonstick cooking spray
4	(6-ounce) tilapia fillets
¼	cup sliced natural almonds (with brown skin still on)
1	small onion, chopped
1	(12-ounce) bag fresh green beans, trimmed
1	(10-ounce) package sliced white mushrooms
2	tablespoons water

1. Preheat oven to 425°F. From 1 lemon, grate 1 teaspoon peel and squeeze 3 tablespoons juice; cut second lemon into wedges. In cup, mix lemon peel and 1 tablespoon juice, 1 tablespoon oil, ¼ teaspoon salt and ⅛ teaspoon pepper.

2. Spray 13 x 9-inch glass baking dish with nonstick spray; place tilapia, dark side down. Drizzle tilapia with lemon mixture; press almonds on top. Bake 15 minutes or until tilapia turns opaque.

3. Meanwhile, in 12-inch skillet, heat remaining 1 tablespoon oil on medium-high 1 minute. Add onions and cook 5 to 6 minutes or until golden, stirring occasionally. Stir in green beans, mushrooms, water, ¼ teaspoon salt, and ⅛ teaspoon pepper. Cook about 6 minutes or until most of liquid evaporates and green beans are tender-crisp. Toss with remaining 2 tablespoons lemon juice. Serve bean mixture and lemon wedges with tilapia.

Each serving: About 315 calories, 33g protein, 15g carbohydrate, 15g total fat (1g saturated), 5g fiber, 380mg sodium

SEARED SALMON WITH SWEET POTATOES

Simple salmon and sweet potatoes become a gourmet meal in minutes when topped with an easy, tangy, lemon-caper sauce and spiked with a hit of spicy cayenne pepper.

ACTIVE TIME: 15 minutes   **TOTAL TIME:** 30 minutes
MAKES: 4 servings

1	pound sweet potatoes, peeled and cut into ½-inch cubes
¼	cup water
⅜	teaspoon salt
¼	teaspoon freshly ground black pepper
1	(6-ounce) bag baby spinach
⅛	teaspoon cayenne pepper
2	(5-ounce) skinless center-cut salmon fillets
1	lemon
1	cup dry white wine
2	teaspoons capers, rinsed
¼	cup chopped fresh flat-leaf parsley

1. In large microwave-safe bowl, combine sweet potatoes, water, and ¼ teaspoon each salt and black pepper. Cover with vented plastic wrap; microwave on High 9 minutes or until tender, stirring halfway through. Add spinach; cover again and microwave 2 minutes longer.

2. Meanwhile, sprinkle cayenne and remaining teaspoon salt on salmon. In 12-inch nonstick skillet on medium heat, cook salmon 10 minutes or until knife pierces center easily, turning over halfway through. (Instant-read thermometer inserted horizontally into center of salmon should register 145°F.) Transfer to plate. From lemon, finely grate ½ teaspoon peel onto fish; into cup, squeeze 1 tablespoon juice.

3. To skillet, add wine and capers. Boil on high heat 2 minutes or until liquid is reduced by half, scraping browned bits from pan. Remove from heat; stir in lemon juice and parsley.

4. Divide sweet potato–spinach mixture among plates; top with fish. Spoon wine sauce over fish.

Each serving: About 300 calories, 31g protein, 22g carbohydrate, 9g total fat (1g saturated), 4g fiber, 430mg sodium

MUSTARD-DILL SALMON WITH HERBED POTATOES

A light and creamy sauce adds piquant flavor to succulent salmon.

ACTIVE TIME: 20 minutes   **TOTAL TIME:** 30 minutes
MAKES: 4 servings

12	ounces small red potatoes, cut into 1-inch chunks
12	ounces small white potatoes, cut into 1-inch chunks
½	teaspoon salt
3	tablespoons chopped fresh dill
½	teaspoon coarsely ground black pepper
Nonstick cooking spray	
4	(6-ounce) salmon fillets
2	tablespoons low-fat mayonnaise
1	tablespoon white wine vinegar
2	teaspoons Dijon mustard
¾	teaspoon sugar

1. In a 3-quart saucepan, heat potatoes, salt, and enough water to cover to boiling over high heat. Reduce heat to low; cover and simmer until potatoes are fork-tender, about 15 minutes. Drain potatoes and toss with 1 tablespoon dill and ¼ teaspoon pepper; keep potatoes warm.

2. Meanwhile, preheat boiler and place rack at closest position to heat source. Grease rack in broiling pan with nonstick spray. Place salmon on rack; sprinkle with ⅛ teaspoon pepper. Broil until just opaque throughout, 8 to 10 minutes. (Instant-read thermometer inserted horizontally into salmon should register 145°F.)

3. While salmon is broiling, prepare sauce: In small bowl, mix mayonnaise, vinegar, mustard, sugar, remaining 2 tablespoons dill, and remaining ⅛ teaspoon pepper.

4. Serve salmon with sauce and potatoes.

Each serving: About 350 calories, 37g protein, 32g carbohydrate, 7g total fat (2g saturated), 3g fiber, 290mg sodium

TIP

To round out this meal, sauté snow peas in a nonstick skillet with 1 teaspoon vegetable oil for a healthy side dish. Finish with our Raspberry Soufflé (page 446) for a company-worthy 425-calorie dinner.

SALMON OVER SWEET AND SOUR CABBAGE

In this spa-style supper, slow-simmered red cabbage, studded with blackberries, delivers a day's supply of vitamin C—a nutrient linked with lower stroke risk.

ACTIVE TIME: 10 minutes   **TOTAL TIME:** 40 minutes
MAKES: 4 servings

2	teaspoons olive oil
1	medium sweet onion, chopped
1	(2-pound) head red cabbage, sliced
1/2	teaspoon salt, plus 1/8 teaspoon
1/4	teaspoon pepper, plus 1/8 teaspoon
1/2	cup dry red wine
2	tablespoons balsamic vinegar
1/2	pint blackberries
4	(6-ounce) skinless center-cut salmon fillets

Fresh parsley leaves

1. In 12-inch skillet, heat oil on medium-high. Add onion; cook 3 minutes or until just tender, stirring. Add cabbage and 1/4 teaspoon each salt and freshly ground black pepper. Cook 3 minutes or until just starting to wilt, stirring.

2. Add wine and vinegar. Heat to boiling. Cover; simmer on medium 25 minutes or until tender, stirring occasionally. Remove from heat; stir in blackberries and 1/4 teaspoon salt.

3. Meanwhile, preheat broiler. Line jelly-roll pan with foil. Sprinkle 1/8 teaspoon each salt and freshly ground black pepper on top of salmon. Transfer to pan. Broil 7 minutes or until just opaque throughout.

4. Divide cabbage among serving plates; top with salmon and parsley.

Each serving: About 335 calories, 35g protein, 20g carbohydrate, 13g total fat (2g saturated), 6g fiber, 478mg sodium

TARRAGON-RUBBED SALMON WITH NECTARINE SALSA

Fresh nectarine salsa, made with jalapeño chiles, fresh lime juice, and chopped cilantro, livens up any grilled dish, especially succulent salmon fillets. Pair with grilled asparagus to up the fiber.

ACTIVE TIME: 20 minutes   **TOTAL TIME:** 30 minutes
MAKES: 4 servings

2	tablespoons chopped red onion
2	large ripe nectarines, chopped
1	small red pepper, chopped
1	jalapeño chile, finely chopped
2	tablespoons fresh lime juice
1	tablespoon chopped fresh cilantro
½	teaspoon salt
1	tablespoon dried tarragon
¼	teaspoon coarsely ground black pepper
4	(6-ounce) skinless salmon fillets
1	teaspoon olive oil, plus more for greasing the grill

1. Grease clean grill grate. Prepare outdoor grill for covered, direct grilling on medium.

2. Meanwhile, in cup, place chopped red onion; cover with cold water and let sit 10 minutes. (This will take some of the sharpness out of the raw onion.) In medium bowl, stir together remaining salsa ingredients: nectarines, red pepper, jalapeño, lime juice, cilantro, and ¼ teaspoon salt; set aside.

3. In small bowl, combine tarragon, ¼ teaspoon salt, and ¼ teaspoon coarsely ground black pepper. Brush salmon with oil and rub with tarragon mixture to coat both sides.

4. Place salmon on hot grill grate. Cover grill and cook salmon 8 to 10 minutes or until it turns opaque throughout, turning once with large spatula. Transfer to platter.

5. Drain onion well. Stir onion into nectarine mixture. Serve nectarine salsa with grilled salmon.

Each serving: About 305 calories, 35g protein, 14g carbohydrate, 12g total fat (2g saturated), 2g fiber, 365mg sodium

SEARED SALMON WITH EDAMAME SALAD

Flat-tummy all-star edamame puts in an appearance in this healthy meal.

ACTIVE TIME: 30 minutes   **TOTAL TIME:** 40 minutes
MAKES: 4 servings

Edamame Salad

1	(16-ounce) bag frozen shelled edamame (green soybeans)
1	tablespoon vegetable oil
1/8	teaspoon ground black pepper
1	(8-ounce) bunch radishes, each cut in half and thinly sliced
1	cup loosely packed fresh cilantro leaves, chopped

Salmon

1	(1½-pound) salmon fillet, with skin
1/8	teaspoon cayenne pepper

1. Prepare outdoor grill for direct grilling over medium-low heat.

2. Prepare salad: Cook edamame as label directs; drain. Rinse edamame with cold running water to stop cooking and drain again.

3. In medium bowl, whisk oil and pepper until blended. Add edamame, radishes, and cilantro and toss until evenly coated. Cover and refrigerate salad up to 1 day if not serving right away. (Makes about 4 cups.)

4. Sprinkle salmon with pepper and place, skin side down, on grill and cook until just opaque throughout, 10 to 12 minutes. Serve with edamame salad.

Each serving (salmon): About 200 calories, 34g protein, 0g carbohydrate, 6g total fat (2g saturated), 0g fiber, 84mg sodium

---

Each serving (1 cup salad): About 164 calories, 13g protein, 11g carbohydrate, 9g total fat (0g saturated), 6g fiber, 29mg sodium

SALMON PROVENÇAL WITH ZUCCHINI

Salmon is brimming with omega-3 fatty acids, which improve the ratio of good to bad cholesterol and also lower heart-damaging triglycerides.

TOTAL TIME: 30 minutes
MAKES: 4 servings

1	tablespoon olive oil
4	pieces skinless salmon fillet
¼	teaspoon salt
⅛	teaspoon ground black pepper
1	(28-ounce) can whole tomatoes in juice
1	small onion, chopped
¼	cup Kalamata olives
1	tablespoon capers
3	medium zucchini
2	tablespoons water
1	tablespoon fresh lemon juice

1. In 12-inch skillet, heat oil on medium-high until hot. Evenly season salmon on both sides with ¼ teaspoon salt and ⅛ teaspoon ground black pepper. Add salmon to skillet and cook 3 minutes. Reduce heat to medium; turn salmon over and cook 3 to 5 minutes longer or until opaque throughout.

2. Meanwhile, drain tomatoes, reserving ¼ cup juice. Chop tomatoes.

3. Transfer salmon to plate; cover with foil to keep warm. To same skillet, add onions and cook 5 minutes or until tender. Stir in tomatoes with reserved juice; heat to boiling. Cook 2 minutes or until sauce thickens, stirring. Remove skillet from heat; stir in olives and capers.

4. While tomato sauce is cooking, cut each zucchini lengthwise in half, then cut crosswise into ¼-inch-thick slices.

5. In microwave-safe medium bowl, place zucchini and 2 tablespoons water. Cover with vented plastic wrap and cook in microwave on High 5 minutes or until just fork-tender. Drain zucchini; add lemon juice and toss to combine.

6. Place salmon on individual dinner plates; top with tomato-olive-caper mixture and serve with zucchini.

Each serving: About 350 calories, 38g protein, 15g carbohydrate, 16g total fat (2g saturated), 5g fiber, 585mg sodium

COLD POACHED SALMON WITH WATERCRESS SAUCE

One of the best warm-weather entrées around. Fast and easy, and you don't even have to turn on the oven.

ACTIVE TIME: 15 minutes   **TOTAL TIME:** 25 minutes, plus cooling
MAKES: 4 servings

1	medium lemon
4	(6-ounce) salmon steaks, 1 inch thick
³/₄	teaspoon salt
½	teaspoon coarsely ground black pepper
1	medium onion, thinly sliced
	Watercress Sauce

1. From lemon, squeeze juice; reserve for Watercress Sauce. Set lemon rinds aside. Rub salmon steaks evenly with salt and pepper.

2. In 12-inch skillet, heat ½ inch water to boiling over high heat. Add salmon, onion, and lemon rinds; heat to boiling. Reduce heat; cover and simmer until fish is just opaque throughout, 5 to 8 minutes. With slotted spatula, transfer fish to platter. Let cool 30 minutes, or cover and refrigerate to serve later.

3. Meanwhile, prepare Watercress Sauce (recipe below).

4. Remove skin and bones from salmon, if you like. Serve with sauce.

Each serving (without sauce): About 274 calories, 30g protein, 0g carbohydrate, 16g total fat (3g saturated), 0g fiber, 231mg sodium

WATERCRESS SAUCE

In blender or in food processor with knife blade attached, puree ½ **bunch watercress**, tough stems trimmed (1 cup), ½ **cup Greek yogurt, 1 tablespoon fresh lemon juice, 1 teaspoon chopped fresh tarragon** or ⅛ **teaspoon dried tarragon, 1½ teaspoons sugar**, and **1 teaspoon salt** until smooth. Cover and refrigerate. Makes about ½ cup sauce.

Each serving: (1 tablespoon): About 20 calories, 2g protein, 2g carbohydrate, 1g total fat (0g saturated), 0g fiber, 253mg sodium

BROILED SALMON STEAKS

Broiling is a quick—and easy—way to get healthful, flavorful salmon steaks onto the dinner table in less than 15 minutes.

ACTIVE TIME: 3 minutes   **TOTAL TIME:** 13 minutes
MAKES: 4 servings

4   (6-ounce) salmon steaks, 1 inch thick
1   teaspoon vegetable oil
Pinch of salt
Pinch of ground black pepper

1. Preheat broiler. Rub both sides of salmon steaks with oil and sprinkle with salt and pepper.

2. Place salmon on rack in broiling pan. Place pan in broiler, 4 inches from heat source. Broil salmon 5 minutes, then turn and broil until fish is just opaque throughout, about 5 minutes longer.

Each serving: About 284 calories, 30g protein, 0g carbohydrate, 17g total fat (3g saturated), 0g fiber, 123mg sodium

"BBQ" SALMON AND BRUSSELS BAKE

Combine two super-healthy, flat-tummy-friendly foods in one tasty bake.

ACTIVE TIME: 15 minutes   **TOTAL TIME:** 30 minutes
MAKES: 6 servings

2	tablespoons brown sugar
1	teaspoon garlic powder
1	teaspoon onion powder
1	teaspoon smoked paprika
3	tablespoons olive oil
1¼	pound Brussels sprouts, trimmed and halved
1¼	teaspoon salt
¼	teaspoon pepper
1	side of salmon (about 3½ pounds)

Snipped chives, for garnish

1. Preheat oven to 450°F. Line large rimmed baking sheet with foil. In small bowl, stir together brown sugar, garlic powder, onion powder, smoked paprika, and 2 tablespoons oil.

2. On another large rimmed baking sheet, toss Brussels sprouts with remaining 1 tablespoon oil and ¼ teaspoon each salt and pepper. Roast sprouts 5 minutes.

3. Meanwhile, cut salmon into 10 fillets; arrange skin side down on foil-lined baking sheet. Brush rub all over salmon; sprinkle with 1 teaspoon salt. Roast salmon with Brussels sprouts 15 minutes or until sprouts are tender and salmon is just cooked through, stirring sprouts once halfway through. Reserve 4 smaller salmon fillets. Serve remaining salmon with Brussels sprouts. Garnish with chives.

Each serving: 280 calories, 35g protein, 11g carbohydrate, 11g total fat (2g saturated), 3g fiber, 380mg sodium

SALMON WITH GREEK YOGURT AND SAUTÉED KALE

Eat like a Viking with this Nordic-inspired hearty salmon dish. In addition to promoting a flat tummy and weight loss, research has shown salmon also helps lower blood pressure.

ACTIVE TIME: 15 minutes
TOTAL TIME: 30 minutes
MAKES: 4 servings

1	tablespoon canola oil
12	ounces wild mushrooms, sliced
3/4	teaspoon salt, plus 1/8 teaspoon
1	bunch kale, trimmed and chopped
4	(5-ounce) skinless salmon fillets
1/4	teaspoon pepper
1/2	cup Greek yogurt
1	tablespoon prepared horseradish, drained
1	green onion, finely chopped, plus more for garnish
2	teaspoons spicy brown mustard

1. Arrange oven rack 6 inches from broiler heat source. Preheat broiler.

2. In 6-quart saucepot heat oil on medium-high. Add mushrooms and ½ teaspoon salt. Cook 5 minutes or until beginning to soften. Add kale and cook 5 to 7 minutes or until stems are tender, stirring occasionally.

3. Meanwhile, arrange salmon on foil-lined baking sheet; sprinkle with ¼ teaspoon salt and pepper. Broil 6 to 8 minutes or until cooked.

4. Stir together yogurt, horseradish, green onion, mustard, and ⅛ teaspoon salt. Serve salmon over greens, topped with yogurt sauce. Garnish with additional green onions if desired.

Each serving: About 290 calories, 36g protein, 13g carbohydrate, 11g total fat (2g saturated), 4g fiber, 522mg sodium

ALMOND-CRUSTED CREOLE SALMON

If you like, swap finely chopped pistachios or pecans for almonds.

ACTIVE TIME: 15 minutes **TOTAL TIME:** 30 minutes
MAKES: 4 servings

1	pound green beans, trimmed
1	tablespoon olive oil
1/4	teaspoon salt
1/4	teaspoon pepper
1/3	cup Greek yogurt
2	teaspoons Creole seasoning
1	teaspoon grated lemon peel
4	(6-ounce) skinless salmon fillets
1/4	cup almonds, coarsely chopped
Nonstick cooking spray	

1. Preheat oven to 450°F.

2. Line large rimmed baking sheet with foil.

3. In large bowl, toss green beans, olive oil, salt, and pepper. Arrange baking sheet and bake 10 minutes.

4. In bowl, stir together yogurt, Creole seasoning, and grated lemon peel. Spread onto 4 salmon fillets; top with almonds.

5. Push beans to one side of baking sheet; place salmon on other side. Spray salmon with cooking spray. Bake 12 minutes or until salmon is cooked through and beans are tender.

Each serving: About 340 calories, 40g protein, 10g carbohydrate, 16g total fat (3g saturated), 4g fiber, 220mg sodium

SPICY GRILLED SALMON

With a little tin foil, this fancy meal can be made right on the grill.

ACTIVE TIME: 10 minutes
TOTAL TIME: 25 minutes
MAKES: 4 servings

4	(6-ounce) salmon fillets
4	tablespoons low-sodium hoisin sauce
½	teaspoon crushed red pepper
1½	pounds cauliflower florets
1	tablespoon oil
¼	teaspoon salt
¼	cup chopped peanuts

Chopped fresh cilantro

1. Prepare outdoor grill for direct grilling over medium-low heat.

2. Place salmon in centers of 4 foil sheets. Brush each with 1 tablespoon hoisin sauce; sprinkle each with ⅛ teaspoon crushed red pepper.

3. Toss cauliflower with oil and salt. Arrange around each fillet. Seal packets; grill 15 minutes or until cauliflower is tender. Garnish with peanuts and cilantro.

Each serving: About 400 calories, 43g protein, 15g carbohydrate, 19g total fat (3g saturated), 4g fiber, 433mg sodium

PAN-SEARED TUNA

This is a great way to cook tuna steaks: Raise the temperature of the oil in the pan to very hot and sear the fish very quickly. The oil in the marinade moistens the fish but adds hardly any fat at all.

ACTIVE TIME: 10 minutes   **TOTAL TIME:** 16 minutes, plus marinating
MAKES: 4 servings

4	large lemons
6	tablespoons olive oil
6	tablespoons chopped fresh parsley
½	teaspoon salt
¼	teaspoon ground black pepper
4	(5-ounce) tuna steaks, ¾ inch thick

1. From lemons, grate 1 teaspoon peel and squeeze ⅔ cup juice. In 9-inch square baking dish, with wire whisk, whisk lemon peel and juice, 3 tablespoons oil, 5 tablespoons parsley, salt, and pepper until mixed. Add tuna, turning to coat. Cover and refrigerate 45 minutes to marinate, turning occasionally.

2. In 10-inch cast-iron skillet or other heavy skillet, heat remaining 3 tablespoons oil over medium-high heat until hot. Add tuna and cook until pale pink in center (medium), about 3 minutes per side, or until desired doneness. Transfer to plates and sprinkle with remaining 1 tablespoon parsley.

Each serving: About 246 calories, 30g protein, 1g carbohydrate, 13g total fat (2g saturated), 0g fiber, 341mg sodium

STOP THE CART FOR FATTY FISH

Omega-3 fats are good for your heart, but they can also be a boon to your waistline. In a multicenter study involving 232 overweight volunteers on a reduced-calorie diet, researchers found that when the dieters ate a meal rich in fatty fish, they felt fuller longer than those who had eaten a leaner fish, such as cod.

The reason? High levels of omega-3s may prompt the body to produce more leptin—the hormone that signals fullness. And this may lead you to eat less food throughout the day, scientists hypothesize. One easy way to get these good-for-you fats: Use canned salmon, which is less expensive than fresh.

THAI SHRIMP

Spoon this chunky shrimp-and-vegetable mixture over brown rice.

ACTIVE TIME: 30 minutes   **TOTAL TIME:** 45 minutes
MAKES: 4 servings

2	medium limes
3	teaspoons vegetable oil
1	small onion, finely chopped
1	small red pepper, thinly sliced
2	teaspoons peeled, grated fresh ginger
1/8	to 1/4 teaspoon cayenne pepper
4	ounces medium mushrooms, cut into quarters
1/2	teaspoon salt
1	(13¾- to 15-ounces) can light coconut milk
1	pound large shrimp, shelled and deveined
2	ounces snow peas, strings removed and cut into 2 x 1/4-inch matchsticks
1/3	cup loosely packed fresh cilantro leaves

1. From limes, with vegetable peeler, peel six 1 x ¾-inch strips of peel; squeeze 2 tablespoons juice. Set aside.

2. In nonstick 12-inch skillet, heat 2 teaspoons oil over medium heat. Add onion and cook until tender, about 5 minutes. Add sliced red pepper and cook 1 minute. Stir in ginger and cayenne; cook 1 minute. Transfer onion mixture to small bowl.

3. In same skillet, heat remaining 1 teaspoon oil over medium heat. Add mushrooms and salt and cook until tender and lightly browned, about 5 minutes. Stir in coconut milk, lime peel and juice, and onion mixture and heat to boiling. Add shrimp and cook until shrimp are opaque throughout, about 2 minutes. Stir in snow peas and cilantro.

Each serving: About 222 calories, 20g protein, 11g carbohydrate, 11g total fat (4g saturated), 1g fiber, 456mg sodium

SHRIMP WITH BABY PEAS

Frozen peas come to the rescue in this quick and healthful dinner.

TOTAL TIME: 10 minutes
MAKES: 1 serving

1	teaspoon olive oil
3	ounces shrimp
2	tablespoons white wine or low-sodium chicken broth
1	cup frozen baby peas, thawed
1	cup cooked whole wheat linguine
1	tablespoon Parmesan cheese
1	tablespoon chopped fresh parsley

Pepper

Heat olive oil in pan, and sauté shrimp until almost cooked through (about 3 minutes). Add wine or broth and peas. Cook until peas are heated through. Pour shrimp and pea mixture over linguine; toss with cheese and top with parsley. Season with pepper to taste.

Each serving: About 470 calories, 30g protein, 68g carbohydrate, 9g total fat (2g saturated), 12g fiber, 585mg sodium

SESAME SHRIMP AND ASPARAGUS STIR-FRY

This Asian-inspired stir-fry is just as tasty as any you'd find dining out, and by making this dish at home you cut the fat by 23 grams and save nearly 700 calories!

ACTIVE TIME: 20 minutes
TOTAL TIME: 25 minutes
MAKES: 4 servings

1	cup brown rice
1½	tablespoons low-sodium soy sauce
1	tablespoon seasoned rice vinegar
1	tablespoon grated, peeled fresh ginger
1	tablespoon sesame seeds
2	tablespoons vegetable oil
1	pound asparagus, trimmed and cut diagonally into 2-inch pieces
1	pint cherry tomatoes
1	pound large shrimp, cleaned, deveined, and cooked
1	teaspoon Asian sesame oil

1. Cook rice as label directs.

2. Meanwhile, in cup, stir together soy sauce, rice vinegar, and ginger; set aside.

3. In 12-inch skillet over medium-high heat, toast sesame seeds about 4 minutes or until golden. Transfer to small bowl.

4. In same skillet, heat vegetable oil over medium-high heat until hot. Add asparagus and cook 5 minutes or until tender-crisp, stirring frequently. Add tomatoes and cook 2 minutes, stirring frequently. Stir soy-sauce mixture and shrimp into asparagus mixture; cook 1 minute to heat through. Remove skillet from heat; stir in sesame oil.

5. To serve, spoon rice onto 4 dinner plates; top with shrimp mixture and sprinkle with toasted sesame seeds.

Each serving: About 400 calories, 28g protein, 45g carbohydrate, 12g total fat (1g saturated), 5g fiber, 586mg sodium

SCALLOP AND ASPARAGUS STIR-FRY

Tossing this dish with chopped basil just before serving adds a pleasing touch of fresh flavor. With brown rice, you have a complete meal.

ACTIVE TIME: 20 minutes
TOTAL TIME: 35 minutes
MAKES: 4 servings

1	pound sea scallops
2	tablespoons low-sodium soy sauce
1	tablespoon minced, peeled fresh ginger
2	tablespoons vegetable oil
2	garlic cloves, thinly sliced
1½	pounds asparagus, trimmed and cut into 2-inch pieces
¼	teaspoon cayenne pepper
½	cup loosely packed fresh basil leaves, chopped, plus additional leaves

1. Pull off and discard tough crescent-shaped muscle from each scallop. In bowl, toss scallops with 1 tablespoon soy sauce and ginger.

2. In 12-inch skillet, heat 1 tablespoon oil over medium-high heat. Add garlic and cook, stirring often, until golden. With slotted spoon, transfer garlic to medium bowl.

3. Add asparagus and cayenne to skillet and cook, stirring frequently (stir-frying), until asparagus is tender-crisp, about 7 minutes. Transfer asparagus to bowl with garlic.

4. Add remaining 1 tablespoon oil to skillet; add scallop mixture and stir-fry until scallops are just opaque throughout, 3 to 5 minutes.

5. Return asparagus and garlic to skillet, along with remaining 1 tablespoon soy sauce; heat through. Add chopped basil, tossing to combine. Spoon mixture onto warm platter and top with basil leaves.

Each serving: About 204 calories, 24g protein, 10g carbohydrate, 8g total fat (1g saturated), 2g fiber, 487mg sodium

PAN-FRIED SCALLOPS

Try these during the fall and winter months, when small bay scallops are in season. Otherwise, substitute sea scallops and increase the cooking time accordingly.

TOTAL TIME: 5 minutes
MAKES: 4 servings

1	pound bay scallops
2	tablespoons olive oil
½	teaspoon salt
2	tablespoons chopped fresh parsley
4	lemon wedges

Pat scallops dry with paper towels. In 12-inch skillet, heat oil over medium-high heat until hot. Add scallops to skillet and sprinkle with salt. Cook, stirring, until just opaque throughout, about 4 minutes. Add parsley and toss. Serve with lemon wedges.

Each serving: About 160 calories, 19g protein, 3g carbohydrate, 8g total fat (1g saturated), 0g fiber, 473mg sodium

SCALLOPS PROVENÇAL

A hint of orange peel gives this tomato sauce a flavor reminiscent of southern France. If you wish, make the sauce in advance and reheat at serving time. You can substitute bay scallops for the sea scallops.

ACTIVE TIME: 20 minutes   **TOTAL TIME:** 40 minutes

MAKES: 4 servings

1	(8-ounce) large leek
2	tablespoons olive oil
2	garlic cloves, finely chopped
1	(14- to 16-ounce) can tomatoes, chopped
½	teaspoon freshly grated orange peel

Pinch of cayenne pepper

1	pound sea scallops
¼	cup all-purpose flour
¼	teaspoon salt

1. Cut off roots and trim dark green tops from leek; cut lengthwise in half, then crosswise into thin slices. Rinse in large bowl of cold water, swishing to remove sand; transfer to colander to drain, leaving sand in bottom of bowl.

2. In nonstick 10-inch skillet, heat 1 tablespoon oil over medium heat. Add leek and garlic and cook, stirring frequently, until leek is tender, about 7 minutes. Add tomatoes with their juice, orange peel, and cayenne; heat to boiling. Reduce heat and simmer until sauce has thickened slightly, about 5 minutes.

3. Meanwhile, pull off and discard tough crescent-shaped muscle from each scallop. Pat scallops dry with paper towels. Cut each scallop horizontally in half, if large.

4. In 12-inch skillet, heat remaining 1 tablespoon oil over medium-high heat until hot. Place flour on waxed paper and coat scallops with flour, shaking off excess. Sprinkle salt on scallops. Add scallops to skillet and cook, stirring, until just opaque throughout and lightly golden, about 4 minutes. Stir in sauce and heat through.

Each serving: About 227 calories, 21g protein, 17g carbohydrate, 8g total fat (1g saturated), 2g fiber, 502mg sodium

MUSSELS WITH TOMATOES AND WHITE WINE

This saucy dish should be served with a slice of good crusty whole-grain bread for dipping. (See photograph on page 304.)

ACTIVE TIME: 20 minutes   **TOTAL TIME:** 45 minutes
MAKES: 4 servings

1	tablespoon olive or vegetable oil
1	small onion, chopped
2	garlic cloves, finely chopped
1/4	teaspoon cayenne pepper
1	(14- to 16-ounce) can tomatoes
3/4	cup dry white wine
4	pounds large mussels, scrubbed and debearded
2	tablespoons chopped fresh parsley

1. In nonreactive 5-quart Dutch oven, heat oil over medium heat. Add onion and cook until tender and golden, 6 to 8 minutes. Add garlic and cayenne and cook 30 seconds longer. Stir in tomatoes with their juice and wine, breaking up tomatoes with side of spoon. Heat to boiling; boil 3 minutes.

2. Add mussels; heat to boiling. Reduce heat; cover and simmer until mussels open, about 5 minutes, transferring mussels to large bowl as they open. Discard any mussels that have not opened. Pour mussel broth over mussels and sprinkle with parsley.

Each serving: About 208 calories, 18g protein, 12g carbohydrate, 6g total fat (2g saturated), 3g fiber, 554mg sodium

MOULES A LA MARINIERE

Prepare as above, substituting **butter** for olive oil, if you like, and **⅓ cup chopped shallots** for onion. Omit crushed red pepper and tomatoes; use **1½ cups dry white wine**. Proceed as directed.

BUYING AND STORING FISH
AND SHELLFISH

- The surface of a whole fish should glisten but not look slimy. The gills should be bright red with no tinge of brown. The eyes should not be sunken.

- Fish fillets and steaks should appear moist and have no gaps in the flesh. The piece of fish should feel firm. The meat of dark fish, such as tuna, should not contain any rainbow streaks.

- Mollusks (including clams, mussels, and oysters) must be purchased alive because their viscera deteriorate quickly once dead. Tightly closed shells indicate the mollusks are alive, but if you tap a gaping shell and it closes, it's also fine. Mollusks sold out of their shells, like scallops and squid, should be as sweet smelling as an ocean breeze.

- Crustaceans, including crabs and lobsters, should be purchased alive from a store. Fresh shrimp should also be subjected to the sniff test; black spots on the shell mean the shrimp are over the hill.

- Keep fish and shellfish as cold as possible. Have the seafood you purchase packed in ice, or place it in the same bag as your frozen food.

- Store fish on ice or in the coldest part of the refrigerator, where the temperature is between 35°F and 40°F.

- It is especially important to keep oily fish, such as mackerel and bluefish, as cold as possible. Their high fat content means they can go rancid quickly.

- If you must freeze seafood, be sure it is very fresh, and wrap it tightly in plastic wrap and heavy-duty foil. Freeze for up to three months.

- Shellfish should also be placed in the coldest part of the refrigerator. Store live clams, mussels, and oysters in a large bowl covered with a wet towel; use within one day.

Lemony Crab Linguine (page 377)

9 | PASTA

You might suspect that pasta and other carb-centric dishes are the first to be kicked off a flat-tummy meal plan. That is simply not the case.

Carbohydrates, including pasta dishes, are a great source of energy and should be incorporated into your diet. But it is important to eat pasta dishes earlier in the day as your body will burn the energy instead of storing it.

When making pasta dishes, use fiber-rich, whole-grain varieties. Whole wheat pasta is a delicious substitution for regular pasta in any of your favorite dishes. If you are still trying to avoid wheat or have a gluten intolerance, consider bean- or lentil-based varieties, now available at many grocery stores.

Pasta is always welcomed at the dinner table. It pairs beautifully with delicate spring veggies in Whole-Grain Rotini with Asparagus and Snap Peas (page 347). Farmers' Market Pasta (page 366) features farmers' market fare like green beans, corn, and cherry tomatoes that have developed a lovely char and flavor on the grill. Plus, Creamy Mushroom Cavatappi (page 358) call for beautiful mushrooms that are great in the fall and winter months. During the chilly winter months, who doesn't enjoy a bowl of pasta topped with a meaty sauce like Slow-Braised Beef Ragu (page 382). When pasta is in the kitchen, everyone will enjoy.

WHOLE-GRAIN ROTINI WITH ASPARAGUS AND SNAP PEAS

Fresh snap peas and asparagus lighten up a pasta dinner (and add plenty of vitamins). Choosing whole-grain pasta helps triple the cholesterol-lowering fiber.

ACTIVE TIME: 10 minutes   **TOTAL TIME:** 20 minutes
MAKES: 4 servings

1	(13¼-ounce) package whole-grain rotini or fusilli pasta
8	ounces asparagus, ends trimmed, cut into 1-inch pieces
1	(8-ounce) bag snap peas
1	tablespoon olive oil
1	small onion, chopped
1	lemon
½	cup freshly grated Pecorino-Romano cheese
¼	cup loosely packed fresh basil leaves, thinly sliced
½	teaspoon salt
¼	teaspoon coarsely ground black pepper

1. In large saucepot, cook pasta as label directs, but add asparagus and snap peas when 3 minutes of cooking time remain.

2. Meanwhile, in 10-inch nonstick skillet, heat oil on medium until hot. Add onion and cook 10 to 12 minutes or until tender and browned. From lemon, grate 1 teaspoon peel and squeeze 2 tablespoons juice.

3. Reserve ½ cup pasta cooking water; drain pasta and vegetables. In large serving bowl, toss pasta and vegetables with cooking water, onion, lemon peel, and juice, cheese, basil, salt, and pepper.

Each serving: About 405 calories, 18g protein, 72g carbohydrate, 8g total fat (2g saturated), 9g fiber, 545mg sodium

RUSTIC PASTA TOSS WITH TUNA AND TOMATOES

This heart-smart pasta salad is loaded with farm-stand squash, zucchini, and tomatoes. Just combine the raw veggies with canned tuna and campanelle pasta for a beat-the-heat—and beat-the-clock—meal.

ACTIVE TIME: 15 minutes **TOTAL TIME:** 30 minutes
MAKES: 6 servings

1	pound whole-grain campanelle or fusilli pasta
2	medium zucchini
1	medium yellow squash
1	pint cherry or grape tomatoes
¼	cup pitted Kalamata olives
¼	cup fresh flat-leaf parsley leaves
3	tablespoons red wine vinegar
¼	cup extra-virgin olive oil
1	clove garlic, crushed with press
¼	teaspoon salt
⅛	teaspoon ground black pepper
2	(5-ounce) cans tuna in water, drained

1. In large saucepot, cook pasta as label directs.

2. Meanwhile, trim zucchini and squash, cut into quarters lengthwise, then cut into thin slices crosswise. Slice tomatoes in half. Slice olives and finely chop parsley.

3. In large bowl, whisk vinegar, oil, garlic, ¼ teaspoon salt, and ⅛ teaspoon freshly ground black pepper; stir in tomatoes.

4. Drain pasta well. Add to tomato mixture along with tuna, zucchini, squash, olives, and parsley. Toss until well mixed.

Each serving: About 465 calories, 21g protein, 66g carbohydrate, 12g total fat (2g saturated), 7g fiber, 435mg sodium

TIP

> If you're lucky enough to find some nice, ripe regular tomatoes, substitute 2 pounds of them for the cherry tomatoes called for here. Chop them in step 2 and add along with the other vegetables at the end. Their extra juices will add more moisture to the sauce.

ORANGE-FENNEL PASTA WITH PORK

Here's another quick and easy whole-grain pasta sauce that's great for fast weeknight meals. Serve with spinach and a green salad.

TOTAL TIME: 10 minutes
MAKES: 1 serving

2	teaspoons olive oil
1	garlic clove, crushed with garlic press
¼	teaspoon salt
¼	teaspoon coarsely ground black pepper
1	teaspoon freshly grated orange peel
½	teaspoon fennel seeds, crushed
1	cup cooked whole-grain pasta
2	tablespoons chopped fresh parsley
3	ounces baked or grilled pork tenderloin

In 10-inch skillet, heat olive oil over medium heat. Add crushed garlic clove, salt, and pepper, and cook 30 seconds. Stir in orange peel and crushed fennel seeds. Stir in cooked pasta and parsley. Heat through and top with pork.

Each serving: About 390 calories, 30g protein, 40g carbohydrate, 13g total fat (3g saturated), 5g fiber, 550mg sodium

PICKING PASTA

Opt for 100 percent whole-grain pasta. Keep in mind that some whole-grain pastas are chewier and grittier and some shapes taste better than others. There are plenty to choose from, so if at first you don't succeed, try (another brand), try (another shape) again. Or, since some whole grain is better than none at all, choose multigrain pasta, which is healthier than white pasta.

PASTA WITH PEAS, ONION, AND SALMON

Healthy, delicious, speedy to make—what more could you ask for?

TOTAL TIME: 15 minutes
MAKES: 1 serving

2	teaspoons olive oil
1	small onion, chopped
2	tablespoons water
1	cup cooked whole-grain pasta
1	cup frozen peas, thawed
1	tablespoon grated Parmesan cheese
3	ounces broiled salmon

In 10-inch skillet, heat olive oil over medium heat. Add onion and water and cook until onion is tender and golden, about 10 minutes. Stir in pasta and peas. Heat through and top with grated cheese and salmon.

Each serving: About 525 calories, 37g protein, 62g carbohydrate, 15g total fat (3g saturated), 11g fiber, 147mg sodium

PASTA WITH TOMATOES, LEMON, AND CHICKEN

This bright dish is perfect for late summer, when tomatoes and basil are at their peak.

ACTIVE TIME: 5 minutes   **TOTAL TIME:** 20 minutes or more
MAKES: 1 serving

1½	pounds ripe tomatoes
¼	cup loosely packed fresh mint leaves, chopped
¼	cup loosely packed fresh basil leaves, chopped
1	garlic clove, crushed with garlic press
1	teaspoon freshly grated lemon peel
1	teaspoons olive oil
¼	teaspoon salt
¼	teaspoon ground black pepper
1	cup cooked whole-grain pasta
3	ounces baked or grilled chicken breast

In serving bowl, combine tomatoes, mint, basil, garlic, lemon peel, olive oil, salt, and pepper. Let stand at least 15 minutes or up to 1 hour at room temperature to blend flavors. Add pasta to tomato mixture and toss well. Top with sliced chicken breast.

Each serving: About 480 calories, 40g protein, 64g carbohydrate, 10g total fat (2g saturated), 13g fiber, 593mg sodium

CREAMY VEGAN LINGUINE WITH WILD MUSHROOMS

This recipe proves that you don't need cream for a truly decadent pasta dish.

ACTIVE TIME: 10 minutes **TOTAL TIME:** 20 minutes
MAKES: 6 servings

1	pound whole-grain linguine or fettuccine
6	tablespoons olive oil
12	ounces mixed mushrooms, thinly sliced
3	cloves garlic, finely chopped
¼	cup nutritional yeast
½	teaspoon salt
¾	teaspoon coarsely ground black pepper
2	green onions, thinly sliced on an angle

1. Cook linguine as label directs, reserving ¾ cup pasta cooking water before draining. Return drained linguine to pot.

2. Meanwhile, in 12-inch skillet, heat oil on medium-high. Add mushrooms and garlic; cook 5 minutes or until mushrooms are browned and tender, stirring. Transfer to pot with cooked, drained linguine along with nutritional yeast, reserved cooking water, salt, and pepper. Toss until well combined. Garnish with green onions.

Each serving: About 405 calories, 14g protein, 60g carbohydrate, 15g total fat (2g saturated), 8g fiber, 182mg sodium

WHOLE-GRAIN SHELLS WITH GOAT CHEESE AND WALNUTS

A substantial vegetarian dish, this pasta showcases the winning combination of goat cheese and walnuts, which provide protein and healthy omega-3s.

ACTIVE TIME: 10 minutes **TOTAL TIME:** 25 minutes
MAKES: 6 servings

½	cup walnuts, chopped
2	garlic cloves, chopped
1	tablespoon olive oil
⅛	teaspoon salt, plus ¼ teaspoon, plus more for salting the water
⅛	teaspoon ground black pepper, plus ¼ teaspoon
1	box (13¼ ounces) medium whole-grain shells
1	pound frozen peas
6	ounces goat cheese, softened

1. Heat large covered saucepot of salted water to boiling over high heat.

2. Meanwhile, in 8- to 10-inch skillet, combine walnuts, garlic, and oil. Cook on medium until golden and fragrant, stirring occasionally. Stir in ⅛ teaspoon each salt and pepper.

3. Add pasta to boiling water in pot. Cook 1 minute less than minimum time that label directs, stirring occasionally. Add peas; cook 1 minute longer. Reserve 1 cup pasta cooking water. Drain pasta and peas; return to pot. Add goat cheese, half of reserved cooking water, and remaining ¼ teaspoon each salt and pepper. If mixture is dry, toss with additional cooking water. To serve, top with garlic-and-walnut mixture.

Each serving: About 430 calories, 20g protein, 59g carbohydrate, 15g total fat (5g saturated), 9g fiber, 350mg sodium

SPINACH AND WHITE BEAN PASTA

Start with prewashed bagged spinach and you can whip up this fiber-packed dish in a snap.

TOTAL TIME: 10 minutes

MAKES: 1 serving

2	cloves chopped garlic
1/2	tablespoon olive oil
1/4	cup canned white beans (navy, cannellini, or Great Northern), rinsed and drained
1	cup cooked multigrain pasta
2	cups spinach
1	tablespoon grated Parmesan cheese

Sauté garlic in olive oil. Stir in beans and cook, stirring occasionally, until heated through. Spoon onto pasta and toss with spinach, stirring until wilted. Top with Parmesan cheese.

Each serving: About 350 calories, 16g protein, 55g carbohydrate, 9g total fat (2g saturated), 10g fiber, 291mg sodium

ORECCHIETTE WITH MORELS AND PEAS

Brown butter makes the perfect, delicate sauce for this spring pasta.

ACTIVE TIME: 25 minutes   **TOTAL TIME:** 35 minutes
MAKES: 6 servings

³/₄	teaspoon kosher salt, plus more for salting the water
3	tablespoons unsalted butter
3	garlic cloves, chopped
3	ounces fresh morel mushrooms, about 1 cup (or ½ ounce dried and reconstituted), quartered lengthwise and well-rinsed
1	pound whole-grain orecchiette pasta
8	ounces sugar snap peas, strings removed
1	cup fresh or frozen (thawed) peas
¼	cup grated Parmesan
1½	cups pea shoots
½	cup microgreens

Shaved Parmesan, for garnish

1. Heat a large, covered pot of salted water to boiling on high.

2. In an 8-inch skillet, heat butter on medium until light brown and foaming, swirling occasionally; about 3 minutes. Add garlic and morels; cook 2 minutes, stirring occasionally. Remove from heat.

3. Cook pasta according to package instructions. Remove ½ cup pasta water 4 minutes before pasta is done; set aside. Add sugar snap peas and peas to boiling water. Continue cooking until pasta is al dente and vegetables are tender. Drain and return to pot.

4. Add mushroom mixture along with Parmesan, pea shoots, microgreens, ¼ cup reserved pasta water, and ¾ teaspoon salt; stir until well-combined, adding more cooking water if necessary. Divide among serving bowls; garnish with shaved Parmesan.

Each serving: About 380 calories, 14g protein, 64g carbohydrate, 8g total fat (4g saturated), 6g fiber, 396mg sodium

CREAMY MUSHROOM CAVATAPPI

If you're craving creamy pasta, whip up this quick and easy dish instead of heading out for fettuccine Alfredo. You'll save a whopping 1,100 calories and 89 grams of fat.

ACTIVE TIME: 15 minutes   **TOTAL TIME:** 30 minutes
MAKES: 6 servings

12	ounces whole wheat cavatappi (penne can be substituted)
2	teaspoons olive oil
1	(4- to 6-ounce) small onion, chopped
1	(8-ounce) package sliced cremini mushrooms
1	tablespoon cornstarch
1½	cups low-fat (1%) milk
½	cup grated Parmesan cheese, plus additional for serving
¼	teaspoon salt, plus more for salting the water
¼	teaspoon ground black pepper
1	(10-ounce) package frozen peas

1. Heat large covered saucepot of salted water to boiling on high. Add pasta and cook as label directs.

2. Meanwhile, in 12-inch skillet, heat oil on medium until hot. Add onion and cook 3 minutes or until beginning to soften. Increase heat to medium-high, and stir in mushrooms; cook 8 to 10 minutes or until mushrooms are golden and most liquid has evaporated, stirring frequently. Transfer mushroom mixture to small bowl.

3. In 2-cup liquid measuring cup, whisk cornstarch into milk; add to same skillet and heat to boiling on medium, whisking frequently. Boil 1 minute, stirring constantly to prevent scorching. Remove skillet from heat and whisk in Parmesan, salt, and pepper.

4. Place peas in colander. Pour pasta over peas; drain and return to saucepot. Stir in mushroom mixture, and cheese sauce; toss to coat. Serve with freshly grated Parmesan.

Each serving (1½ cup): About 335 calories, 15g protein, 57g carbohydrate, 6g total fat (2g saturated), 8g fiber, 308mg sodium

FETTUCCINE WITH MUSHROOM SAUCE

The combination of dried porcini and fresh shiitake mushrooms gives this sauce a rich, earthy flavor.

ACTIVE TIME: 20 minutes   **TOTAL TIME:** 25 minutes, plus standing
MAKES: 6 servings

1/2	cup boiling water
1	(1/2-ounce) package dried porcini mushrooms
2	tablespoons olive oil
1	medium onion, chopped
2	garlic cloves, finely chopped
8	ounces shiitake mushrooms, stems removed and caps thinly sliced
12	ounces white mushrooms, trimmed and thinly sliced
1/2	teaspoon salt
1/4	teaspoon freshly ground black pepper
1 1/4	cups chicken broth
1	pound fresh whole-grain fettuccine
2	tablespoons butter, cut into pieces (optional)
1/4	cup chopped fresh parsley

1. In small bowl, pour boiling water over porcini mushrooms; let stand about 15 minutes. With slotted spoon, remove porcini, reserving liquid. Rinse mushrooms to remove any grit, then chop. Strain mushroom liquid through sieve lined with paper towels; set aside.

2. In 12-inch skillet, heat 1 tablespoon oil over low heat. Add onion and garlic and cook, stirring frequently, until onion is tender. Add shiitake mushrooms; increase heat to medium and cook, stirring, 5 minutes. Add remaining 1 tablespoon oil, white and porcini mushrooms, salt, and pepper; cook until mushrooms are tender, about 7 minutes. Add reserved mushroom liquid and cook, stirring frequently, until liquid has evaporated, about 2 minutes. Add broth and heat to boiling; cook until broth has reduced by one-third.

3. Meanwhile, in large saucepot, cook pasta as label directs. Drain. In warm serving bowl, toss pasta with mushroom sauce, butter if using, and parsley.

Each serving (without butter): About 295 calories, 13g protein, 44g carbohydrate, 8g total fat (2g saturated), 6g fiber, 291mg sodium

SPAGHETTI WITH GARLIC AND OIL

The classic combination of garlic and oil gives this simple pasta its heady flavor. Serve with lots of freshly grated Parmesan or Pecorino-Romano cheese.

ACTIVE TIME: 5 minutes   **TOTAL TIME:** 30 minutes

MAKES: 6 servings

1	(16-ounce) package whole-grain spaghetti or linguine
1/4	cup olive oil
1	large garlic clove, finely chopped
1/8	teaspoon cayenne pepper (optional)
3/4	teaspoon salt
1/4	teaspoon coarsely ground pepper
2	tablespoons chopped fresh parsley

1. In large saucepot, cook pasta as label directs. Drain, reserving ½ cup cooking water.

2. Meanwhile, in 1-quart saucepan, heat oil over medium heat. Add garlic and cook just until golden, about 1 minute; add cayenne pepper if using, and cook 30 seconds longer. Remove saucepan from heat; stir in salt and black pepper. In warm serving bowl, toss pasta with sauce and parsley, using cooking water to moisten pasta as necessary.

Each serving: About 390 calories, 12g protein, 62g carbohydrate, 13g total fat (2g saturated), 8g fiber, 255mg sodium

EASY ADD-INS FOR GARLIC AND OIL SAUCE

Spaghetti with Garlic and Oil (page 360) is just the starting point for many delicious possibilities.

- Add 4 to 6 coarsely chopped anchovy fillets in oil, drained (or 1 to 1½ teaspoons anchovy paste), and 2 tablespoons capers, drained, to cooked garlic-oil mixture; reduce heat and stir until anchovies break up, about 30 seconds.

- Add ½ cup Gaeta, Kalamata, or green Sicilian olives, pitted and chopped, to cooked garlic-oil mixture; reduce heat and stir until olives are heated through, about 1 minute.

- Add 2 to 3 ounces crumbled firm low-fat goat cheese to tossed pasta; toss again.

- Substitute 2 to 4 tablespoons chopped fresh basil, oregano, chives, or tarragon for parsley.

- Add ⅓ cup chopped dried tomatoes to pasta with garlic-oil mixture and parsley; toss.

LINGUINE WITH FRESH TOMATO SAUCE

If the ripe summer tomatoes you use taste a bit acidic, simply add 1 teaspoon sugar to the sauce. If using juicy beefsteak tomatoes instead of meaty plum tomatoes, simmer the sauce uncovered for about 20 minutes to allow the excess juices to evaporate.

ACTIVE TIME: 15 minutes **TOTAL TIME:** 45 minutes
MAKES: 6 servings

1	tablespoon olive oil
1	small onion, chopped
2	pounds ripe plum tomatoes or beefsteak tomatoes, peeled and coarsely chopped
$1/2$	teaspoon salt
3	tablespoons butter, cut into pieces, or olive oil
2	tablespoons chopped fresh sage or $1/2$ cup chopped fresh basil
1	(16-ounce) package whole-grain linguine or penne

1. In nonstick 10-inch skillet, heat oil over medium heat. Add onion and cook until tender and golden, about 10 minutes. Add tomatoes with their juice and salt; heat to boiling over high heat. Reduce heat; cover and simmer, stirring and breaking up tomatoes with side of spoon, until sauce has thickened, 15 to 20 minutes. Stir in olive oil and sage.

2. Meanwhile, in large saucepot, cook pasta as label directs. Drain. In warm serving bowl, toss pasta with sauce.

Each serving: About 410 calories, 14g protein, 69g carbohydrate, 12g total fat (5g saturated), 9g fiber, 225mg sodium

WHOLE WHEAT PENNE GENOVESE

An onion-flecked white bean sauté adds heft to this fresh and healthy pesto pasta dish, making it light yet satisfying.

TOTAL TIME: 30 minutes
MAKES: 6 servings

12	ounces whole wheat penne or rotini
1½	cups packed fresh basil leaves
1	clove garlic
3	tablespoons water
3	tablespoons olive oil
¼	teaspoon salt, plus more for salting the water
¼	teaspoon freshly ground black pepper
½	cup freshly grated Pecorino-Romano cheese
1	(4- to 6-ounce) small onion, chopped
1	(15- to 19-ounce) can white kidney beans (cannellini), rinsed and drained
1	pint grape tomatoes, each cut into quarters

1. Heat large covered saucepot of salted water to boiling over high heat. Add pasta and cook as label directs.

2. Meanwhile, make pesto: In food processor with knife blade attached, blend basil, garlic, water, 2 tablespoons oil, ¼ teaspoon salt, and pepper until pureed, stopping processor occasionally and scraping bowl with rubber spatula. Add Romano; pulse to combine. Set aside.

3. In 12-inch skillet, heat remaining 1 tablespoon oil on medium until very hot; add onion and cook 5 to 7 minutes or until beginning to soften. Stir in white beans, and cook 5 minutes longer, stirring occasionally.

4. Reserve ¼ cup pasta cooking water. Drain pasta and return to saucepot; stir in white-bean mixture, pesto, cut-up tomatoes, and reserved cooking water. Toss to coat.

Each serving (1⅓ cup): About 375 calories, 15g protein, 59g carbohydrate, 10g total fat (2g saturated), 9g fiber, 435mg sodium

SPAGHETTI WITH ROASTED TOMATOES

Oven-roasted tomatoes have a sweet, intense flavor that is hard to resist. They make a terrific pasta sauce. If you like, you can use 3 pints of whole grape tomatoes to replace the plum tomatoes; reduce the roasting time to 20 to 30 minutes. No need to peel!

ACTIVE TIME: 10 minutes   **TOTAL TIME:** 1 hour, 10 minutes, plus cooling
MAKES: 6 servings

2	tablespoons olive oil
3	pounds (16 medium) ripe plum tomatoes, cut lengthwise in half
6	garlic cloves, not peeled
1	(16-ounce) package whole-grain spaghetti or linguine
3/4	teaspoon salt
1/4	teaspoon coarsely ground black pepper

Freshly grated Pecorino-Romano cheese (optional)

1. Preheat oven to 450°F. Brush jelly-roll pan with 1 tablespoon oil. Arrange tomatoes, cut side down, in pan; add garlic. Roast tomatoes and garlic until tomatoes are well browned and garlic has softened, 50 to 60 minutes.

2. When cool enough to handle, peel tomatoes over medium bowl to catch any juices. Place tomatoes in bowl; discard skins. Squeeze garlic to separate pulp from skins. Add garlic to tomatoes.

3. Meanwhile, in large saucepot, cook pasta as label directs. Drain.

4. With back of spoon, crush tomatoes and garlic. Stir in salt, pepper, and remaining 1 tablespoon oil. Serve sauce at room temperature or transfer to saucepan and heat through over low heat. In warm serving bowl, toss pasta with sauce. Serve with Romano, if you like.

Each serving: About 390 calories, 14g protein, 71g carbohydrate, 8g total fat (1g saturated), 9g fiber, 265mg sodium

RADIATORE WITH ARUGULA AND CHERRY TOMATOES

No need to cook the arugula in this easy dish; it quickly wilts when tossed with the hot pasta and sauce.

ACTIVE TIME: 15 minutes   **TOTAL TIME:** 40 minutes
MAKES: 4 servings

1	tablespoon olive oil
1	garlic clove, crushed with garlic press
1	pound cherry tomatoes, cut into quarters
1/2	teaspoon salt
1/4	teaspoon coarsely ground black pepper
1	(16-ounce) package whole-grain radiatore or rotini
2	(10-ounce) bunches arugula, trimmed
1/4	cup freshly grated Parmesan cheese

1. In nonstick 10-inch skillet, heat olive oil over medium heat. Add garlic and cook, stirring, 30 seconds. Add tomatoes, salt, and pepper and cook until tomatoes are warmed through, 1 to 2 minutes longer.

2. Meanwhile, in large saucepot, cook pasta as label directs. Drain. In warm serving bowl, toss pasta with arugula and Parmesan.

Each serving: About 475 calories, 21g protein, 90g carbohydrate, 7g total fat (2g saturated), 11g fiber, 373mg sodium

KNOW YOUR PASTA

Choose the right sauce for your pasta. Here are some tried-and-true guidelines:

- Thin pastas, such as capellini and vermicelli, should be dressed with delicate, light sauces that will cling to the skinny strands.
- Fettuccine and linguine are excellent with light meat, vegetable, and seafood sauces.
- Tubular pastas are great with meat sauces: The nuggets of meat nestle right inside the tubes. Chunky vegetable or olive sauces are also a good match for macaroni-type pastas as well as for baked dishes.
- Tiny pastas are best saved for soups or combined with other ingredients.

FARMERS' MARKET PASTA

Grilled summer produce meets pasta for a colorful, appealing dinner or al fresco brunch.

TOTAL TIME: 45 minutes, plus cooling
MAKES: 8 servings

1	pound whole-grain campanelle or penne pasta
$\frac{1}{2}$	small red onion, very thinly sliced
$\frac{1}{2}$	pound green beans, trimmed
1	teaspoon plus $\frac{1}{4}$ cup extra-virgin olive oil
$\frac{1}{8}$	teaspoon salt, plus $\frac{3}{4}$ teaspoon
4	large ears corn, husked
$\frac{1}{3}$	cup sherry vinegar
$\frac{1}{4}$	cup fresh lemon juice
1	clove garlic, crushed with press
$\frac{1}{4}$	teaspoon ground black pepper
12	ounces multicolored cherry tomatoes, cut into halves
$\frac{1}{4}$	cup fresh basil leaves, finely chopped

1. Heat outdoor grill on medium-high. Cook pasta as label directs. In medium bowl, soak onion in ice water at least 30 minutes.

2. Meanwhile, fold 12 x 30-inch sheet of foil in half. In large bowl, toss green beans with 1 teaspoon oil and $\frac{1}{8}$ teaspoon salt. Place beans in center of foil. Crimp edges of foil to seal tightly. Grill 15 minutes, turning over once halfway through. Grill corn 8 to 10 minutes, or until charred in spots, turning occasionally.

3. Transfer bean packet and corn to cutting board; let cool. In large bowl, whisk together vinegar, lemon juice, garlic, remaining $\frac{1}{4}$ cup oil, $\frac{3}{4}$ teaspoon salt, and black pepper. Add cooked pasta and tomatoes to bowl, tossing to combine.

4. When cool enough to handle, slice beans into 2-inch lengths and cut corn kernels off cob; add to bowl with pasta along with basil, tossing until well combined. Drain soaked onions well. Pat dry with paper towel and add to pasta, tossing. Pasta can be covered and refrigerated up to 1 day ahead.

Each serving: About 345 calories, 12g protein, 59g carbohydrate, 10g total fat (1g saturated), 7g fiber, 239mg sodium

GARLICKY BROCCOLI PASTA

Serving pasta with garlic and broccoli is a time-honored tradition and with good reason: It is absolutely delicious.

ACTIVE TIME: 15 minutes   **TOTAL TIME:** 45 minutes

MAKES: 6 servings

1	(16-ounce) package whole-grain orecchiette or fusilli
1	(1-pound) bunch broccoli
2	tablespoons extra-virgin olive oil
3	garlic cloves, thinly sliced
¼	cup water
½	teaspoon salt
½	cup freshly grated Pecorino Romano cheese

1. In large saucepot, cook pasta as label directs.

2. Meanwhile, trim broccoli. Coarsely chop stems and florets. You should have about 5 cups broccoli.

3. In nonstick 12-inch skillet, heat oil over medium heat until hot. Add garlic and cook, stirring, until golden, 2 to 3 minutes. Stir in broccoli, water, and salt. Cover and cook, stirring occasionally, until broccoli is tender, 8 to 10 minutes.

4. Drain pasta, reserving ½ cup pasta cooking water. Return pasta to saucepot. Add cheese, broccoli mixture, and reserved cooking water to pasta; toss until well combined.

Each serving: About 370 calories, 14g protein, 61g carbohydrate, 8g total fat (2g saturated), 8g fiber, 395mg sodium

WHOLE WHEAT PASTA WITH GARLICKY GREENS

This delicious, heart-healthy dish makes a great first course, or a light lunch or supper on its own.

ACTIVE TIME: 15 minutes   **TOTAL TIME:** 35 minutes
MAKES: 6 servings

1	large (1-pound) bunch broccoli rabe
1	(½-pound) bunch Swiss chard
1	pound whole wheat penne or ziti
2	tablespoons extra-virgin olive oil
3	garlic cloves, finely chopped
¼	teaspoon cayenne pepper
½	cup water
½	teaspoon salt, plus more for salting the water
½	cup freshly grated Parmesan

1. Heat large covered saucepot of salted water to boiling over high heat.

2. Meanwhile, trim and discard tough stem ends from broccoli rabe and Swiss chard. Coarsely chop tender stems and leaves. You should have about 20 cups chopped greens.

3. Add pasta to boiling water and cook as label directs. While pasta cooks, in nonstick 12-inch skillet, heat oil over medium heat until hot. Add garlic and cayenne pepper; cook 2 minutes or until garlic is golden, stirring. Stir half of greens, all of water, and salt into garlic in skillet. Increase to medium-high heat; cover and cook 2 to 3 minutes or until greens in skillet wilt. Stir in remaining greens; cover and cook 10 to 12 minutes or until greens are tender, stirring occasionally.

4. Drain pasta, reserving ¼ cup of cooking water. Return pasta to saucepot. Add Parmesan, greens mixture, and reserved cooking water to pasta in saucepot; toss until well combined.

Each serving: About 360 calories, 16g protein, 60g carbohydrate, 8g total fat (2g saturated), 8g fiber, 505mg sodium

GRILLED RATATOUILLE PASTA

Here's more proof that grilled summer veggies and whole-grain pasta are a winning combination for great taste and a figure to match.

ACTIVE TIME: 35 minutes   **TOTAL TIME:** 50 minutes
MAKES: 6 servings

³/₄	teaspoon salt, plus more for salting the water
3	tablespoons red wine vinegar
3	tablespoons extra-virgin olive oil
2	cloves garlic
1	medium red onion
2	medium zucchini
1	large eggplant
2	large orange or yellow peppers
1	pound ripe plum tomatoes
1	pound whole-grain gemelli or elbow pasta
1	tablespoon Dijon mustard
2	tablespoons chopped fresh flat-leaf parsley leaves
¼	teaspoon pepper

1. Prepare outdoor grill for direct grilling on medium-high. Heat covered 6-quart pot of salted water to boiling on high.

2. In small bowl, whisk vinegar, oil, and garlic

3. Cut onion crosswise into ½-inch thick slices. Trim zucchini and eggplant; cut diagonally into ½-inch-thick slices. Brush half of vinegar mixture on one side of onion, zucchini, eggplant, peppers, and tomatoes.

4. Grill tomatoes 6 minutes, zucchini and eggplant 10 minutes, and peppers and onion 12 minutes, or until all vegetables are tender and charred, turning over once. Transfer vegetables to cutting board. Cool slightly, then cut into ½-inch pieces.

5. Meanwhile, cook pasta in boiling water as label directs. Drain; return to pot.

6. Stir mustard into remaining vinegar mixture. Toss with pasta along with parsley, vegetables, ¾ teaspoon salt, and black pepper.

Each serving: About 400 calories, 14g protein, 72g carbohydrate, 9g total fat (1g saturated), 11g fiber, 408mg sodium

LASAGNE TOSS WITH VEGGIES

If only lasagna, that perennial family favorite, didn't take 2½ hours to prepare and bake (and that's not counting the 15 minutes it needs once it's out of the oven to settle so it's easier to serve)! Luckily our streamlined vegetable version clocks in at just 30 minutes from saucepot to pasta bowl, without losing any of the robust flavors of the original.

ACTIVE TIME: 15 minutes   **TOTAL TIME:** 30 minutes
MAKES: 6 servings

1	(16-ounce) package whole-grain lasagna noodles
2	teaspoons olive oil
12	ounces sliced cremini mushrooms
1	medium zucchini, diced
½	cup dry red wine
1	(24-ounce) jar low-sodium marinara sauce
1	(6-ounce) bag baby spinach
¾	cup low-fat ricotta cheese
½	cup fresh basil, chopped
⅓	cup freshly grated Pecorino-Romano cheese
¼	teaspoon coarsely ground black pepper
⅓	cup shredded low-fat mozzarella cheese

1. In a large saucepot, cook lasagna noodles as label directs, but increase cooking time by 2 to 3 minutes or until just tender.

2. Meanwhile, in 12-inch skillet, heat oil over medium-high heat. Add mushrooms and zucchini; cook 5 minutes. Add wine; cook 2 to 3 minutes or until almost evaporated. Stir in marinara; heat to boiling. Simmer on low 5 minutes. Stir in baby spinach until wilted.

3. In bowl, stir ricotta with basil, Romano, and pepper; set aside.

4. Drain noodles; return to saucepot. Add sauce and mozzarella; toss well. Spoon onto 6 warm plates; top with dollops of ricotta mixture.

Each serving: About 480 calories, 24g protein, 76g carbohydrate, 12g total fat (4g saturated), 10g fiber, 314mg sodium

SEAFOOD FRA DIAVOLO

Packed with shrimp, mussels, and rings of tender squid, this pasta is a flat-tummy-conscious seafood lover's dream.

ACTIVE TIME: 25 minutes   **TOTAL TIME:** 1 hour, 25 minutes
MAKES: 6 servings

8	ounces cleaned squid
1	tablespoon olive oil
1	large garlic clove, finely chopped
¼	teaspoon cayenne pepper
1	(28-ounce) can low-sodium plum tomatoes
¾	teaspoon salt
1	dozen mussels, scrubbed and debearded
8	ounces medium shrimp, shelled and deveined
1	(16-ounce) package whole-grain linguine or spaghetti
¼	cup chopped fresh parsley

1. Rinse squid and pat dry with paper towels. Slice squid bodies crosswise into ¼-inch rings. Cut tentacles into several pieces if they are large.

2. In nonreactive 4-quart saucepan, heat oil over medium heat. Add garlic and cayenne pepper; cook just until fragrant, about 30 seconds. Stir in tomatoes with their juice and salt, breaking up tomatoes with side of spoon. Heat to boiling over high heat. Add squid and heat to boiling. Reduce heat; cover and simmer 30 minutes. Remove cover and simmer 15 minutes longer. Increase heat to high. Add mussels; cover and cook 3 minutes. Stir in shrimp; cover and cook until mussels open and shrimp are opaque throughout, about 2 minutes longer. Discard any mussels that have not opened.

3. Meanwhile, in large saucepot, cook pasta as label directs. Drain. In warm serving bowl, toss pasta with seafood mixture and parsley.

Each serving: About 445 calories, 27g protein, 72g carbohydrate, 7g total fat (1g saturated), 10g fiber, 559mg sodium

LINGUINE WITH RED CLAM SAUCE

If you wish, substitute two (10-ounce) cans of whole baby clams plus ¼ of the clam liquid for the littleneck clams.

ACTIVE TIME: 20 minutes   **TOTAL TIME:** 1 hour, 20 minutes
MAKES: 6 servings

Marinara Sauce (page 375)

½	cup dry white wine
2	dozen littleneck clams, scrubbed
1	(16-ounce) package whole-grain linguine
1	tablespoon butter, cut into pieces (optional)
¼	cup chopped fresh parsley

1. Prepare Marinara Sauce.

2. In nonreactive 12-inch skillet, heat wine to boiling over high heat. Add clams; cover and cook until clams open, 5 to 10 minutes, transferring clams to bowl as they open. Discard any clams that have not opened. Strain clam broth through sieve lined with paper towels; reserve ¼ cup. When cool enough to handle, remove clams from shells and coarsely chop. Discard shells.

3. Meanwhile, in large saucepot, cook pasta as label directs. Drain.

4. In same clean 12-inch skillet, combine marinara sauce, reserved clam broth, and clams; cook over low heat until heated through. In warm serving bowl, toss pasta with sauce and butter, if using. Sprinkle with parsley and serve.

Each serving: About 420 calories, 19g protein, 72g carbohydrate, 8g total fat (1g saturated), 10g fiber, 517mg sodium

MARINARA SAUCE

This sauce is very versatile. Top each serving with a spoonful of ricotta cheese for a creamy treat, or add ¼ to ½ teaspoon crushed red pepper instead of herbs in step 1 for arrabbiata sauce.

ACTIVE TIME: 5 minutes
TOTAL TIME: 35 minutes
MAKES: 4 servings

2	tablespoons olive oil
1	small onion, chopped
1	garlic clove, finely chopped
1	(28-ounce) can plum tomatoes
2	tablespoons low-sodium tomato paste
2	tablespoons chopped fresh basil or parsley (optional)

Salt to taste

1. In nonreactive 3-quart saucepan, heat oil over medium heat; add onion and garlic and cook, stirring, until onion is tender, about 5 minutes.

2. Stir in tomatoes with their juice, tomato paste, basil if using, and salt. Heat to boiling, breaking up tomatoes with side of spoon. Reduce heat; partially cover and simmer, stirring occasionally, until sauce has thickened slightly, about 20 minutes. Use to coat 1 pound whole-grain pasta.

Each serving: About 115 calories, 2g protein, 12g carbohydrate, 7g total fat (1g saturated), 2g fiber, 436mg sodium

> **TIP**
>
> Have a serving of leftover sauce? For a quick meal, you can add 3 ounces of baked or grilled chicken and 2 cups of steamed and chopped broccoli to your marinara pasta. Top with a tablespoon of Parmesan cheese.

LINGUINE WITH TUNA AND CHILES

Packed with summer veggies, this pasta has a little bit of kick.

TOTAL TIME: 25 minutes
MAKES: 4 servings

12	ounces whole-grain linguine
3	tablespoons extra-virgin olive oil
3	garlic cloves, finely chopped
2	small fresh chiles, thinly sliced
2	medium zucchini, thinly sliced
8	ounces mixed mushrooms, thinly sliced
½	teaspoon kosher salt

Freshly ground black pepper

1	(6-ounce) jar tuna packed in olive oil, drained

1. Cook linguine as label directs, reserving ½ cup cooking water. Drain. In 10-inch skillet on medium, heat olive oil; add garlic and chiles. Cook 2 minutes, stirring.

2. Add zucchini, mushrooms, salt, and pepper. Cook 5 minutes, stirring. Remove from heat.

3. In pasta pot, toss cooked pasta, zucchini mixture, and tuna, adding reserved cooking water as needed.

Each serving: About 530 calories, 25g protein, 76g carbohydrate, 17g total fat (3g saturated), 11g fiber, 394mg sodium

LEMONY CRAB LINGUINE

This zesty seafood pasta makes a quick weekday dinner but crab makes it special enough for company. (See photograph on page 344.)

TOTAL TIME: 20 minutes
MAKES: 4 servings

¼	cup olive oil
3	cloves garlic, thinly sliced
1	tablespoon fresh thyme
8	ounces lump crabmeat
1	lemon
½	teaspoon salt
½	teaspoon pepper
1	pound whole-grain linguine, cooked
¼	cup pasta cooking water
⅓	cup sliced pickled peppers

Lemon wedges

1. In skillet, combine olive oil, garlic, and fresh thyme. Cook on medium 3 minutes, stirring.

2. Add lump crab, grated zest and juice of 1 lemon, salt, and pepper.

3. Toss crab mixture with cooked linguine, pasta cooking water, and sliced pickled peppers.

4. Serve with lemon wedges.

Each serving: About 475 calories, 22g protein, 65g carbohydrate, 16g total fat (2g saturated), 5g fiber, 604mg sodium

PUTTANESCA FRESCA

Freshen up (and slim down) your pasta with this fresh take on the classic puttanesca sauce.

TOTAL TIME: 35 minutes
MAKES: 6 servings

1	pound skinless, boneless chicken breasts
3	tablespoons extra-virgin olive oil

Kosher salt to taste

Black pepper to taste

1	pound tomatoes, chopped
¼	cup pitted Kalamata olives, chopped
¼	cup packed fresh parsley, chopped
1	tablespoon capers, drained and chopped
2	cloves garlic, crushed with press
1	tablespoon red wine vinegar
1	pound whole-grain rigatoni, cooked

1. Heat grill to medium. Toss chicken with 1 tablespoon olive oil, salt, and pepper. Grill 15 to 20 minutes or until cooked through, turning once.

2. Combine tomatoes, Kalamata olives, parsley, capers, garlic, remaining olive oil, red wine vinegar, and salt.

3. Thinly slice chicken; add to bowl with tomatoes, along with rigatoni, tossing until well combined.

Each serving: About 420 calories, 27g protein, 58g carbohydrate, 11g total fat (2g saturated), 7g fiber, 160mg sodium

CHICKEN AND ARTICHOKE PASTA

This quick and slimming pasta dish is perfect for a weeknight meal.

TOTAL TIME: 15 minutes
MAKES: 4 servings

Nonstick cooking spray

1½	cups chopped marinated artichoke hearts
1	cup chopped tomatoes
4	tablespoons chopped Kalamata olives
4	cups chopped skinless, boneless white breast meat
4	cups whole-grain penne
4	tablespoons feta cheese
8	tablespoons chopped fresh basil

Ground black pepper

Sprinkle of salt

1. In a skillet coated with cooking spray, combine artichoke hearts, tomatoes, olives, and chicken, and cook until warmed through.

2. Serve over penne and top with feta cheese and basil. Season with pepper and salt.

Each serving: About 515 calories, 54g protein, 45g carbohydrates, 14g total fat (4g saturated), 6g fiber, 584mg sodium

CLASSIC BOLOGNESE SAUCE

A staple in Bologna, Italy, this tomato-based meat sauce, mellowed by long simmering, is well worth the time. Freeze leftovers in small batches.

ACTIVE TIME: 10 minutes   **TOTAL TIME:** 1 hour, 35 minutes
MAKES: 6 servings

2	tablespoons olive oil
1	medium onion, chopped
1	carrot, peeled and finely chopped
1	stalk celery, finely chopped
1½	pounds lean (90%) ground beef
½	cup dry red wine
1	(28-ounce) can low-sodium plum tomatoes, chopped
1¼	teaspoon salt
¼	teaspoon ground black pepper
⅛	teaspoon ground nutmeg

1. In nonreactive 5-quart Dutch oven, heat oil over medium heat. Add onion, carrot, and celery and cook, stirring occasionally, until tender, about 10 minutes.

2. Add ground beef and cook, breaking up meat with side of spoon, until no longer pink. Stir in wine and heat to boiling. Stir in tomatoes with their juice, salt, pepper, and nutmeg. Heat to boiling over high heat. Reduce heat and simmer, stirring occasionally, 1 hour.

Each serving: About 275 calories, 24g protein, 8g carbohydrate, 16g total fat (5g saturated), 3g fiber, 512mg sodium

SLOW-BRAISED BEEF RAGU

Hearty, rich beef ragu is a classic sauce that pairs perfectly with satisfying whole-grain pappardelle.

ACTIVE TIME: 15 minutes   **TOTAL TIME:** 10 hours, 15 minutes
MAKES: 8 servings

3	stalks celery
1	medium carrot
1	medium onion
4	cloves garlic
1	tablespoon olive oil
1	beef chuck roast (3 to 4 pounds), trimmed and cut into quarters
¾	teaspoon salt
½	teaspoon pepper
¼	cup low-sodium tomato paste
1	(14-ounce) can diced tomatoes
1	cup dry red wine
2	sprigs fresh rosemary
1	pound cooked whole-grain pappardelle

Finely chopped fresh parsley

Grated Parmesan cheese

1. In food processor, pulse celery, carrot, onion, and garlic until finely chopped, scraping down side of bowl occasionally.

2. In large skillet, heat oil on medium-high until hot. Sprinkle beef all over with ½ teaspoon each salt and pepper. Add beef to skillet; cook 6 to 8 minutes or until browned on all sides, turning occasionally. Transfer beef to 6- to 7-quart slow-cooker bowl.

3. To same skillet, add vegetable mixture and ¼ teaspoon salt. Reduce heat to medium. Cook 5 minutes, stirring occasionally. Add tomato paste; cook 1 minute, stirring. Stir in diced tomatoes and wine. Cook 2 minutes, stirring and scraping up browned bits. Pour mixture over beef. Add rosemary. Cover and cook on low 10 hours or until very tender.

4. Transfer beef to cutting board. Discard fat from cooking liquid. Remove chunks of fat from beef. Shred beef into bite-size chunks and return to cooking liquid. Serve tossed with pappardelle; garnish with parsley and Parmesan.

Each serving: About 480 calories, 48g protein, 48g carbohydrates, 11g total fat (4g saturated), 7g fiber, 354mg sodium

PENNE WITH BRUSSELS SPROUTS AND ROASTED PEPPERS

This hearty pasta is full of an array of bright textures and flavors.

TOTAL TIME: 20 minutes
MAKES: 6 servings

1	pound whole-grain penne pasta
2	tablespoons olive oil
1	pound Brussels sprouts, trimmed and quartered
1/2	teaspoon salt
1/2	teaspoon pepper
2	medium shallots
1/2	cup golden raisins
1/2	cup dry white wine
1/2	cup roasted red peppers, chopped
1	teaspoon grated lemon peel

1. Cook penne pasta as label directs, reserving 1/2 cup pasta water before draining.

2. Meanwhile, in 12-inch deep skillet, heat oil on medium-high. Add Brussels sprouts, along with salt and pepper. Cover and cook 5 minutes (do not stir). Reduce heat to medium. Add shallots and golden raisins. Cook 2 minutes, stirring occasionally. Add white wine; cook 2 minutes, scraping up browned bits. To sprouts, add cooked pasta, roasted peppers, lemon zest, and reserved pasta water.

Each serving: About 385 calories, 14g protein, 76g carbohydrate, 6g total fat (1g saturated), 10g fiber, 231mg sodium

> **TIP**
> Don't have wine? Not a problem. Substitute 1 tablespoon lemon juice and enough water to equal 1/2 cup.

Quick-Braised Spring Vegetables (page 395)

10 | SIDES

Usually rich in vegetables, side dishes have a head start when it comes to being filled with flat-tummy all-stars. But the recipes in this chapter go one step further, making sure to avoid fatty preparations like frying or adding heavy cream that can turn a perfectly healthy vegetable into a diet saboteur.

We'll show you how to prepare all kinds of seasonal vegetables like Quick-Braised Spring Vegetables (page 395) and Sweet Leeks and Fennel (page 406) in the winter. With a drizzle of olive oil Spice-Roasted Carrots (page 396) and Herb-Roasted Veggie Salad (page 405) can be transformed in the oven. Plus, Crunchy Carrot Coleslaw (page 394) has a great vinaigrette that can be tossed on any bed of greens for a delicious side. Apple Cider Greens (page 397) uses the health-trend hero, apple cider vinegar, to braise fibrous greens. We will also share slimmed-down recipes for traditional vegetable favorites like Lean Green Bean Casserole (page 392) and Light Latkes (page 431). Finally, we have included tons of ideas for preparing greens and asparagus, so you will always have an option. Cooking with season produce means your meals will always be fresh and incorporating these vegetables into your weekly menus will also ensure that your grocery bill will stay within budget.

KALE SALAD

This hearty winter salad is not only good for you—it's delicious!

TOTAL TIME: 20 minutes
MAKES: 6 servings

2	tablespoons fresh lemon juice
2	tablespoons extra-virgin olive oil
⅛	teaspoon salt
1	bunch kale
⅓	cup chopped roasted salted almonds
¼	cup pitted and sliced jarred green olives
½	cup pitted dates

1. In large bowl, whisk together lemon juice, extra-virgin olive oil, and salt. Remove and discard stems and ribs from kale. Very thinly slice leaves; add to bowl with vinaigrette, tossing to coat. Let stand 10 minutes.

2. Add almonds, olives, and dates, cut into slivers. Toss to combine.

Each serving: 180 calories, 5g protein, 22g carbohydrate, 10g total fat (1g saturated), 4g fiber, 190mg sodium

CORN AND AVOCADO SALAD

Flat-tummy all-stars lime and cilantro are the perfect pairing for sweet corn, garden-ripe tomatoes, and avocado.

TOTAL TIME: 10 minutes
MAKES: 4 servings

2	cups fresh corn kernels or 1 (10-ounce) package frozen whole-kernel corn, thawed
1	(6- to 8-ounce) ripe medium tomato, cut into ½-inch pieces
2	tablespoons chopped fresh cilantro
2	tablespoons fresh lime juice
1	tablespoon olive oil
¼	teaspoon salt
¼	teaspoon sugar
1	ripe medium avocado

Lettuce leaves (optional)

In medium bowl, combine corn, tomato, cilantro, lime juice, oil, salt, and sugar. Just before serving, cut avocado in half; remove seed and peel. Cut avocado into ½-inch pieces; toss with corn mixture. Serve on lettuce leaves, if you like.

Each serving: 180 calories, 3g protein, 19g carbohydrate, 9g total fat (1g saturated), 5g fiber, 196mg sodium

FLAT-TUMMY HABIT

EAT VEGGIES OR SALAD AS A FIRST COURSE

Try this: Before dinner, open a bag of frozen edamame (green soybeans), a flat-tummy all-star, zap them in the microwave, and serve them, still in the pod, as a starter. Or begin your meal with a simple mixed green salad with a few pumps of low-calorie spray dressing. You're likely to eat much less during your meal.

CARROT AND ZUCCHINI RIBBONS

Southwestern seasonings make this quick side salad a great complement to summer's grilled foods.

TOTAL TIME: 20 minutes

MAKES: 4 servings

1	tablespoon fresh lime juice
1	teaspoon vegetable oil
1/8	teapoon chipotle chili powder
1/4	teaspoon salt
1/4	teaspoon ground black pepper
3	peeled carrots
1	large zucchini
1/4	cup fresh cilantro leaves

In large bowl, whisk together lime juice, vegetable oil, chipotle chili powder, salt, and ground black pepper. Use vegetable peeler to shave carrots into long ribbons. Stop peeling at core and discard. Shave zucchini into ribbons; stop peeling at seeds and discard. Cut all ribbons in half. Add ribbons and cilantro leaves to dressing; toss until evenly coated.

Each serving: 40 calories, 1g protein, 7g carbohydrate, 1g total fat (0g saturated), 2g fiber, 183mg sodium

LEMONY BEAN DUO

Wax and green beans are tossed in a simple dressing and garnished with lemon and mint.

TOTAL TIME: 35 minutes
MAKES: 6 servings

¼	cup fresh mint leaves
12	ounces green beans, trimmed
12	ounces wax beans, trimmed
½	teaspoon salt
1	tablespoon extra-virgin olive oil
1	teaspoon ground black pepper
½	lemon

Finely chop mint leaves; set aside. In large saucepot of boiling water, cook green beans and wax beans with ¼ teaspoon salt for 7 to 8 minutes or until just crisp-tender. Drain well. In large bowl, toss warm beans with olive oil, chopped mint, ¼ teaspoon salt, and ground black pepper. Transfer to large shallow serving bowl. Grate lemon peel directly over beans.

Each serving: 55 calories, 1g protein, 7g carbohydrate, 1g total fat (0g saturated), 2g fiber, 183mg sodium

LEAN GREEN BEAN CASSEROLE

Don't let the holidays derail your diet. About 30 million households will serve this dish on Thanksgiving. Too bad it's not as good for you as it tastes. We switched to low- and reduced-sodium broth, and traded canned french-fried onions for oven-fried ones, trimming the total fat by 8 grams and dropping the sodium by 257 milligrams. Seconds, anyone?

ACTIVE TIME: 30 minutes   **TOTAL TIME:** 45 minutes
MAKES: 8 servings

Olive-oil nonstick cooking spray

1	(12-ounce) large onion, cut into $\frac{1}{2}$-inch-thick slices and separated into rings
5	tablespoons all-purpose flour
$\frac{3}{8}$	teaspoon salt
$1\frac{1}{2}$	pounds green beans, trimmed
1	tablespoon butter
1	large shallot, finely chopped
1	(10-ounce) container sliced cremini or white mushrooms
$\frac{1}{4}$	teaspoon ground black pepper
1	cup low-sodium chicken broth
$\frac{1}{2}$	cup low-fat (1%) milk

1. Preheat oven to 425°F. Line large baking sheet with foil; spray with nonstick spray. In bowl, toss onion with 2 tablespoons flour and $\frac{1}{8}$ teaspoon salt. Spread onion in single layer on prepared foil; spray onion with nonstick spray. Bake 14 minutes; toss to rearrange, then spray again. Bake 15 minutes or until crisp.

2. Meanwhile, in 5-quart saucepot, heat 3 quarts water to boiling on high. Add beans and cook, uncovered, 5 minutes or until tender-crisp. Drain beans in colander; rinse under cold water. Drain.

3. In 4-quart saucepan, melt butter on medium. Add shallot; cook 2 minutes, stirring. Add mushrooms; cook 7 to 8 minutes or until tender, stirring often. Stir in remaining $\frac{1}{4}$ teaspoon salt, $\frac{1}{4}$ teaspoon pepper, and remaining 3 tablespoons flour; cook 1 minute. Add broth and milk; heat to boiling on high, stirring. Reduce heat to low; cook 2 minutes. Add beans.

4. Transfer mixture to 2-quart baking dish; bake 15 minutes. Stir mixture; top with onion. Bake 5 minutes more or until sauce is bubbly.

Each serving (1 cup): About 95 calories, 56 protein, 16g carbohydrate, 2g total fat (0g saturated), 4g fiber, 285mg sodium

CRUNCHY CARROT COLESLAW

A mix of cabbage and carrots gives this slaw its crunch; cider vinegar and a little cayenne deliver a bite.

TOTAL TIME: 10 minutes
MAKES: 4 servings

⅓	cup fresh orange juice
¼	cup apple cider vinegar
2	tablespoons sugar
2	tablespoons Dijon mustard
1	tablespoon vegetable oil
1	teaspoon salt
¼	teaspoon dried mint
⅛	teaspoon cayenne pepper
1	(16-ounce) bag shredded cabbage
1	(10-ounce) bag shredded carrots

In large bowl, with wire whisk, mix orange juice, cider vinegar, sugar, mustard, vegetable oil, salt, dried mint, and cayenne until blended. Add cabbage and carrots; toss well. Serve slaw at room temperature, or cover and refrigerate until ready to serve.

Each serving: 65 calories, 1g protein, 12g carbohydrate, 2g total fat (0g saturated), 2g fiber, 385mg sodium

QUICK-BRAISED SPRING VEGETABLES

This healthy side dish is like gathering the whole spring garden into one recipe. (See photograph on page 384.)

TOTAL TIME: 25 minutes
MAKES: 6 servings

1	spring onion, or 4 green onions, trimmed and sliced
2	cloves garlic, finely chopped
3	tablespoons olive oil
3	tablespoons low-sodium chicken broth or water
8	ounces asparagus, trimmed and cut into 1½-inch pieces
1	cup shelled fresh fava beans (from about 1 pound pods), peeled, or sugar snap peas, trimmed and halved crosswise
1	cup shelled fresh English peas (from about 1 pound peas in the pod) or frozen peas (thawed)
½	head (about 2 cups) escarole, torn into bite-size pieces
½	cup loosely packed baby spinach leaves
½	cup loosely packed fresh basil leaves
1	tablespoon finely grated lemon peel
1	tablespoon fresh lemon juice
Kosher salt	
1	tablespoon finely chopped fresh chives
Parmesan cheese, grated, for serving	

1. In heavy 12-inch skillet, combine spring onion, garlic, oil, and broth; heat to simmering on medium heat. Cover; cook about 2 minutes, or until onion softens slightly.

2. Add asparagus, fava beans, and peas and sauté 2 to 3 minutes, or until beans and peas are heated through. Add escarole, spinach, and basil; sauté 2 to 3 minutes, or until escarole wilts and asparagus is crisp-tender.

3. Stir in lemon peel and juice. Season to taste with kosher salt. Transfer to serving platter; sprinkle with chives and grated Parmesan. Serve immediately.

Each serving: About 120 calories, 5g protein, 10g carbohydrate, 4g total fat (1g saturated), 4g fiber, 250mg sodium

SPICE-ROASTED CARROTS

This is a great recipe for holiday dinners or company.

ACTIVE TIME: 15 minutes

TOTAL TIME: 1 hour, 15 minutes

MAKES: 8 servings

8	large carrots
3	tablespoons olive oil
2	tablespoons packed fresh oregano leaves
1	teaspoon smoked paprika
½	teaspoon ground nutmeg
½	teaspoon salt
¼	teaspoon pepper
2	tablespoons butter
1	tablespoon red wine vinegar
⅓	cup roasted salted pistachios

1. Preheat oven to 450°F.

2. In roasting pan, toss carrots with oil, oregano, paprika, nutmeg, salt, and pepper. Roast 1 hour or until tender but not falling apart. Transfer to serving platter. Drizzle with butter and vinegar and garnish with pistachios.

Each serving: About 165 calories, 3g protein, 16g carbohydrate, 11g total fat (3g saturated), 5g fiber, 295mg sodium

APPLE CIDER GREENS

This green side dish is brimming with flat-tummy all-stars!

ACTIVE TIME: 30 minutes
TOTAL TIME: 1 hour, 5 minutes
MAKES: 8 servings

12	ounces mustard greens
12	ounces collard greens
12	ounces Swiss chard
2	garlic cloves, thinly sliced
1	tablespoon olive oil
2/3	cup apple cider
1	tablespoon apple cider vinegar
3/4	teaspoon salt
1	cup red cooking apples, unpeeled and cut into 3/4-inch chunks

1. Remove and discard stems from mustard greens. Trim stem ends from collard greens and Swiss chard and remove stems from leaves; cut stems into 1-inch pieces. Cut all leaves into 2-inch pieces; rinse and drain well.

2. In 5-quart saucepot over high heat, sauté garlic in olive oil over high heat 30 seconds to 1 minute or until golden, stirring constantly. Add as many leaves and stems as possible, apple cider, cider vinegar, and salt, stirring to wilt greens. Add remaining greens in batches; reduce heat to medium; cover and cook 15 minutes.

3. Stir in apples and cook, partially covered, 10 minutes longer or until stems are very tender and most liquid has evaporated, stirring occasionally. With slotted spoon, transfer to serving bowl.

Each serving: 60 calories, 2g protein, 10g carbohydrate, 2g total fat (0g saturated), 3g fiber, 310mg sodium

STIR-FRYING GREENS

One of the best ways to serve nutritious greens is to stir-fry them, which cooks them just enough to mellow their flavor but retains their bright color. Tough, bitter greens, such as broccoli rabe and collard greens, should be blanched first to tenderize them and to remove some of their bitterness.

PREPARATION: Discard discolored leaves and trim thick stem ends; slice or tear leaves, if necessary. To blanch (if recommended), add greens to 6 quarts boiling water; cook, uncovered, as directed (begin timing as soon as greens are added), then drain. Now you're ready to let things sizzle.

STIR-FRYING: In 12-inch skillet or wok, heat 1 tablespoon olive oil over high heat until hot. Add 2 garlic cloves, crushed with flat side of chef's knife. Cook, stirring frequently (stir-frying), until golden. Add $\frac{1}{8}$ teaspoon salt and stir-fry as directed on page 399. Discard garlic, if desired.

TYPE OF GREENS	PREPARATION	BLANCH	STIR-FRY
Beet Greens (1 pound)	Wash	No	5 minutes
Bok Choy (pak choi, pak choy, Chinese mustard stems, and cabbage)	Wash and slice leaves into 1-inch-wide slices	No	5 minutes
Broccoli Rabe (rape, rapini, broccoli di rape)	Wash; trim stems	5 minutes	5 minutes
Chicory (curly endive)	Wash; tear leaves into bite-size pieces	No	5 minutes
Collard Greens	Wash and discard stems; cut leaves into 1-inch pieces	3 minutes	5 minutes
Dandelion Greens	Wash	3 minutes	5 minutes
Escarole (broad-leaf endive)	Wash and tear leaves	No	5 minutes
Kale (all varieties)	Wash; discard stems and center ribs. Cut leaves into 1-inch wide slices	5 minutes	5 minutes
Mustard Greens	Wash	5 minutes	5 minutes
Napa or Chinese cabbage, celery cabbage	Wash	No	3 minutes
Spinach	Wash thoroughly	No	3 minutes
Swiss Chard	Wash and thinly slice stems. Cut leaves into 1-inch-wide slices	No	3 minutes
Watercress	Wash	No	3 minutes

HONEYED RADISHES AND TURNIPS

Tired of the same old, same old? Try this bright, unusual vegetable combination.

ACTIVE TIME: 10 minutes **TOTAL TIME:** 30 minutes
MAKES: 8 servings

1	tablespoon butter
1	small shallot, finely chopped
12	ounces radishes, trimmed and cut in halves or quarters
12	ounces small turnips, trimmed, peeled, and each cut into 8 wedges
$\frac{1}{3}$	cup water
2	teaspoons honey
$\frac{1}{4}$	teaspoon salt
$\frac{1}{8}$	teaspoon ground black pepper
1	tablespoon thinly sliced mint leaves, plus sprigs
1	tablespoon chopped chives

1. In 12-inch skillet, melt butter on medium-high. Add shallot and cook 2 minutes or until golden and tender, stirring occasionally. Add radishes and turnips; stir until well coated. Stir in water, honey, salt, and black pepper. Heat to boiling. Reduce heat to medium-low; cover and cook 15 minutes.

2. Uncover and cook 7 to 10 minutes longer or until most of liquid has evaporated, stirring often. Remove from heat and stir in mint leaves and chives. Garnish with sprigs of mint.

Each serving: 70 calories, 1g protein, 10g carbohydrate, 3g total fat (1g saturated fat), 3g fiber, 190mg sodium

TROPICAL RADICCHIO SLAW

Switch up mayo-based sides with this fresh slaw.

ACTIVE TIME: 5 minutes
TOTAL TIME: 15 minutes
MAKES: 12 servings

2	medium heads radicchio, cut into quarters from top to bottom
2	tablespoons vegetable oil
2	cups finely chopped fresh pineapple
1/4	cup packed basil leaves, chopped
2	tablespoons orange juice
1/2	teaspoon kosher salt
1/2	teaspoon freshly ground black pepper

1. Brush cut sides of radicchio with vegetable oil. Grill on cut sides, covered, on medium for 8 minutes, turning once to other cut side. Transfer to cutting board; cool.

2. Slice very thinly; toss with pineapple, basil, orange juice, salt, and pepper. Serve immediately or refrigerate, covered, up to 1 day.

Each serving (½ cup): 40 calories, 5g carbohydrate, 2g total fat (0g saturated), 1g fiber, 85mg sodium

SESAME-GINGER SPROUTS

Lively, spicy ginger enhances this Asian-inspired side dish.

ACTIVE TIME: 15 minutes   **TOTAL TIME:** 30 minutes
MAKES: 4 servings

1	(10-ounce) container Brussels sprouts
1	tablespoon low-sodium soy sauce
1	teaspoon grated, peeled fresh ginger
1/2	teaspoon Asian sesame oil
1 1/2	teaspoons olive oil
1	small onion
1	tablespoon water

Trim stems and yellow leaves from Brussels sprouts, and cut each sprout lengthwise into quarters. In cup, stir together soy sauce, ginger, and sesame oil. In nonstick 12-inch skillet, heat olive oil over medium heat. Add onion, cut in half and thinly sliced, and cook 5 minutes or until softened, stirring occasionally. Increase heat to medium-high; add sprouts and water; cover and cook 5 minutes or until sprouts begin to soften and brown, stirring once. Remove cover and cook 5 minutes longer or until sprouts are tender-crisp, stirring frequently. Remove skillet from heat; stir in soy sauce mixture.

Each serving: 65 calories, 3g protein, 10g carbohydrate, 3g total fat (0g saturated), 3g fiber, 165mg sodium

GINGER-JALAPENO SLAW

Red and green cabbage costar in this Asian-accented slaw.

TOTAL TIME: 10 minutes, plus chilling

MAKES: 8 servings

⅓	cup seasoned rice vinegar
1	tablespoon extra-virgin olive oil
2	teaspoons grated, peeled fresh ginger
½	teaspoon salt
2	seeded and minced jalapeño chiles
6	cups (1 pound) thinly sliced green cabbage
3	cups (8 ounces) ounces sliced red cabbage
1½	cups finely shredded carrots (about 3 carrots)
2	green onions, thinly sliced

In large bowl, whisk vinegar, olive oil, ginger, salt, and jalapeño chiles until blended. Add green and red cabbage, carrots, and green onions; toss well to coat with dressing. Cover and refrigerate slaw 1 hour before serving to allow flavors to blend.

Each serving: 65 calories, 1g protein, 10g carbohydrate, 2g total fat (0g saturated), 2g fiber, 480mg sodium

HERB-ROASTED VEGGIE SALAD

This satisfying salad is packed with meaty vegetables like Brussels sprouts, broccoli, and carrots.

ACTIVE TIME: 15 minutes
TOTAL TIME: 35 minutes
MAKES: 8 servings

1	pound broccoli florets
1	pound carrots, cut into 1-inch wedges
1/2	cup olive oil
1/2	plus 1/8 teaspoon salt
1	pound Brussels sprouts, trimmed and halved
3	medium shallots, sliced
1	cup fresh cilantro, finely chopped
1/2	cup fresh mint, finely chopped
3	tablespoons fresh lemon juice

1. Preheat oven to 450°F. Toss broccoli, carrots, ¼ cup oil, and ½ teaspoon salt; arrange in single layer on large rimmed baking sheet and roast 10 minutes. Toss Brussels sprouts, shallots, remaining ¼ cup oil and ¼ teaspoon salt. Arrange in single layer on another large rimmed baking sheet; add to oven with other vegetables. Roast 20 minutes or until all vegetables are tender and golden brown, stirring once halfway through. (Vegetables can be roasted up to 1 day ahead. Cool slightly; cover and refrigerate.)

2. Meanwhile, stir together cilantro, mint, lemon juice, and ⅛ teaspoon salt.

3. Toss vegetables with herb dressing. Serve warm or at room temperature.

Each serving: About 190 calories, 4g protein, 15g carbohydrate, 14g total fat (2g saturated), 6g fiber, 250mg sodium

SWEET LEEKS AND FENNEL

This tasty relish is the perfect accompaniment to grilled meat.

ACTIVE TIME: 5 minutes
TOTAL TIME: 40 minutes
MAKES: 48 servings

1	tablespoon extra-virgin olive oil
2	medium leeks, thinly sliced
1	large fennel bulb, cored and thinly sliced
¼	teaspoon kosher salt
¼	teaspoon sugar
½	cup Dijon mustard

1. In a 12-inch skillet, heat olive oil on medium-low. Add leeks, fennel, salt, and sugar. Cook, covered, 20 to 30 minutes or until very soft, stirring occasionally. Remove from heat.

2. Stir in Dijon. Serve immediately or refrigerate, covered, up to 3 days.

Each serving (2 tablespoons): 20 calories, 3g carbohydrate, 1g total fat (0g saturated), 1g fiber, 180mg sodium

MAPLE SQUASH

Nothing evokes the fall season like butternut squash. Here we toss it with a mix of maple syrup and spices for a hint of heat and smoke flavor, then roast it, which concentrates the vegetable's natural sweetness.

ACTIVE TIME: 5 minutes   **TOTAL TIME:** 35 minutes
MAKES: 8 servings

1	(2-pound) package peeled and cubed butternut squash
1	tablespoon olive oil
¼	teaspoon salt
⅓	cup maple syrup
½	teaspoon pumpkin-pie spice

Pinch of cayenne pepper

Preheat oven to 425°F. Line 15½ x 10½-inch jelly-roll pan with foil. Place butternut squash in pan; drizzle with olive oil, sprinkle with salt, and toss to combine. Roast 15 minutes. Meanwhile, in 1-cup liquid measuring cup, stir maple syrup with pumpkin-pie spice and cayenne. Toss squash with maple mixture. Continue roasting until fork-tender, 15 to 20 minutes longer. Spoon squash, along with any pan juices, into serving dish.

Each serving: 100 calories, 1g protein, 22g carbohydrate, 2g total fat (0g saturated), 2g fiber, 80mg sodium

RAINBOW VEGGIE KEBABS

Don't want to grill? Roast the veggies instead: Toss with all the oil and spices on large, rimmed baking sheets, then pop in the oven at 425°F for 15 to 20 minutes. Squeeze lime over veggies before serving.

ACTIVE TIME: 20 minutes **TOTAL TIME:** 30 minutes

MAKES: 10 servings

1	teaspoon ground cumin
½	teaspoon ground coriander
½	teaspoon smoked paprika
1	teaspoon salt
2	pounds small green and yellow summer squash, cut into 1-inch chunks
1	pint grape tomatoes
6	tablespoons extra-virgin olive oil
12	ounces small broccoli florets
8	ounces cremini or button mushrooms, halved if large
1	lime

1. Heat grill to medium. In a small bowl, combine cumin, coriander, paprika, and salt; set aside.

2. In a large bowl, toss squash and tomatoes with 2 tablespoons oil. In another bowl, toss broccoli with 1 tablespoon oil. In third bowl, toss mushrooms with 1 tablespoon oil. Thread vegetables onto skewers. (If using bamboo skewers, soak them 30 minutes first.)

3. Grill broccoli and mushrooms 6 to 10 minutes, turning over once. Grill squash and tomatoes 6 to 8 minutes, turning over once. Transfer skewers to a large platter or cutting board and squeeze lime juice all over vegetables. Drizzle with remaining 2 tablespoons oil, then sprinkle all over with half of spice mixture. Cover platter tightly with foil; let stand, covered, at least 5 minutes before serving. Sprinkle with additional spice mixture, if desired.

Each serving: 110 calories, 3g protein, 8g carbohydrate, 9g total fat (1g saturated), 3g fiber, 210mg sodium

ROASTED ASPARAGUS

Easy and with tasty results, oven-roasting is sure to become a favorite way to enjoy this flat-tummy all-star vegetable.

ACTIVE TIME: 10 minutes   **TOTAL TIME:** 30 minutes
MAKES: 6 servings

2   pounds asparagus, trimmed
1   tablespoon olive oil
½   teaspoon salt
¼   teaspoon coarsely ground black pepper
Freshly grated lemon peel (optional)
Lemon wedges

1. Preheat oven to 450°F.

2. In large roasting pan (17 x 11½ inches), toss asparagus, oil, salt, and pepper until coated.

3. Roast asparagus, shaking pan occasionally, until tender and lightly browned, about 20 minutes. Sprinkle with grated lemon peel, if you like, and serve with lemon wedges.

Each serving: About 50 calories, 4g protein, 5g carbohydrate, 3g total fat (0g saturated), 2g fiber, 195mg sodium

GRILLED ASPARAGUS

Grilling asparagus is one of the simplest and tastiest ways to enjoy this late-spring vegetable.

ACTIVE TIME: 5 minutes   **TOTAL TIME:** 10 minutes
MAKES: 4 servings

1	pound medium asparagus
1	tablespoon olive oil
1/8	teaspoon salt
1/8	teaspoon coarsely ground black pepper

1. Prepare outdoor grill for covered, direct grilling on medium.

2. Trim ends from asparagus. Place asparagus on jelly-roll pan; brush with olive oil, and sprinkle with salt and pepper. Transfer asparagus to grill topper or vegetable basket on hot grill grate. Cover grill and cook asparagus 6 to 8 minutes or until lightly charred and tender, turning occasionally. Serve warm or at room temperature.

Each serving: About 40 calories, 1g protein, 2g carbohydrate, 4g total fat (0g saturated), 1g fiber, 69mg sodium

SESAME STIR-FRIED ASPARAGUS

Thin asparagus is the ideal candidate for stir-frying.

ACTIVE TIME: 15 minutes

TOTAL TIME: 20 minutes

MAKES: 4 servings

1	tablespoon vegetable oil
½	teaspoon Asian sesame oil
1	pound thin asparagus, trimmed and cut on diagonal into 1-inch pieces
¼	teaspoon salt
1	tablespoon sesame seeds, toasted

In 10-inch skillet, heat vegetable and sesame oils over high heat until hot. Add asparagus and sprinkle with salt; cook, stirring frequently (stir-frying), until tender-crisp, about 5 minutes. Transfer to serving bowl and sprinkle with toasted sesame seeds.

Each serving: About 70 calories, 3g protein, 4g carbohydrate, 5g total fat (1g saturated), 1g fiber, 145mg sodium

ASPARAGUS KNOW-HOW

AVAILABILITY: Almost year-round

PEAK SEASON: March through May

BUYING TIPS: Look for bright green, firm, crisp stalks with compact tips and no trace of brown or rust. Buy evenly sized stalks for uniform cooking. White asparagus, imported from Europe, is an expensive delicacy.

TO STORE: Asparagus is very perishable. Stand the stalks in ½ inch of cold water in a container. Refrigerate up to two days.

TO PREPARE: Hold the base of each asparagus spear in one hand and bend back the stalk; the end will break off at the spot where the stalk becomes too tough to eat. Discard the tough portion. Rinse well to remove any sand. Some cooks like to peel asparagus, but this is a matter of personal choice. Leave asparagus whole or cut diagonally into 1- to 2-inch pieces.

TO COOK: Asparagus can be boiled, steamed, stir-fried, roasted, or grilled. Serve hot, room temperature, or cold. To boil, in a 12-inch skillet, heat 1 inch of water to boiling over high heat. Add asparagus and ½ teaspoon salt; heat to boiling. Reduce heat to medium-high and cook, uncovered, until barely tender, 5 to 10 minutes (depending on the thickness of asparagus); drain. If serving cold, rinse under cold running water to stop cooking; drain again.

SAUCES FOR ASPARAGUS

For everyday meals, most green vegetables need little more than a drizzle of melted butter or olive oil or a squeeze of lemon juice, and asparagus is no exception. For more festive occasions, it's nice to dress it up. Here are some suggestions:

TAHINI DRESSING

Try this sesame-paste dressing on sautéed or broiled chicken or salads, as well as on asparagus.

TOTAL TIME: 10 minutes **MAKES:** About 8 servings

⅓	cup tahini (sesame seed paste)	1	tablespoon honey (optional)
2	tablespoons fresh lemon juice	½	small garlic clove, minced
4	teaspoons low-sodium soy sauce	½	teaspoon ground black pepper

In small bowl, with wire whisk, mix tahini, lemon juice, soy sauce, honey if using, garlic, and pepper until smooth. Cover and refrigerate up to 2 days.

Each serving (1 tablespoon): About 60 calories, 2g protein, 3g carbohydrate, 5g total fat (1g saturated), 1g fiber, 100mg sodium

JAPANESE MISO VINAIGRETTE

Miso comes in different colors and flavor varieties, but any one will make a tasty dressing.

TOTAL TIME: 10 minutes **MAKES:** About 16 servings

2	tablespoons miso (fermented soybean paste)	1	tablespoon peeled, minced fresh ginger
½	cup rice vinegar	1	tablespoon sugar
¼	cup extra-virgin olive oil		

In small bowl, with wire whisk, stir miso into vinegar until smooth. In blender, combine miso mixture, oil, ginger, and sugar; puree until smooth. Transfer to small bowl or jar. Cover and refrigerate up to 3 days.

Each serving (1 tablespoon): About 38 calories, 0g protein, 1g carbohydrate, 4g total fat (0g saturated), 0g fiber, 78mg sodium

TOMATO-MISO DRESSING

Use on grilled veggies, like asparagus and zucchini, or grilled salmon.

TOTAL TIME: 10 minutes, plus cooling   **MAKES:** 24 servings

¼	cup canola oil	8	ounces tomatoes, chopped
1	small shallot, sliced	3	tablepoons miso
1	jalapeño chile, sliced	3	tablespoons rice vinegar
1	clove garlic	1	tablespoon water

In 10-inch skillet, cook canola oil, shallot, jalapeño, and garlic on medium 3 to 4 minutes or until slightly browned, stirring. Add tomatoes. Cook 5 minutes, stirring. Cool. Blend with miso, rice vinegar, and water.

Each serving (1 tablespoon): About 30 calories, 0g protein, 1g carbohydrate, 2g total fat (0g saturated), 0g fiber, 81mg sodium

CLASSIC FRENCH VINAIGRETTE

Dijon mustard gives this vinaigrette smoothness and just the right amount of zing.

TOTAL TIME: 5 minutes   **MAKES:** About 12 servings

¼	cup red wine vinegar	½	teaspoon coarsely ground black pepper
1	tablespoon Dijon mustard		
¾	teaspoon salt	½	cup extra-virgin olive oil

In medium bowl, with wire whisk, mix vinegar, mustard, salt, and pepper until blended. In thin, steady stream, whisk in oil until blended. Cover and refrigerate up to 1 week.

Each serving (1 tablespoon): About 82 calories, 0g protein, 0g carbohydrate, 9g total fat (1g saturated), 0g fiber, 175mg sodium

MUSTARD-SHALLOT VINAIGRETTE

Prepare as directed for Classic French Vinaigrette (above) but add 1 tablespoon minced shallot. Cover and refrigerate up to 1 day.

BALSAMIC VINAIGRETTE

Prepare as directed for Classic French Vinaigrette (above) but replace red wine vinegar with balsamic vinegar and reduce mustard to 1 teaspoon.

ASPARAGUS WITH LEMON CREAM

Serve alongside scrambled eggs and sliced tomatoes at your next brunch.

ACTIVE TIME: 20 minutes
TOTAL TIME: 30 minutes
MAKES: 6 servings

1¼	teaspoons salt
2	pounds asparagus
1	lemon
½	cup plain, unsweetened Greek yogurt
2	tablespoons heavy cream
¼	teaspoon pepper
1	tablespoon snipped fresh chives

1. Heat large covered saucepot of water to boiling on high. Fill large bowl with ice and water.

2. Add 1 teaspoon salt, then asparagus, to boiling water. Cook, uncovered, 4 minutes or until bright green and a knife pierces easily through stalks. With tongs, transfer directly to bowl of ice water. When asparagus is cool, drain well; roll between paper towels to dry completely. Asparagus can be refrigerated in airtight container or resealable plastic bag up to overnight.

3. From lemon, grate 1 teaspoon peel and squeeze 2 tablespoons juice into small bowl. Whisk in yogurt, heavy cream, and ¼ teaspoon each salt and freshly ground black pepper. Sauce can be refrigerated in airtight container up to 3 days.

4. Spoon sauce over asparagus and garnish with chives.

Each serving: About 55 calories, 4g protein, 5g carbohydrate, 3g total fat (2g saturated), 2g fiber, 134mg sodium

ROASTED SWEET AND SOUR BRUSSELS SPROUTS

Sweet and tangy balsamic vinegar is the surprise ingredient in this Chinese-inspired side. (See photograph on page 8.)

ACTIVE TIME: 10 minutes   **TOTAL TIME:** 55 minutes
MAKES: 12 servings

3	pounds Brussels sprouts, trimmed and halved
2	tablespoons olive oil
1/4	cup low-sodium soy sauce
1/4	cup balsamic vinegar
1/4	cup brown sugar
1/2	teaspoon ground ginger
1/4	teaspoon black pepper
1/4	cup loosely packed fresh parsley leaves, finely chopped

1. Preheat oven to 450°F. On 2 large rimmed baking sheets, toss sprouts with oil; spread out in single layers. Roast 20 to 25 minutes or until deep golden brown, stirring and rotating sheets on oven racks halfway through.

2. Meanwhile, in 2-quart saucepan, heat soy sauce, vinegar, brown sugar, ginger, and black pepper to boiling on medium-high. Reduce heat to maintain simmer; simmer 12 to 15 minutes or until syrupy. Remove from heat. Toss sprouts with parsley and enough sauce to coat. Serve remaining sauce on the side.

Each serving: About 90 calories, 4g protein, 15g carbohydrate, 3g total fat, (0g saturated), 4g fiber, 210mg sodium

SAVORY MUSHROOM MEDLEY WITH THYME

These buttery mushrooms get an herby boost from fresh thyme leaves.

ACTIVE TIME: 20 minutes   **TOTAL TIME:** 40 minutes
MAKES: 8 servings

4	tablespoons butter
2	large shallots, finely chopped
1	pound white mushrooms, trimmed and quartered
8	ounces shiitake mushrooms, stems removed, cut into 1-inch-thick slices
8	ounces oyster mushrooms, cut in half if large
2	cloves garlic, finely chopped
1	teaspoon fresh thyme leaves, plus sprigs for garnish
½	teaspoon salt
¼	teaspoon black pepper

In deep 12-inch skillet, heat butter on medium-high. Add shallots; cook, stirring, 1 minute. Stir in mushrooms, garlic, thyme, salt, and black pepper; cook 12 to 15 minutes or until mushrooms are tender and browned and liquid has evaporated, stirring frequently.

Each serving: About 85 calories, 3g protein, 7g carbohydrate, 6g total fat (4g saturated), 1g fiber, 205mg sodium

SWEET 'N' TANGY PASTA SALAD WITH CREAMY BALSAMIC DRESSING

Your next BBQ doesn't have to be a calorie blow-out with this diet-conscious pasta salad.

TOTAL TIME: 10 minutes
MAKES: 12 servings

For the Creamy Balsamic Dressing

1	cup reduced-calorie mayo
½	cup balsamic vinegar
¼	cup extra-virgin olive oil
2	cloves garlic, pressed

Kosher salt

Black pepper

For the Salad

1	pound whole-grain rotini, cooked, slightly cooled
3	ribs celery, thinly sliced
3	carrots, shredded
1	red pepper, chopped
5	ounces arugula
2	(15-ounce) can cannellini beans, rinsed and drained

1. Make the dressing: Combine the mayo, balsamic vinegar, olive oil, garlic, salt, and pepper in a small container. Close the container and shake until mixed.

2. Make the salad: In a large bowl, combine the rotini, celery, carrots, red pepper, arugula, and cannellini beans. Add the dressing and toss to combine.

Each serving: About 290 calories, 11g protein, 46g carbohydrate, 8g total fat (1g saturated), 9g fiber, 283mg sodium

QUINOA TABBOULEH

This filling dish (quinoa has 5 grams of fiber per cup) is great for summer gatherings. Pair with grilled chicken or refrigerate and serve cold.

ACTIVE TIME: 20 minutes
TOTAL TIME: 40 minutes
MAKES: 12 servings

1½	cups quinoa, rinsed
1	cup packed fresh mint leaves
1	cup packed fresh parsley leaves
¼	cup lemon juice
¼	cup extra-virgin olive oil
½	teaspoon salt
½	teaspoon black pepper
1	(14-ounce) can garbanzo beans, rinsed and drained
12	ounces tomatoes, seeded and chopped
4	ounces feta cheese, cut into ½-inch cubes

1. Cook quinoa as label directs; spread on a large platter to cool completely.

2. Meanwhile, in food processor, pulse mint, parsley, lemon juice, oil, salt, and pepper until very finely chopped, occasionally scraping down side of bowl.

3. Transfer herb mixture to large bowl. Add chickpeas, tomatoes, feta, and cooked quinoa; toss to combine. Makes about 7 cups.

Each serving: About 190 calories, 7g protein, 22g carbohydrate, 9g total fat (3g saturated), 4g fiber, 4240mg sodium

BLACK-EYED PEA SAUTÉ

Start with a can of low-fat, high-protein, black-eyed peas for this spiced, slender side dish.

TOTAL TIME: 5 minutes
MAKES: 4 servings

1	small onion, chopped
1	teaspoon olive oil
1	clove garlic, crushed with press
1	(15-ounce) can black-eyed peas, drained and rinsed
1	to 2 tablespoons chopped pickled jalapeño chiles

In nonstick skillet, brown onion in olive oil. Stir in garlic and cook 1 minute. Stir in black-eyed peas and heat through. Remove from heat and stir in jalapeño chiles.

Each serving: About 100 calories, 5g protein, 17g carbohydrate, 2g total fat (0g saturated), 4g fiber, 226mg sodium

HOLIDAY HERB ROAST POTATOES

No need to drown your spuds in cheese and butter. This is a light alternative to traditional high-fat, creamy potato side dishes.

ACTIVE TIME: 15 minutes **TOTAL TIME:** 45 minutes
MAKES: 6 servings

2	tablespoons butter
1	tablespoon chopped fresh parsley
$1/2$	teaspoon freshly grated lemon peel
$1/2$	teaspoon salt
$1/8$	teaspoon coarsely ground black pepper
$1/2$	pounds small red potatoes, cut in half

1. Preheat oven to 450°F.

2. In 3-quart saucepan, melt butter over medium-low heat together with parsley, lemon peel, salt, and pepper. Remove saucepan from heat; add potatoes and toss well to coat.

3. Place potato mixture in center of 24 x 18-inch sheet of heavy-duty aluminum foil. Fold edges over and pinch to seal tightly.

4. Place package in jelly-roll pan and bake until potatoes are tender when they are pierced (through foil) with knife, about 30 minutes.

Each serving: About 125 calories, 2g protein, 20g carbohydrate, 4g total fat (2g saturated), 2g fiber, 241mg sodium

OVEN FRIES

You won't miss the fat in these hand-cut "fries." They bake beautifully with a spritz of nonstick cooking spray and a sprinkle of salt and pepper.

ACTIVE TIME: 10 minutes
TOTAL TIME: 30 minutes
MAKES: 4 servings

Nonstick cooking spray

3	(8-ounce) medium baking potatoes
½	teaspoon salt
¼	teaspoon coarsely ground black pepper

1. Preheat oven to 500°F. Spray two 15½ x 10½-inch jelly-roll pans or large baking sheets with nonstick cooking spray.

2. Scrub potatoes well, but do not peel. Cut each potato lengthwise in half, then cut lengthwise into ¼-inch-thick slices. Place potatoes in medium bowl and toss with salt and pepper.

3. Divide potato slices between pans and spray potatoes with nonstick cooking spray. Roast potatoes until tender and lightly browned, about 20 minutes, rotating pans between upper and lower racks halfway through.

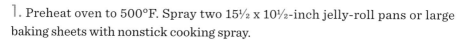

Each serving: 130 calories, 4g protein, 28g carbohydrate, 1g total fat (0g saturated), 3g fiber, 305mg sodium

PARISIAN POTATO SALAD

This creamy side dish incorporates French flavors into every bite.

ACTIVE TIME: 20 minutes
TOTAL TIME: 45 minutes
MAKES: 10 servings

3	pounds Yukon gold potatoes, peeled and cut into 1-inch chunks
³/₄	cup plain, unsweetened Greek yogurt
3	tablespoons extra-virgin olive oil
2	tablespoons grainy mustard
1	teaspoon salt, plus more for salting the water
1	teaspoon pepper
4	stalks celery, thinly sliced
½	cup cornichon pickles, drained and thinly sliced
½	small red onion, very thinly sliced
5	large hard-cooked eggs, coarsely chopped
¼	cup finely chopped parsley

1. To a large saucepot of salted water, add potatoes. Partially cover; heat to boiling on high. Reduce heat to maintain simmer. Cook 12 to 15 minutes or until potatoes are tender. Drain well; let cool 10 minutes.

2. Meanwhile, in a large bowl, stir yogurt, oil, mustard, salt, and pepper. Add potatoes to dressing; toss until well-coated.

3. Fold in celery, pickles, and red onion. Then gently fold in eggs and parsley. Serve immediately or refrigerate, covered, up to 1 day.

Each serving: 215 calories, 8g protein, 26g carbohydrate, 9g total fat (3g saturated), 2g fiber, 410mg sodium

LIGHT POTATO SALAD

This slimmed-down barbecue and picnic favorite saves a tidy sum of calories and fat over the traditional, mayo-loaded side dish—without sacrificing any of the flavor.

ACTIVE TIME: 25 minutes   **TOTAL TIME:** 35 minutes, plus chilling
MAKES: 10 servings

3	pounds Yukon Gold potatoes, peeled and cut into 1-inch chunks
1 1/4	teaspoons salt
3/4	cup low-fat buttermilk
1/4	cup light mayonnaise
2	tablespoons snipped fresh dill
2	tablespoons apple cider vinegar
1	tablespoon Dijon mustard
2	green onions, thinly sliced
1/4	teaspoon coarsely ground black pepper

1. In 4-quart saucepan, combine potatoes, 1 teaspoon salt, and enough water to cover. Heat to boiling on high. Reduce heat to medium-low, cover, and simmer 10 minutes or until potatoes are just fork-tender.

2. Meanwhile, in large bowl, whisk buttermilk with mayonnaise, dill, vinegar, mustard, green onions, remaining 1/4 teaspoon salt, and pepper.

3. Drain potatoes well. Toss hot potatoes with buttermilk mixture until coated. (Mixture will look very loose before chilling.) Cover and refrigerate potato salad at least 2 hours (or overnight), stirring gently after 1 hour, to blend flavors.

Each serving: About 135 calories, 3g protein, 25g carbohydrate, 2g total fat (0g saturated), 2g fiber, 164mg sodium

MASHED POTATOES WITH BROWNED ONIONS

A caramelized onion topping makes mashed potatoes even more irresistible. Who knew that was possible? Consider making extra browned onions—they may be as popular as the potatoes!

ACTIVE TIME: 15 minutes   **TOTAL TIME:** 45 minutes
MAKES: 6 servings

3	tablespoons butter
1	pound Spanish onions, each cut in half, then thinly sliced
2	teaspoons apple cider vinegar
3	medium baking potatoes (8 ounces each), peeled, each cut into quarters
1/2	cup low-fat (1%) milk, warmed
3/4	teaspoon salt
1/4	teaspoon ground black pepper

1. In 12-inch skillet, melt butter over medium-low heat. Add onions, stirring to coat. Cover and cook 10 minutes or until onions soften, stirring occasionally. Uncover; increase heat to medium and cook 15 minutes longer or until onions are very soft, browned, and reduced to ¾ cup, stirring frequently. Stir in vinegar and set aside.

2. Meanwhile, in 3-quart saucepan, place potatoes and enough water to cover; heat to boiling over high heat. Reduce heat to low; cover and simmer 15 to 20 minutes or until potatoes are tender. Reserve ¼ cup potato cooking water. Drain potatoes.

3. In saucepan, with masher, mash potatoes until smooth. Gradually add warm milk, mashing potatoes until fluffy. Add some reserved potato cooking water if necessary. Stir in salt and pepper.

4. Spoon mashed potatoes into serving bowl and top with onion mixture. Stir before serving.

Each serving: 75 calories, 3g protein, 27g carbohydrate, 7g total fat (2g saturated), 3g fiber, 385mg sodium

SWEET POTATO AND CAULIFLOWER MASH

The combination of sweet potatoes and cauliflower creates a savory, cozy winter side dish loaded with nutrients.

ACTIVE TIME: 20 minutes   **TOTAL TIME:** 1 hour
MAKES: 12 servings

3	pounds sweet potatoes, peeled and cut into 1-inch chunks
3	tablespoons salt, plus ¼ teaspoon
1	large cauliflower, cut into florets (about 8 cups)
⅓	cup olive oil
6	leaves fresh sage
2	cloves garlic, crushed with press
¼	cup low-fat (1%) milk

1. In 7- to 8-quart saucepot, combine sweet potatoes, enough cold water to cover by 1 inch, and 3 tablespoons salt. Partially cover and heat to simmering on high. Remove cover and add cauliflower. Simmer 15 minutes or until vegetables are very tender but not falling apart, stirring occasionally.

2. Meanwhile, in 1-quart saucepot, heat oil on medium-low. Add sage and garlic. Cook 4 to 5 minutes or until garlic is golden, stirring occasionally. Remove from heat. Remove and discard sage leaves.

3. Drain vegetables well; return to empty pot. In batches, in food processor, puree vegetables until smooth; transfer to large bowl. To pureed vegetables, add oil mixture, milk, and ¼ teaspoon salt, stirring to combine.

Each serving: About 140 calories, 3g protein, 19g carbohydrate, 7g total fat (1g saturated), 4g fiber, 180mg sodium

BROCCOLI GRATIN

We've trimmed the fat from a family favorite by using creamy Yukon Gold potatoes as the base of this dish. They make the traditional use of heavy cream and milk unnecessary.

ACTIVE TIME: 10 minutes   **TOTAL TIME:** 30 minutes
MAKES: 8 servings

1	pound broccoli florets
1	pound Yukon Gold potatoes, peeled and cut into 1-inch chunks
2	cups water
Pinch of ground nutmeg	
³/₄	cup freshly grated Parmesan cheese
¹/₂	teaspoon salt
¹/₄	teaspoon coarsely ground black pepper

1. In 4-quart saucepan, place broccoli, potatoes, and water. Cover and heat to boiling over high heat. Reduce heat to medium-low; cover and cook until potatoes and broccoli are very tender, 17 to 20 minutes, stirring once halfway through cooking.

2. Meanwhile, preheat broiler and set rack 6 inches from source of heat.

3. Drain vegetables in colander set over large bowl, reserving ¹/₄ cup cooking water. Return vegetables to saucepan. With potato masher or slotted spoon, coarsely mash vegetables, adding some reserved vegetable cooking water if mixture seems dry. Stir in nutmeg, ¹/₄ cup Parmesan, salt, and pepper.

4. In broiler-safe shallow 1- to 1¹/₂-quart baking dish, spread vegetable mixture; sprinkle with remaining ¹/₂ cup Parmesan. Place dish in oven and broil until cheese is browned, 2 to 3 minutes. The unbroiled casserole can be refrigerated up to 1 day. Just bake it 10 minutes before broiling as directed in the recipe.

Each serving: 95 calories, 6g protein, 13g carbohydrate, 3g total fat (2g saturated), 2g fiber, 305mg sodium

LIGHT LATKES

Potato latkes are a Hanukkah tradition, since they're cooked in oil, the sacred fuel central to the story of the menorah's lighting. Alas, that oil adds to the fat and calories in these crispy patties. This year, try our lighter twist, which we baked instead.

ACTIVE TIME: 20 minutes
TOTAL TIME: 50 minutes
MAKES: 12 servings

Canola-oil nonstick cooking spray

2	large egg whites
3	tablespoons snipped fresh chives
2	tablespoons all-purpose flour
1	tablespoon fresh lemon juice
3/4	teaspoon salt
1/4	teaspoon ground black pepper
2 1/2	pounds baking potatoes (4 medium), peeled

Applesauce (optional)

1. Preheat oven to 450°F. Spray very large baking sheet (20 x 14 inches) or 2 smaller ones with canola-oil nonstick cooking spray.

2. In large bowl, with fork, mix egg whites, chives, flour, lemon juice, salt, and pepper. In food processor with shredding disk attached, or on coarse side of box grater, shred potatoes. Place potatoes in colander in sink; squeeze out liquid. Stir potatoes into egg mixture.

3. Drop potato mixture by generous ⅓ cups, about 2 inches apart, onto prepared baking sheet to make 12 mounds. Press each mound slightly to flatten into a 3-inch round.

4. Bake latkes 15 minutes. With wide metal spatula, turn latkes over and bake 15 minutes or longer or until browned and crisp on both sides. Serve with applesauce, if you like.

Each serving (1 latke): About 65 calories, 2g protein, 15g carbohoydrate, 0g total fat (0g saturated), 1g fiber, 160mg sodium

Healthy Makeover Strawberry Ice Cream (page 435)

11 | DESSERTS

Fruit-based desserts are a sweet solution to any sugar craving. Besides offering nutrients, fruits are low in calories so you can indulge without blowing a day of good eating. You'll find plenty of fruity delights in this chapter.

Whether they're loaded with antioxidants, like Balsamic Berries (page 434) and Bold Berry Granita (page 438), or fiber-rich, like Banana Quick Bread (page 460) and Creamy Banana Sorbet (page 453), these desserts will satisfy and slim you down. Craving chocolate? Dig into our Dark Chocolate and Banana Sundae (page 463). And if you need a pick-me-up, Coffee Granita (page 462) will give you the extra jolt you're looking for.

Who says you can't have a flat tummy and dessert? Not us!

BALSAMIC BERRIES

At just over 100 calories, this flat-tummy all-star treat is totally legal.

TOTAL TIME: 5 minutes
MAKES: 1 serving

1	cup sliced strawberries
½	tablespoon melted butter

Balsamic vinegar
Coarsely ground black pepper

Toss strawberries with butter to coat. Stir in a splash of balsamic vinegar and a pinch of coarsely ground black pepper.

Each serving: About 110 calories, 1g protein, 14g carbohydrate, 6g total fat (4g saturated), 3g fiber, 49mg sodium

FOUR THINGS YOU DIDN'T KNOW ABOUT BERRIES

Berries can add important nutrients to desserts and more. Here's how:

1. 1 cup strawberries equals as much vitamin C as 1 cup orange juice

2. 1 cup blueberries equals as many antioxidants as 4½ cups red cabbage

3. 1 cup raspberries equals as much fiber as 2 cups cooked oatmeal

4. 1½ cups blackberries equals as much potassium as 2 cups fresh spinach

HEALTHY MAKEOVER STRAWBERRY ICE CREAM

This delectable four-ingredient treat whips up in 10 minutes and freezes into scoopable sweetness in an hour. (See photograph on page 432.)

TOTAL TIME: 10 minutes, plus freezing
MAKES: 3½ cups or 7 servings

16	ounces frozen strawberries
1	cup 2% plain unsweetened Greek yogurt
¼	cup sugar
½	teaspoon vanilla extract

Fresh strawberries, sliced, for garnish

1. In food processor with knife blade attached, pulse 1 cup frozen strawberries until finely chopped. Transfer chopped berries to large metal bowl.

2. In food processor, puree yogurt, sugar, vanilla, and remaining frozen strawberries until smooth. Transfer to bowl with frozen strawberries; stir until well combined. Cover and freeze about 1 hour, until firm but not hard. Garnish with fresh strawberries.

Each serving (½ cup): About 70 calories, 3g protein, 14g carbohydrate, 1g total fat (0g saturated fat), 1g fiber, 10mg sodium

ROSY PEACH MELBA

Less is more! This combination of juicy peaches and berries in a sweet rosé syrup calls for only 5 basic ingredients.

ACTIVE TIME: 15 minutes   **TOTAL TIME:** 20 minutes
MAKES: 8 servings

³/₄	cup sugar
1	cup water
4	large ripe peaches, pitted and cut into wedges
¹/₂	pint raspberries
1¹/₂	cups rosé or blush wine
3	tablespoons fresh lemon juice

Mint sprigs for garnish

1. In 1-quart saucepan, heat sugar and water to boiling over high heat; boil 1 minute. Pour syrup into large bowl; cool to room temperature.

2. To bowl with syrup, add peaches, raspberries, wine, and lemon juice; stir gently to combine. Cover and refrigerate at least 2 hours or overnight. Garnish with mint to serve.

Each serving: About 155 calories, 1g protein, 31g carbohydrate, 0g total fat (0g saturated), 2g fiber, 3mg sodium

RASPBERRY-LEMONADE GRANITA

Be sure to use a metal baking pan, not a glass baking dish, when making granita; it will freeze more efficiently. For a variation, layer the granita in wineglasses with fresh raspberries and top each with an emerald-green mint sprig just before serving.

TOTAL TIME: 20 minutes, plus freezing
MAKES: About 16 servings

2	to 3 lemons
3/4	cup sugar
3	cups water
1	pint raspberries

1. From lemons, grate 1 teaspoon peel and squeeze ¼ cup juice.

2. In 1-quart saucepan, heat sugar, lemon peel, and 1½ cups water to boiling over high heat, stirring to dissolve sugar. Remove saucepan from heat; stir in raspberries. Cool sugar syrup to room temperature.

3. In food processor with knife blade attached, blend mixture until pureed. With back of spoon, press puree through sieve into bowl; discard seeds. Stir in lemon juice and remaining 1½ cups water. Pour into 13 x 9-inch metal baking pan.

4. Cover, freeze, and scrape mixture as directed for granitas (page 439).

5. Serve granita right away, spooning shards into chilled dessert dishes or wine goblets. Or cover and freeze up to 1 month. To serve, let stand about 5 minutes at room temperature to soften slightly.

Each serving: About 45 calories, 0g protein, 11g carbohydrate, 0g total fat (0g saturated fat), 0mg sodium

BOLD BERRY GRANITA

Frosty, fruity, and fat-free, this heat-beating Italian ice doesn't require any special equipment.

ACTIVE TIME: 20 minutes   **TOTAL TIME:** 25 minutes, plus cooling and freezing
MAKES: About 10 servings

1	cup water
½	cup sugar
1	to 2 lemons
1	pound strawberries, hulled
1½	cups raspberries (about ¾ pint)

Fresh mint sprigs for garnish (optional)

1. Make sugar syrup: In 2-quart saucepan, heat water and sugar to boiling on high, stirring until sugar dissolves. Reduce heat to low and simmer, uncovered, 5 minutes. Set aside to cool slightly, about 5 minutes.

2. Meanwhile, from lemons, grate 2 teaspoons peel and squeeze ¼ cup juice. In food processor with knife blade attached, blend strawberries and raspberries until pureed. With back of spoon, press puree through sieve into medium bowl; discard seeds.

3. Stir sugar syrup, lemon juice, and lemon peel into berry puree. Pour into 9-inch-square metal baking pan.

4. Cover, freeze, and scrape as directed for granitas (page 439). Garnish with mint, if you like. Serve immediately.

Each serving: About 60 calories, 1g protein, 15g carbohydrate, 0g total fat (0g saturated fat), 2g fiber, 0mg sodium

GRANITAS

Cover and freeze the granita mixture until partially frozen, about 2 hours. Stir with a fork to break up the chunks. Cover and freeze until completely frozen, at least 3 hours or up to overnight. To serve, let the granita stand at room temperature until slightly softened, about 15 minutes. Use a metal spoon to scrape across the surface of the granita, transferring the ice shards to chilled dessert dishes or wine goblets without packing them.

INDULGE IN BERRIES!

All fruits are great on the flat-tummy diet, but berries are a special stand-out. High in fiber, filled with antioxidants, and rich in minerals that beat bloat, they also provide a little extra hydration. Raspberries and blueberries are the most helpful, since they're low in natural sugar and high in vitamin C. Here's what you need to know to incorporate them into your diet:

AVAILABILITY: Year-round, depending on variety

PEAK SEASON: June through October

BUYING TIPS: Berries should be plump, uniformly colored, and free of stems and leaves. Avoid bruised berries and cartons that are stained with berry juice. Beware of moldy berries and don't be tempted by the dewy-looking water-sprayed berries at the market; the moisture will only make them decay faster.

To Store

Berries are very perishable and can deteriorate within twenty-four hours of purchase. You can store them in their baskets for a brief period, but to keep them for more than two days, place the (unwashed) berries in a paper towel–lined jelly-roll or baking pan, cover loosely with paper towels, and refrigerate.

To freeze berries, wash and drain, then spread in a single layer in a jelly-roll pan and place in the freezer. Once they're frozen, transfer to a heavy-duty zip-tight plastic bag and freeze for up to one year. Do not thaw or rinse frozen berries before using. Extend the cooking time ten to fifteen minutes for berry pies and five to ten minutes for muffins and quick breads.

To Prepare

Rinse fresh berries just before serving. Remove hulls from strawberries (with a huller or a small knife) and any stems from the other berry varieties; drain well.

BLACKBERRIES: For the best flavor, buy deeply colored berries. Choose large maroon boysenberries for their rich, tart taste; deep red loganberries, which are long and tangy; medium to large purple marionberries, which have small seeds and an intense flavor; and large black olallieberries, whose flavor ranges from sweet to tart.

BLUEBERRIES: The silvery "bloom" on this berry is a natural protective coating and a sign of freshness. Only buy berries that still have their bloom. Blueberries range in color from purplish blue to almost black. Wild blueberries, also called lowbush berries, are pea-sized and quite tart; they hold their shape well in baked goods. Look for cultivated berries June through August; wild berries are most easily found along the coasts in August and September. Refrigerate in their baskets for up to ten days.

CURRANTS: Currants are red, white, and black. Red and white currants, found in farmers' markets in July and August, are sweet enough to eat out of hand and are often used in summer puddings. Black currants are made into liqueurs, syrups, and jams.

DEWBERRIES: Dewberries resemble blackberries in appearance and flavor, but they grow on trailing, ground-running vines.

GOOSEBERRIES: Ranging in color from green (the most common) to amber to red, tart gooseberries are usually cooked into jams, sauces, or pies. The Chinese (Cape) gooseberry is an entirely different species that is covered with a balloonlike papery husk (peel the shell back for a dramatic-looking dessert garnish). Gooseberries are available in June and July. You'll most likely find them in farmers' markets.

RASPBERRIES: Red raspberries are the most common, but also look for sweet apricot-colored berries and sweet-tart black raspberries in produce or farmers' markets. If red raspberries have darkened to a dusky shade, they are past their prime. There are two peak seasons: June and July and September and October.

STRAWBERRIES: Choose bright red berries with fresh green stems still attached: Pale or yellowish white strawberries are unripe and sour. Strawberries do not ripen after they are picked. Local strawberries are available from April to July, but strawberries are found year-round.

FRESH FRUIT WITH RASPBERRY-LIME DIPPING SAUCE

Flat-tummy all-star Greek yogurt has the rich texture of sour cream, making it perfect for sauces.

TOTAL TIME: 20 minutes
MAKES: About 8 servings

1	cup raspberries
1	lime
1½	cups reduced-fat Greek yogurt
¼	cup packed light brown sugar

Assorted fresh fruit for dipping, such as strawberries, grapes, cut-up melon, banana or kiwi slices, and plum, peach, nectarine, pear, and/or apricot wedges

1. Place raspberries in sieve set over bowl. With back of spoon, mash and press raspberries through sieve into bowl; discard seeds. From lime, grate 1 teaspoon peel and squeeze 1 tablespoon juice.

2. Add lime peel and juice, yogurt, and brown sugar to raspberry puree and stir to combine. If not serving right away, cover and refrigerate up to 1 day.

3. To serve, spoon sauce into serving bowl and place on large platter. Arrange fruit on same platter.

Each serving (¼ cup): About 55 calories, 3g protein, 10g carbohydrate, 1g total fat (1g saturated), 0g fiber, 15mg sodium

STRAWBERRY-RHUBARB CRISP

This sweet-tart confection is just as tasty as Grandma's strawberry-rhubarb pie—but with one-fifth the calories. A whole-grain crumble slashes the fat, while a splash of citrus enhances the sweetness of the berries, making up for almost 2 cups of sugar. Got a spoon? Dig in!

ACTIVE TIME: 15 minutes   **TOTAL TIME:** 1 hour, plus cooling

MAKES: 8 servings

1	small orange
1	pound strawberries, hulled and each cut in half
10	ounces rhubarb, trimmed and cut into 1/2-inch-thick slices
1/4	cup granulated sugar
1	tablespoon cornstarch
1/3	cup old-fashioned oats, uncooked
1/3	cup packed dark brown sugar
1/4	cup whole wheat flour

Pinch of salt

3	tablespoons butter, slightly softened

1. Preheat oven to 375°F. From orange, grate peel and divide between two large bowls; squeeze 1/4 cup orange juice into small measuring cup.

2. In one large bowl with peel, combine strawberries, rhubarb, and granulated sugar until well mixed. To measuring cup with juice, add cornstarch; stir until well mixed. Stir juice mixture into fruit mixture until well combined. Pour into 9-inch glass or ceramic pie plate; spread filling in even layer.

3. In other large bowl with peel, combine oats, brown sugar, flour, and salt. With pastry blender or with fingertips, blend in butter until mixture forms coarse crumbs with some pea-size pieces remaining.

4. Sprinkle oat mixture evenly over strawberry mixture. Place pie plate on foil-lined baking sheet to catch any drips. Bake 45 minutes or until topping is golden brown and fruit filling is hot and bubbling.

5. Cool strawberry-rhubarb crisp on wire rack until filling is set but still slightly warm, at least 1 hour.

Each serving: 155 calories, 2g protein, 27g carbohydrate, 5g total fat (3g saturated), 2g fiber, 70mg sodium

BERRIES IN RED WINE

This simple dessert is a healthy, refreshing end to a meal.

TOTAL TIME: 15 minutes, plus chilling
MAKES: About 6 servings

⅓	cup sugar
1	stick cinnamon
2	cups red wine
1	pound strawberries
1	pint raspberries

1. In 1-quart saucepan, heat sugar, cinnamon, and ½ cup wine to boiling on medium-high. Boil 2 minutes.

2. Place strawberries and raspberries in medium bowl. Pour remaining 1½ cups wine and wine mixture over berries. Cover berry mixture, and refrigerate 1 to 3 hours to blend flavors.

3. To serve, ladle berries with wine into wine goblets or dessert bowls.

Each serving: 140 calories, 1g protein, 24g carbohoydrate, 0g total fat (0g saturated), 4g fiber, 5mg sodium

RASPBERRY SOUFFLE

This impressive fat-free dessert is easier to make than you think; just fold store-bought raspberry fruit spread into beaten egg whites and bake. To get a head start, prepare and refrigerate the soufflé mixture in the soufflé dish up to 3 hours ahead, then bake it as directed just before serving.

ACTIVE TIME: 20 minutes
TOTAL TIME: 35 minutes
MAKES: 6 servings

²/₃	cup seedless raspberry spreadable fruit (no-sugar-added) jam
1	tablespoon fresh lemon juice
4	large egg whites
½	teaspoon cream of tartar
1	teaspoon vanilla extract
2	tablespoons sugar

1. Preheat oven to 375°F. In large bowl, with wire whisk, beat raspberry fruit spread with lemon juice; set aside.

2. In small bowl, with mixer on high speed, beat egg whites and cream of tartar until whites begin to mound. Beat in vanilla. Gradually add sugar, beating until sugar dissolves and whites stand in stiff peaks when beaters are lifted.

3. With rubber spatula, fold ⅓ of whites into raspberry mixture until well blended, then fold in remaining whites. Spoon mixture into 1½-quart soufflé dish; gently spread evenly.

4. Bake 15 to 18 minutes or until soufflé is puffed and lightly browned. Serve immediately.

Each serving: 75 calories, 3g protein, 16g carbohoydrate, 0g total fat (0g saturated), 1g fiber, 35mg sodium

MIXED BERRY BLITZ

Freeze summer's best produce for a tart and refreshing ice cold treat. (See photograph on page 449.)

TOTAL TIME: 15 minutes, plus 6 to 8 hours freezing
MAKES: 6 to 8 pops

8	ounces strawberries
½	cup water
½	cup sugar
1	tablespoon lemon juice
6	ounces blackberries

1. Blend strawberries and ¼ cup each water and sugar with lemon juice until smooth; transfer to liquid measuring cup. Wash and dry blender. Blend blackberries and ¼ cup each water and sugar until smooth.

2. Fill ice pop molds halfway with strawberry mixture. Add blackberry mixture to fill molds completely. Insert butter knife or chopstick and stir gently to swirl berry mixture in centers of molds. Add sticks; freeze until solid, about 6 to 8 hours.

Each serving: 75 calories, 1g protein, 19g carbohoydrate, 0g total fat (0g saturated), 2g fiber, 1mg sodium

BEST BERRY FRO-YO POPS

Since it's filled with Greek yogurt, this ultimate summertime treat can also double as breakfast!

TOTAL TIME: 10 minutes, plus 6 to 8 hours freezing
MAKES: 6 to 8 pops

1½	cups low-fat plain unsweetened Greek yogurt	3	tablespoons honey
6	ounces blackberries	2	tablespoons sugar
6	ounces blueberries	1	teaspoon vanilla

Blend yogurt, blackberries, blueberries, honey, sugar, and vanilla until combined but still chunky. Divide among ice pop molds; add sticks. Freeze until solid, about 6 to 8 hours.

Each serving: 100 calories, 5g protein, 19g carbohoydrate, 1g total fat (1g saturated), 2g fiber, 17mg sodium

GINGER FRUIT SMASH POPS

This ice pop gets some serious heat from fresh ginger and cayenne pepper.

TOTAL TIME: 15 minutes, plus 6 to 8 hours freezing
MAKES: 6 to 8 pops

1	cup water	Pinch of cayenne pepper
⅓	cup sugar	Pineapple chunks
1	(4-inch) piece fresh ginger, peeled and sliced	Green grape halves
4	strips lemon peel	Kiwi slices

In small saucepan, heat water, sugar, ginger, lemon peel, and cayenne on high until sugar dissolves, stirring. Transfer to blender and blend until smooth. Strain into liquid measuring cup; discard solids. Fill ice pop molds halfway with ginger syrup. Add small pineapple chunks, green grape halves and kiwi slices to molds. Add remaining ginger syrup to fill molds completely. Add sticks; freeze until solid, about 6 to 8 hours.

Each serving: 55 calories, 0g protein, 14g carbohoydrate, 0g total fat (0g saturated), 1g fiber, 1mg sodium

WATERMELON SLUSHIE

We combined antioxidant-rich pomegranate juice with fresh watermelon and ice to create this ruby-red summer cooler.

TOTAL TIME: 5 minutes

MAKES: 1 serving

2	cups 1-inch pieces seeded watermelon
1/2	cup pomegranate juice
1/2	cup ice cubes

In blender, combine watermelon, pomegranate juice, and ice cubes. Blend until smooth. Pour into tall glass.

Each serving: About 170 calories, 2g protein, 40g carbohydrate, 1g total fat (0g saturated), 2g fiber, 10mg sodium

PEACH AND TOASTED ALMOND GREEK YOGURT

Topping low-fat Greek yogurt with fresh peach slices, toasted almonds, and a drizzle of honey adds natural sweetness that's almost guilt-free.

TOTAL TIME: 5 minutes
MAKES: 1 serving

2	tablespoons sliced almonds
1	peach, sliced
6	ounces low-fat plain, unsweetened Greek yogurt
1	tablespoon honey

Microwave almonds on plate 1 minute or until toasted. Mix sliced peach and honey in bowl; spoon over yogurt. Top with almonds.

Each serving: 300 calories, 18g protein, 41g carbohoydrate, 9g total fat (3g saturated), 4g fiber, 57mg sodium

HONEY-DIPPED FIGS WITH YOGURT

Dessert doesn't get easier than this Greek-inspired yogurt dish.

TOTAL TIME: 5 minutes
MAKES: 6 servings

24	ounces low-fat plain, unsweetened Greek yogurt
12	figs
½	cup honey
¾	cup walnuts, finely chopped

Spoon 6 ounces yogurt into each of four bowls. Top each with 3 figs that have been brushed with honey and coated with walnuts.

Each serving: 330 calories, 13g protein, 49g carbohoydrate, 12g total fat (2g saturated), 4g fiber, 40mg sodium

PINEAPPLE POM FRUIT MELANGE

This herbaceous blend of pineapple, pomegranate seeds, and grapes is much better than your average fruit salad.

ACTIVE TIME: 20 minutes
TOTAL TIME: 25 minutes
MAKES: 8 servings

¼	cup sugar
1	sprig fresh rosemary, slightly bruised with side of knife
½	teaspoon vanilla extract

Pinch of salt

¼	cup water
4	large navel oranges
1	pound fresh pineapple chunks
1	pound large seedless grapes, halved
1½	cups pomegranate seeds

1. In small saucepan, combine sugar, rosemary, vanilla, salt, and water. Heat on medium-high just until sugar dissolves. Remove from heat; cool completely.

2. With sharp paring knife, cut off tops and bottoms of oranges, then cut off peel. Working over large bowl, cut segments out of oranges into bowl; discard membranes. To bowl with orange segments, add pineapple, grapes, pomegranate seeds, and rosemary syrup, tossing until combined. Serve immediately, or cover and refrigerate up to 1 day.

Each serving: About 160 calories, 2g protein, 40g carbohydrate, 0g total fat (0g saturated fat), 4g fiber, 310mg sodium

CREAMY BANANA SORBET

Here's an all-natural frozen treat made with bananas, vanilla, and a touch of maple syrup. Fast, easy, and deliciously creamy, it'll be loved by kids and adults alike.

TOTAL TIME: 5 minutes
MAKES: 6 servings

4	medium very ripe bananas
⅓	cup maple syrup
1	teaspoon vanilla extract

Pinch of salt

1. Peel bananas and place in large self-sealing plastic bag. Freeze overnight or until very firm.

2. Slice frozen bananas. In food processor with knife blade attached, blend bananas with maple syrup, vanilla, and salt until creamy but still frozen, about 2 minutes. Serve immediately.

Each serving: About 115 calories, 1g protein, 20g carbohydrate, 0g total fat (0g saturated), 1g fiber, 25mg sodium

TIP
This is a great way to use up any extra ripe bananas that you may have on hand. Before the bananas begin to brown, peel them and freeze in a large self-sealing bag for up to 1 week. Then, you'll have frozen bananas whenever you want to make this luscious dessert.

POMEGRANATE POACHED PEARS

Poached with added sugar, all these delicate pears need is a dollop of yogurt for one deceptively healthy dessert.

ACTIVE TIME: 10 minutes   **TOTAL TIME:** 30 minutes

MAKES: 6 servings

1	stick cinnamon
4	cups pomegranate juice
6	pears
¼	cup sugar
Plain, unsweetened Greek yogurt	
1	sprig mint

1. Simmer cinnamon stick, pomegranate juice, pears, and sugar in 4-quart saucepan until pears are tender (15 to 25 minutes).

2. Serve with Greek yogurt and a sprig of mint.

Each serving: 240 calories, 2g protein, 59g carbohoydrate, 1g total fat (0g saturated), 6g fiber, 26mg sodium

MELON LIME CUPS

This super-simple dessert is just right on a summer evening.

TOTAL TIME: 5 minutes
MAKES: 4 servings

2	cups 1-inch chunks of honeydew melon
2	cups 1-inch chunks of cantaloupe
2	tablespoons fresh lime juice
1	tablespoon honey
4	twists lime peel

Toss honeydew and cantaloupe with lime juice and honey. Spoon into wine-glasses and garnish with a twist of lime peel.

Each serving: 75 calories, 1g protein, 19g carbohoydrate, 0g total fat (0g saturated), 1g fiber, 28mg sodium

GINGERED "CREAM" AND GRAPES

Here's another super-fast, super-healthy, super-slimming fruit- and yogurt-based dessert. Indulge!

TOTAL TIME: 15 minutes
MAKES: 4 servings

2	cups red and green seedless grapes, halved
³/₄	cup plain, unsweetened Greek yogurt
¹/₄	cup coarsely chopped, crystallized ginger

Spoon grapes into each of four bowls. Top with a dollop of yogurt and sprinkle with ginger.

Each serving: 135 calories, 5g protein, 25g carbohoydrate, 3g total fat (1g saturated), 1g fiber, 22mg sodium

FRUIT COMPOTE WITH ALMONDS

Easy and elegant: Pears poached in fresh orange juice are paired with sliced strawberries. A sprinkling of sliced almonds completes the compote.

TOTAL TIME: 15 minutes, plus chilling
MAKES: 4 servings

1	medium orange
2	small pears, peeled, cored, and chopped
¼	teaspoon almond extract
2	teaspoons sugar
12	ounces (3 cups) strawberries, hulled and cut into quarters
½	ounce sliced blanched almonds (about 2 tablespoons)

1. Into 3-quart saucepan, squeeze juice from orange. Add pears, almond extract, and sugar. Cook over medium-high, stirring occasionally for 5 minutes, or until pears begin to soften.

2. Remove compote from heat and stir in strawberries. Transfer to medium bowl and refrigerate at least 1½ hours, until chilled. Divide among four glasses or serving bowls and top with almonds.

Each serving: About 110 calories, 2g protein, 22g carbohydrate, 2g total fat (0g saturated), 4g fiber, 2mg sodium

SLICED CITRUS WITH LIME

Served on top of plain, unsweetened Greek yogurt, this versatile fruit dish can be eaten for breakfast as well as dessert. It's also a colorful addition to a brunch buffet.

ACTIVE TIME: 20 minutes   **TOTAL TIME:** 25 minutes, plus chilling
MAKES: 6 servings

1	to 2 lemons
1	lime
¼	cup sugar
2	navel oranges
2	clementines
2	red or white grapefruit

1. From lemons, grate 1 teaspoon peel and squeeze 3 tablespoons juice. From lime, grate ½ teaspoon peel and squeeze 1 tablespoon juice.

2. In 1-quart saucepan, combine lemon and lime juices with sugar; bring to boiling over medium-high. Reduce heat to low; simmer 1 minute. Stir in lemon and lime peels, cover, and refrigerate until cold.

3. Meanwhile, cut peel and white pith from navel oranges, clementines, and grapefruit. Slice all fruit crosswise into ¼-inch-thick rounds. Arrange slices on large, deep platter. Spoon syrup over fruit. If not serving right away, cover and refrigerate up to 2 days.

Each serving: About 95 calories, 1g protein, 24g carbohydrate, 0g total fat (0g saturated), 3g fiber, 1mg sodium

FLAT-TUMMY TIP:
REMOVING THE PEEL
AND PITH FROM CITRUS

Here's how to create tiny rounds of orange and other citrus fruits:

1. Using a sharp paring knife, trim off the top and bottom of the citrus fruit to create an even base; set the fruit cut side up on a cutting board.

2. Following the fruit's contour and working from top to bottom, slice between the peel and flesh to remove a strip of the peel and pith. Repeat, working around the fruit, until you've removed all of the peel.

3. If a little pith remains attached to the flesh, trim it off, then slice the citrus as instructed in the recipe.

BANANA QUICK BREAD

Made with white whole wheat flour to up the fiber quotient, our sweet, moist banana bread is a delicious quick breakfast, snack, or dessert.

ACTIVE TIME: 15 minutes   **TOTAL TIME:** 1 hour, 15 minutes
MAKES: 12 servings

Nonstick cooking spray

2	cups white whole wheat flour
1½	teaspoons baking powder
½	teaspoon baking soda
½	teaspoon salt
¼	teaspoon ground cinnamon
½	cup packed brown sugar
2	large egg whites
1	large egg
4	ripe bananas, mashed (1½ cups)
⅓	cup low-fat (1%) buttermilk
3	tablespoons vegetable oil

1. Preheat oven to 350°F. Lightly coat 9 x 5-inch loaf pan with nonstick cooking spray.

2. In medium bowl, whisk together flour, baking powder and soda, salt, and cinnamon.

3. In large bowl, with mixer on medium-high speed, beat sugar, egg whites, and egg until almost doubled in volume. On medium speed, beat in bananas, buttermilk, and oil until well combined.

4. With rubber spatula, gently fold in flour mixture until just combined.

5. Pour batter into prepared pan, smoothing top. Bake 1 hour or until toothpick inserted in center comes out clean.

6. Let cool in pan on wire rack 10 minutes. Remove from pan and let cool completely on wire rack. Can be stored, tightly wrapped, at room temperature up to 3 days or in freezer up to 1 month.

Each serving: 170 calories, 4g protein, 28g carbohydrate, 4g total fat (0g saturated), 3g fiber, 228mg sodium

TIP

White whole wheat flour is milled from an albino variety of wheat. It's as healthy as traditional whole wheat—with the same levels of fiber, nutrients, and minerals—but it has a lighter texture that makes it perfect for baked goods. Gold Medal and King Arthur Flour make it, and there are also health-food-store options to choose from.

COFFEE GRANITA

This quick-fix, satisfying treat weighs in at well under 100 calories per serving!

TOTAL TIME: 10 minutes, plus 5 hours or more freezing time
MAKES: About 10 servings

2/3	cup sugar	1¼	cups whipped cream
2	cups hot espresso		

1. In medium bowl, stir sugar and espresso until sugar has completely dissolved. Pour into 9-inch-square metal baking pan; cool. Cover, freeze, and scrape as directed for granitas (page 439).

2. To serve, let the granita stand at room temperature for about 15 minutes. Use a metal spoon to scrape across the surface of the granita, transferring the ice shards to dessert dishes. Top ½ cup granita with 2 tablespoons whipped cream.

Each serving: 105 calories, 1g protein, 14g carbohoydrate, 5g total fat (3g saturated), 0g fiber, 10mg sodium

ORANGE GRANITA

Whip up this fancy, Italian-style flavored ice with only three ingredients. (See photograph on page 6.)

TOTAL TIME: 1 hour, plus 5 hours freezing time
MAKES: 6 servings

11	large navel oranges	Pinch of salt
½	cups sugar	

1. Cut the top quarter off 6 oranges; set aside. Trim the bottoms so they stand upright. With a small knife and spoon, scrape pulp into a bowl; place the shells in freezer. Into 4-cup measuring cup, squeeze juice from pulp.

2. From 5 more oranges, grate 1 tablespoon peel and squeeze enough juice to make 3 cups in all, including the juice from step 1. Stir in sugar and a pinch of salt to dissolve; pour into a square metal baking pan.

3. Freeze for 5 hours, scraping frozen bits with a fork every hour. To serve, scoop into frozen shells and replace tops.

Each serving: 120 calories, 1g protein, 30g carbohoydrate, 0g total fat (0g saturated), 0g fiber, 21mg sodium

DARK CHOCOLATE AND BANANA SUNDAE

This no-dairy sundae is a deliciously sin-free dessert.

TOTAL TIME: 15 minutes,
  plus 3 hours freezing time
MAKES: 4 servings

4	large ripe bananas, peeled and sliced
2	ounces dark (60% to 70% cacao) chocolate
4	cherries

1. Freeze bananas for 3 hours. Pulse in food processor until smooth, stirring often.

2. Melt dark chocolate. Divide banana puree among 4 bowls; drizzle with chocolate and top each with 1 cherry.

Each serving: About 205 calories, 2g protein, 40g carbohydrate, 6g total fat (3g saturated), 5g fiber, 2mg sodium

METRIC EQUIVALENT CHARTS

The recipes that appear in this cookbook use the standard United States method for measuring liquid and dry or solid ingredients (teaspoons, tablespoons, and cups). The information on this chart is provided to help cooks outside the United States successfully use these recipes. All equivalents are approximate.

METRIC EQUIVALENTS FOR DIFFERENT TYPES OF INGREDIENTS
A standard cup measure of a dry or solid ingredient will vary in weight depending on the type of ingredient. A standard cup of liquid is the same volume for any type of liquid. Use the following chart when converting standard cup measures to grams (weight) or milliliters (volume).

Standard Cup	Fine Powder (e.g., flour)	Grain (e.g., rice)	Granular (e.g., sugar)	Liquid Solids (e.g., butter)	Liquid (e.g., milk)
1	140 g	150 g	190 g	200 g	240 ml
¾	105 g	113 g	143 g	150 g	180 ml
⅔	93 g	100 g	125 g	133 g	160 ml
½	70 g	75 g	95 g	100 g	120 ml
⅓	47 g	50 g	63 g	67 g	80 ml
¼	35 g	38 g	48 g	50 g	60 ml
⅛	18 g	19 g	24 g	25 g	30 ml

USEFUL EQUIVALENTS FOR LIQUID INGREDIENTS BY VOLUME

¼ tsp	=					1 ml
½ tsp	=					2 ml
1 tsp	=					5 ml
3 tsp	= 1 tbsp	=		½ fl oz	=	15 ml
	2 tbsp	= ⅛ cup	=	1 fl oz	=	30 ml
	4 tbsp	= ¼ cup	=	2 fl oz	=	60 ml
	5⅓ tbsp	= ⅓ cup	=	3 fl oz	=	80 ml
	8 tbsp	= ½ cup	=	4 fl oz	=	120 ml
	10⅔ tbsp	= ⅔ cup	=	5 fl oz	=	160 ml
	12 tbsp	= ¾ cup	=	6 fl oz	=	180 ml
	16 tbsp	= 1 cup	=	8 fl oz	=	240 ml
	1 pt	= 2 cups	=	16 fl oz	=	480 ml
	1 qt	= 4 cups	=	32 fl oz	=	960 ml
				33 fl oz	= 1000 ml	= 1 L

USEFUL EQUIVALENTS FOR COOKING/ OVEN TEMPERATURES

	Fahrenheit	Celsius	Gas Mark
Freeze Water	32°F	0° C	
Room Temperature	68°F	20° C	
Boil Water	212°F	100° C	
Bake	325°F	160° C	3
	350°F	180° C	4
	375°F	190° C	5
	400°F	200° C	6
	425°F	220° C	7
	450°F	230° C	8
Broil			Grill

USEFUL EQUIVALENTS FOR DRY INGREDIENTS BY WEIGHT
(To convert ounces to grams, multiply the number of ounces by 30.)

1 oz	=	¹⁄₁₆ lb	=	30g
4 oz	=	¼ lb	=	120g
8 oz	=	½ lb	=	240g
12 oz	=	¾ lb	=	360g
16 oz	=	1 lb	=	480g

USEFUL EQUIVALENTS FOR LENGTH
(To convert inches to centimeters, multiply the number of inches by 2.5.)

1 in	=		2.5cm
6 in	= ½ ft	=	15cm
12 in	= 1 ft	=	30cm
36 in	= 3 ft	= 1 yd	= 90cm
40 in	=		100cm = 1 m

PHOTOGRAPHY CREDITS

© Antonin Achilleos: 197

© Yossy Arefi: 247

© James Baigre: 32, 103, 110, 202, 314, 320, 324, 439

© Monica Buck: 25, 346

Depositphotos © Andrii Gorulko: 62; © Maks Narodenko: 15; © Sedneva: 380

© Tara Donne: 190, 459

Mike Garten: back cover top row, back cover bottom right, 8, 16, 48, 60, 80, 89, 90, 92, 104, 139, 151, 167, 182, 187, 188, 191, 210, 217, 228, 249, 252, 265, 296, 329, 330, 333, 334, 344, 353, 356, 367, 379, 402, 405, 406, 408, 420, 425, 449, 452, 461, 463

© Brian Hagiwara: 243, 273, 304, 307, 323

© Lisa Hubbard: 442

iStock © Monika Adamczyk: 149; © James Alasdair: 77 right; © Aleaimage: 255; © anilakkus: 422; © bergamont: 312; © Bluestocking: 98; © Norman Chan: 20; © Oliver Hoffman: 101; © Valerie Janssen: 113; © kyoshino: 221; © Lisovskaya: 141; © Materio: 207; © Natikka: 198, 436; © Nipaporn Panyacharoen: 115; © Oleksandr Pereprlytsia: 302; © RedHelga: 413; © Keith Tsuji: 77 left

© John Kernick: 396, 429

© Rita Maas: 133, 283, 338

© Kate Mathis: 38, 40, 54, 71, 72, 85, 118, 136, 157, 162, 175, 194, 215, 225, 295, 393, 400, 416, 431, 432, 445, 450

© Joanna Pecha: 44

© Con Poulos: 6, 29, 31, 37, 42, 57, 66, 205, 277, 299

© Emily Kate Roemer: back cover bottom left, 58, 75, 178, 250, 260, 287, 311

© Alan Richardson: 446

© Kate Sears: 144, 168, 216, 235, 363, 391, 454

Shutterstock © 7th Son Studio: 219; © Bienchen-s: 237; © CGissemann: 361; © cobraphotography: 201; © Dionisvera: 79; © eugena-klykova: 95; © Svetlana Lukienko: 398; © Maksim Fesenko: 394; © Joe Gough: 173; © Christian Jung: 279; © Viktar Malyshchyts: 229; © photomaru: 193, 211; © Alexander Raths: 269; © spline_x: 377; © TTL media: 434; © Dani Vincek: 123; © Valentyn Volkov: 161; © Hong Vo: 127; © zkruger: 412

Stocksy United © Trent Lanz: 27

© Curtis Stone: 384

© Ann Stratton: 108, 397, 424

Studio D: Chris Eckert: 7; Emily Kate Roemer: front cover, 3

© Christopher Testino: back cover bottom center, 131

Thinkstock: © miwa_in_oz: 457

© Mark Thomas: 154

© Anna Williams: 222, 259, 274, 370, 386, 451

INDEX

THE GOOD HOUSEKEEPING TRIPLE-TEST PROMISE

At Good Housekeeping, we want to make sure that every recipe we print works in any oven, with any brand of ingredient, no matter what. That's why, in our test kitchens at the **Good Housekeeping Research Institute**, we go all out: We test each recipe at least three times—and, often, several more times after that.

When a recipe is first developed, one member of our team prepares the dish and we judge it on these criteria: it must be **delicious, family-friendly, healthy,** and **easy to make**.

1. The recipe is then tested several more times to fine-tune the flavor and ease of preparation, always by the same team member, using the same equipment.

2. Next, another team member follows the recipe as written, **varying the brands of ingredients** and **kinds of equipment**. Even the types of stoves we use are changed.

3. A third team member repeats the whole process **using yet another set of equipment** and **alternative ingredients**.

By the time the recipes appear on these pages, they are guaranteed to work in any kitchen, including yours. WE PROMISE.